THE
LIFE AND LETTERS OF
THEODORE
WATTS-DUNTON

BY THOMAS HAKE AND
ARTHUR COMPTON-RICKETT

INCLUDING SOME PERSONAL REMINISCENCES
BY CLARA WATTS-DUNTON

WITH SIXTEEN ILLUSTRATIONS

VoL. II.

LONDON : T. C. & E. C. JACK, LIMITED
NEW YORK : G. P. PUTNAM'S SONS
1916

Mrs. Watts-Dunton about the time of her Marriage

CONTENTS

XVI. Mid-Victorian Friendships (I.)—John Nichol, E. Burne-Jones, Sir James Knowles, Mrs. Augusta Webster, E. J. Trelawney, Robert Browning, J. R. Lowell 9

XVII. Mid - Victorian Friendships (II.) — Christina Rossetti 29

XVIII. Mid-Victorian Friendships (III.)—Tennyson . . 51

XIX. Mid-Victorian Friendships (IV.)—George Meredith, W. E. Henley, F. H. Groome, George Borrow . 61

XX. A Day with "Lavengro". 87

XXI. At the Pines 99

XXII. The Midsummer Holiday. 111

XXIII. Last Days 133

XXIV. "Walter Theodore Watts-Dunton and I." By Clara Watts-Dunton 163

XXV. Three Personal Impressions—(a) Mr. Coulson Kernahan; (b) Mr. Herbert Jenkins; (c) Mr. John Lawrence Lambe. 211

XXVI. Watts-Dunton: The Man 247

Appendices 279

Index 337

LIST OF ILLUSTRATIONS

Mrs. Watts-Dunton about the time of her marriage . . . . *Frontispiece*

Algernon Charles Swinburne (æt. 65) . . . 100

Swinburne's room at "The Pines" . . . 112

Drawing-room at "The Pines," showing the sofa where Watts-Dunton used to receive visitors, and on which he died 136

Mrs. Watts-Dunton 164

XVI.

MID-VICTORIAN FRIENDSHIPS.—I.

THE LIFE AND LETTERS OF THEODORE WATTS-DUNTON.

XVI.

MID-VICTORIAN FRIENDSHIPS (I.)—JOHN NICHOL, E. BURNE-JONES, SIR JAMES KNOWLES, MRS. AUGUSTA WEBSTER, E. J. TRELAWNEY, ROBERT BROWNING, J. R. LOWELL.

TO tell of all the notable men and women of letters with whom Swinburne and Watts-Dunton had personal association during those thirty years at The Pines would fill many interesting pages in literary lives of the two poets. Among a score of names special mention may be made of Tennyson, Browning, George Meredith, William Morris, Francis Groome, Borrow, Sir Richard and Lady Burton, Edward Burne-Jones, Benjamin Jowett (whom they used to visit at Oxford, Swinburne passing many an hour over old plays at the Bodleian), Augusta Webster, Sir James Knowles, Anne Proctor, W. E. Henley, and Sir John Skelton. There were also Marion Crawford and many other famous American writers, such as Lowell and Bret Harte. Swinburne's old friend, Dr. John Nichol, Professor of

English Literature in Glasgow University, must not be forgotten. At Balliol College, Oxford, Nichol had an immense influence, as Watts-Dunton soon discovered, on Swinburne's stream of thought. At the very moment when the two house-mates were planning a new departure in their lives on Putney Hill, Nichol wrote to Watts-Dunton from Glasgow :—

" I have just sent a note to Swinburne directed to ' Werter Road,' but as you may be on the move, I send this forward to The Pines. I shall be glad to arrange to spend an evening with you there in November. The long letter I wrote to S. was open to you to read, though not to . . ., and I have to thank you for your kind message. I am very sorry you agree with Swinburne about Byron ; it is one of the points on which we must agree to differ.* . . . Please drop me a line some time before the close of next month to tell me how you are flourishing."

In another letter, after one of his visits to Watts-Dunton and Swinburne at The Pines, he wrote from Carrick, Loch Goil, September 25, 1880 :—

" As I have before thanked you through Swinburne,

* In the article. *Byron,* in *Chambers's Cyclopædia of English Literature,* already referred to, Watts-Dunton has fully expressed his own views as to the poet's place among English bards. Professor Nichol had a special knowledge of the author of *Don Juan,* having written the monograph on Byron in the English Men of Letters series. He died at the age of sixty-one, in 1894.

I must now thank him through you for your joint hospitality, which, for my own behoof, I wish you would some day allow me to return by welcoming you to Scotland—such as it is. I had a few days' rest at Malvern, then proceeded north, reaching Glasgow only this week. We are.now settled here by the sea-shore till the close of October. This place is remote, it may be slow at this season, but it is ' beyond those noises, friended by almost perfect silence,' and out of the reach of reviews whose watchword seems to be damnation by faint and obviously reluctant approval. . . . Give Swinburne my best regards, and tell him I look forward to enjoying Dryden and Pope as much on reading as I did on hearing them."

John Nichol never conquered the belief that " the English critic was slow to do the Scotsman justice," although Watts-Dunton did his utmost to disabuse him of the idea. " There is nothing, my dear fellow," he would say, " nothing whatsoever in the idea that a Scotsman does not fight on equal terms with the Englishman in the great literary cockpit of London. As a matter of fact, I'm strongly of opinion that the Scottish cock is really longer in spur and beak than the English cock : depend upon it, Nichol, he can more than take care of himself."

On one occasion, after a visit to Agnew's, Watts-Dunton gave his impression of some of Burne-Jones's pictures when writing to a friend, though at the same time laying no claim to any great proficiency as an art critic.

" Of course," he says, " they are wonderful from the executive point of view—most wonderful. But a series of large pictures with God knows how many figures and but one pair of open eyes between them (those of Prince Charming in the first picture), is, in my poor judgment, about as huge a mistake as ever was made by any man of genius. Without eyes the human face cannot pretend to exist at all, and as these eyeless faces are all more or less without any sign that blood is moving behind the skin, they might just as well be dead so far as they can give any pleasure to me. To show that sleep is not death (nor even death's brother), there should be more, not less, of what Dick Swiveller calls the ' rosy ' and the ' balmy ' in all artistic renderings of sleep. And then, surely, a fifth picture is needed, a picture with ' eyes,' eyes so full of life on the Princess's part as to be able to assure us that the ghastly sallow girl, ' swaddled out straight ' à la Egyptian mummy, who has so shocked us in the fourth picture, was not really starved to death at all (as she seems to be), but only shamming. . . ."

Watts-Dunton was a frequent guest at Sir James Knowles's attractive house, Queen Anne's Lodge, looking out upon St. James's Park. For many years he and Swinburne contributed largely to the *Nineteenth Century*, and it would have been hard to find a more appreciative editor, as the endless letters from him to Watts-Dunton clearly show. Their correspondence was very voluminous, extending over twenty years. For not only was the author of *Aylwin* a somewhat frequent writer in the *Nineteenth Century*, but all communications regarding Swinburne's work contributed to the journal were " adjusted " by Sir James Knowles and Watts-Dunton; the very proof sheets of his poem, indeed, were seldom sent direct to the author of *Atalanta*.

" Many thanks for your encouraging appreciation of my efforts to help in the arming and drilling of our people," writes Sir James Knowles on February 5, 1900, " without which we shall entirely be overthrown before long. With it, and with forty millions of a fighting race to draw upon, we could hold our own against the world ! Especially I am thankful for what you say about my own few words of warning. . . . Is it not time that you came here to lunch again ? My wife wishes this as well as myself. What answer shall I give her ? "

At the time of Sir James Knowles's death, Watts-Dunton wrote to Mr. W. Wray Skilbeck :—

" I will not try to give full expression to the grief I felt on getting the news yesterday morning of my dear old friend's sudden death. I call him ' my dear old friend ' for a very good reason. It was he who in 1882 persuaded me at last to break the shell of anonymity under which such capabilities as I possessed had been incubating. I, of course, knew him a long time before that, and he had told me that he had been a reader of my anonymous *Athenæum* and *Examiner* essays ever since I began to write, and that he wondered why I had so long been content to remain unknown, except in the inner circle of letters. I told him that anonymity was what especially suited my temperament, and that I never believed that I could do my best in signed essays. However, the fact that he did at last persuade me to write my first signed review essay, and afterwards to become one of his literary contributors, and so open my energies to a wider world, is a very great fact in my own humble life-history. And during a quarter of a century I found him a delightful friend. My wife, too, has always entertained the liveliest feelings of regard for him ever since she first met him, and is deeply grieved at the sad loss that has come upon you all.

" It is a pleasing thought to me that my literary connection with him ended so late in his career that I wrote the very last article in the very last number of the last volume of the great organ during the time that he was acting-editor. I do not mean by this that I think it will be the last article of mine that will appear in the review under whatsoever new editorship it may now pass. . . ."

The first friend among the women of letters that Watts-Dunton ever knew, and the one in whose poetic work he took the greatest interest, was Mrs. Augusta

(1,894)

Webster. He had met her in earlier days at St. Ives ; his father had had business relations with an important firm of Cambridge solicitors in which this lady's husband, Thomas Webster, was a partner. This gentleman not only held in Cambridge a high position in his profession ; he was Fellow and Law Lecturer of Trinity College. Mrs. Webster, however, a woman of genius and keen literary ambition, persuaded him to resign his partnership in the legal firm at Cambridge and migrate to London, there practically to begin life anew ; for it had been her dream since girlhood to mix in literary circles, where she would win a fuller appreciation of her undoubted literary gifts. Watts-Dunton showed himself the " nurse of genius " in her case with unremitting zeal ; for he felt an exceptional desire to do the utmost in his power to aid her in gaining recognition among the writers of her time. He attended her receptions with great regularity, and from time to time he expressed his genuine esteem of her work in the *Athenæum.* Between the years 1881 and 1888 he seldom failed to review in that journal the various books of poems that she published.*

Watts-Dunton has described her as " one of the noble band, represented by George Eliot and Miss Cobbe among others, who, in virtue of lofty purpose, purity of soul, and deep sympathy with suffering humanity, bend their genius, like the rainbow, as a

* For obituary notice of Mrs. Webster by T. Watts-Dunton, see *Athenæum,* Vol. II., 1894.

covenant of love over all flesh that is upon the earth."

So late as within a month of his decease (May 13, 1914) Watts-Dunton wrote to Professor Walker, of St. David's College, Lampeter : " Many thanks for a sight of the typed script of your essay upon Augusta Webster. It is difficult to get magazine editors to read with intelligent literary eyes anything upon a poet that is out of the public ken.   It is a monstrous thing that such poetry as Augusta Webster's should be unknown.   Her name is not even mentioned in the *Encyclopædia Britannica*."

For six years during her childhood Augusta Webster lived with her father, Vice-Admiral George Davies, on board ship in Chichester Harbour, and to this fact can be traced her passion for the sea which is so picturesquely described in some of her poems, of which *A Coarse Morning*, in her volume *A Book of Rhyme*, is an eloquent example.

The case of Augusta Webster is one of many, illustrating Watts-Dunton's ready instinct for work of high quality.   In his long connection with the *Athenæum* he never used its pages to puff an unworthy writer, but often and often he drew attention to talented writers unjustly neglected by the majority.

Yet in the world of letters, as Watts-Dunton would laughingly remark, no one reminded him of the sea more forcibly than that breezy and briny old " Corsair," Edward John Trelawney.   He knew him intimately in his old age, at the time he was living at Pelham

Crescent, and his estimate of him coincided with that of Severn—" an odd fish, glowing and rich in romance, who went mad on reading Byron's *Corsair*."

And yet " no one could fail, however, to admire his agility of limb and brain," Watts-Dunton would admit. " But, compared with Borrow, who was close upon seventy years of age when I first met him—why, Borrow could have walked off with Trelawney under his arm." He once summed up Trelawney's personality in two words—" an opinionated, vain man, who lived on his reputation as the finder of Shelley's body on the shore in the Bay of Spezia ! " And then he would relate, as an illustration of the " Corsair's " marvellous vitality, how, when Swinburne and he one day called upon him in his eightieth year, Trelawney was still so violent, not to say obstreperous, that he got into a heated discussion upon some subject connected with Shelley, and thumped the table with such energy that Watts-Dunton began to fear the consequences not only to the furniture and himself, but to his house-mate as well.

The visitors at The Pines, in fact, whom Watts-Dunton and Swinburne entertained, came not merely from all parts of Great Britain, but from all parts of the world—India, Canada, Australia, China, and Japan. Some letters from strangers humbly asking permission to step within the precincts of the far-famed house on Putney Hill could not be read without a smile. Both Watts-Dunton and his house-mate had endless appeals for some recognition to which it was impossible to send any response.

The influence of the *Athenæum*, it need scarcely be observed, has always been considerable : never was it greater, not only in England but in America and on the Continent, during the twenty-five years when Watts-Dunton was one of its leading critics. Although his contributions were called " reviews," they were regarded more as literary essays that expressed generalizations upon life. Many a writer of the present day has acknowledged his indebtedness to Watts - Dunton's articles, looking out eagerly on his student days each week for a fresh number of the journal. His work began to have some influence on literature even in the *Examiner* days, as Minto observed, and its influence would have been greater still had he published a volume of selections while his essays were attracting wide attention.

Watts-Dunton's success as a writer in the *Examiner*, followed by a still greater success in the *Athenæum*, had naturally led to a desire on every side to win his friendship. And it was not merely on account of his power as a critic : it was only necessary to meet him once in order to discover that he had that indefinable, yet unmistakable gift of personality quite apart from the fact of his being a man of intellect and culture.

" *Aylwin*," he has said, " brought me many friends." But surely they had " arrived," and by the score, years before *Aylwin* was published.

There is no better proof to be found than in his first

letter from Robert Browning, that Watts-Dunton's work on the *Athenæum* was widely recognized at an early period of his connection with that journal. It is dated December 1, 1882, from 19 Warwick Crescent, W.

" MY DEAR MR. WATTS,

" First of all, I ' remember your name ' exceedingly well, and am duly bound to it both for verse and prose to which it has been attached ; and yourself I remember quite as pleasantly, pray be assured !

" Mrs. Proctor is removed to Albert Mansions (I think the huge red building beside the Albert Hall is so styled), at No. 2 of those Mansions, and No. 19 within it.

" Yours very truly,

" ROBERT BROWNING."

The lady referred to in Browning's letter to Watts-Dunton—so famous in mid-Victorian society—Anne B. Proctor, was one whom Watts-Dunton always spoke of as among the most cultured and charming of women. She was an enthusiastic admirer of Rossetti's pictures, and on one memorable occasion, not long before the poet-painter's death, she went with Watts-Dunton to the studio at Cheyne Walk. She told him at the time that it was at Robert Browning's house in Wimpole Street that she first saw a painting of Rossetti's, and that from that time the sight of his masterpieces had formed for her a " gallery of thoughts."

Although Watts-Dunton was but slightly acquainted with Browning in 1882, they subsequently became intimate. But Watts-Dunton was always more in the way of meeting the author of *The Ring and the Book* at literary gatherings than in private life. He wrote some half-dozen critiques in the *Athenæum* on Browning's volumes as they appeared between 1878 and 1894, among which may be mentioned *La Saisiaz* and *Ferishtah's Fancies*.

While writing an essay on the latter volume in the *Athenæum*, certain eccentricities in it, for some reason or another, irritated Watts-Dunton, and he expressed his irritation in his critique something " very like chaff " —to use his own words.* Swinburne, a great admirer of Browning, chided him for it, and he felt that his friend's reproof was right.

" The poems in this volume "—to quote from this article on *Ferishtah's Fancies*—" can only be described as parable-poems, not in the sense that they are capable of being read as parables (as is said to be the case with the *Rubáiyát* of Omar Khayyám), but parable-poems in the sense that they must be read as parables, or they show no artistic *raison d'être* at all. Nor do our English poets know what it is to write a parable-poem. It is to set self-conscious philosophy singing and dancing, like a young Gretry, to the tune of a waterfall. Or rather, it is to imprison the soul of Dinah Morris in the lissome body of Esmeralda, and set the preacher strumming a gypsy's tambourine. Though in the pure

* *Vide* Appendix.

parable the intellectual or ethical motive does not dominate so absolutely as in the case of the pure fable the
form that expresses it, yet it does, nevertheless, so far
govern the form as to interfere with that entire abandon
—that emotional freedom—which seems necessary to the
very existence of song. Indeed, if poetry must, like
Wordsworth's ideal John Bull, ' be free or die ; ' if
she must know no law but that of her own being (as
the doctrine of 'L'art pour l'art' declares) ; if she must
not even seem to know that (as the doctrine of bardic
inspiration implies), but must bend to it apparently in
tricksy sport alone, how can she—' the singing maid
with pictures in her eyes '—mount the pulpit, read the
text, and deliver the sermon ? . . . To sing a real
parable and make it a real song requires a genius of a
very special and peculiar, if somewhat narrow order—
a genius rare, delicate, ethereal, such as can, according
to a certain Oriental fancy, compete with Angels of the
Water-pot in floriculture. Mr. Browning, being so
fond of Oriental fancies, and being, moreover, on terms
of the closest intimacy with a certain fancy-weaving
Ferishtah, must be quite familiar with the story—how,
when the earth was without flowers, men dreamed of
nothing more beautiful than cabbages." Watts-Dunton
then goes on in the review to relate the Persian tale of
Poetry and Cabbages, and tells how the " Angel of the
Water-pot " made flowers.

On the afternoon following the appearance of the
article he was at the Royal Academy private view, when

Lowell came up to him and at once began talking about the review. Lowell, he found, was delighted with it. " But," said he, " you're a brave man to be here, where Browning always comes." Then, looking round the room, he said : " Why, there he is, with his sister, immediately on the side opposite to us. Surely you will slip away, and avoid a meeting."

" Slip away," said Watts-Dunton, " to avoid Browning ! You don't know him as well as I do after all ! Now let me tell you what will occur if we stand here for a minute or two. Miss Browning, whose eyes are looking busily over the room, for people that Browning ought to speak to, in a moment will see you, and in another moment she will see me."

No sooner had he uttered these words than, as Watts-Dunton had predicted, Miss Browning did spot first Lowell and then Watts-Dunton. She turned and whispered in Browning's ear, and Browning came straight across the room to them, and this is what he said, speaking to Watts-Dunton before he spoke to Lowell—a thing which on any other occasion he would scarcely have done.

" Now," said he, " you're not going to put me off with generalities any longer. You promised to write and tell me when you could come to luncheon. You have never done so—you will never do so, unless I fix you with a distinct day. Will you come to-morrow ? "

" I shall be delighted," said Watts-Dunton.

Browning then turned to Lowell, and exchanged a few friendly words with him.

After Browning and Miss Browning had left them, Lowell said, " Well, this is wonderful. How do you explain it ? "

" By Browning's greatness of soul and heart," said Watts-Dunton. " He wishes to make it quite apparent that he feels no anger towards a man who says what he thinks about a poem."

Among the miscellaneous poems in *The Coming of Love*, the sonnet, *To Britain and America, on the Death of James Russell Lowell*, he has left a tribute to the memory of his famous friend, ending with these eloquent lines :—

> " Keep Love's bright sails afloat,
> For Lowell's sake, where once ye strove and smote
> On waves that must unite, not part, your strands."

Discussing Browning with a friend, Watts-Dunton would deplore the emphasis laid in certain directions upon the poet's optimism. " There is no philosophic basis to his optimism," he would complain. " With him it was merely temperamental bias, interesting, doubtless, as a phase in his character, but carrying with it no significance for others. There is something ridiculous about the solemn way in which it is paraded by some of the poet's admirers. Browning makes no serious attempt to defend it. He merely dogmatizes with the cheerful assurance of—" he hesitated for a word.

" —Of a man with a fortunate blood supply," suggested the friend.

" Exactly," chimed in the critic. " That's just it. ' All's right with the world ' just because *I* feel that way. . . ."

" Then you would not call Browning a deep thinker ? "

" Not in the least. An acute dialectician, if you like, with a happy knack of dramatizing different points of view, but no depth of thought. And in his conversation you found no trace even of the acuteness which he assuredly does show in his poetry. I had many chats with Browning, and what struck me most was his *bourgeois* point of view. Tennyson, mind, now, was really profound."

" Yet there is little profundity in his poetry," objected the friend.

" Little acuteness, perhaps ; but he sees more into the heart of things than Browning did. He was a true mystic."

Yet it must not be supposed that Watts-Dunton did not admire Browning's poetry. He deprecated the position into which Browning was forced by Browning Societies as a teacher and thinker, but declared that he thought more highly of some of his work than many professing admirers did. " At his best," he once declared, " when Browning forgets to probe and analyze, he is a supremely great poet. *Meeting at Night* and *Parting at Morning* are magnificent in their romantic realism. As a love poet he is in the very first flight."

He would then declaim *Meeting at Night* and *Parting at Morning* in his lyrically sympathetic voice. At the characteristic lines—

> " . . . the quick sharp scratch
> And the blue spurt of a lighted match "—

he threw back his head, a favourite gesture when particularly interested. " There ! Just see how this intimate and familiar touch of realism heightens the beauty and force of the lyric. Browning's love poetry abounds in these familiar touches that lesser poets would shrink from as impairing the artistic effect of the poem. Browning knew better ; and in boldly using these touches raises the emotional intensity of his poems of passion."

XVII.

MID-VICTORIAN FRIENDSHIPS.—II.

XVII.

Mid-Victorian Friendships (II.)—Christina Rossetti.

THE essay in the *Nineteenth Century* (February 1, 1895), in which Watts-Dunton penned his sketchy *Reminiscences of Christina Rossetti*, was admittedly intended by him to form the nucleus for a biography of the poetess. This was further expanded into a fragmentary study,* which contains some characteristic touches besides the description of the only sunrise Christina Rossetti ever witnessed :—

" I was in the habit of talking about the attractions of Wimbledon Common, which in the early morning was left to the birds and the rabbits to a degree that could scarcely be imagined by people unfamiliar with it. I knew from previous conversations that Christina had never seen the sun rise ; and I believe that it is a phenomenon not commonly observed by poets, and that this is why it so commonly occurs that a poet's description of the cloud pageantry of a sunrise is evidently borrowed from his recollections of the sunsets he

* Hitherto unpublished.

has seen. No doubt, as I said to Christina, the two
are alike in many ways, and yet in many ways are extremely different. Upon a certain occasion she made
up her mind·that a sunrise she would see, and one morning we went out just as the chilly but bewitching shiver
of the dawn breeze began to move, and the eastern sky
began slowly to grow grey. Early as it was, however,
many of the birds were awake, and waiting to see what
we went out to see, as we knew by twitter after twitter
coming from the hedgerows. Christina was not much
interested at first ; but when the grey became slowly
changed into a kind of apple-green crossed by bars of
lilac, and then by bars of pink and gold, and finally,
when the sun rose behind a tall clump of slender elms,
so close together that they looked like one enormous
tree whose foliage was sufficiently thin to allow the
sunbeams to pour through it as through a glittering
lacework of dewy leaves, she confessed that no sunset
could surpass it. And when the sun, growing brighter
still and falling upon the silver sheet of mist in which ·
the cows were lying, turned it into a sheet of gold, and
made each brown patch on each cow's coat gleam like
burnished copper—then she admitted that a sunrise
surpassed a sunset, and was worth getting up to see.
She stood and looked at it, and her lips moved, but in
a whisper that I could not hear. Yet so powerful is
the force of habit, that I greatly doubt whether Christina ever took the trouble to see another sunrise.

" It was my privilege to be thrown much into contact with Christina Rossetti, not only in London and Chelsea, but at Kelmscott Manor, at Aldwick Lodge, Bognor, at Hunter's Forestall near Herne Bay, and at Birchington-on-Sea, where her brother Gabriel died. This being well known, I was immediately after her death urged in several quarters to write upon her, and the result was that I did write some reminiscences of her in the *Nineteenth Century*, and two or three articles upon her in the *Athenæum*.

" Necessarily these were hastily composed, inadequate in expression, and indeed inadequate in everything, and I would willingly have let them remain with the mass of uncollected articles of mine which have been appearing for a quarter of a century, ungathered from the pages where they appeared, but always available to those who may think them worth the trouble of looking them up.

" This is not to be, however. Christina Rossetti, her life and her work, are a subject of such passionate interest to a widening circle of readers, that to refuse any longer to bring out these essays in book form is, I feel, ungracious.

" My first idea was, especially as I am in the midst of work of a different kind altogether, to reprint these essays exactly as they appeared. But on re-reading them, I found that as in parts they overran each other, I could give a more vigorous picture of the poet by blending them and dividing the result into chapters.

" All the indulgence I ask of the reader is that he

will not misunderstand the *raison d'être* of a brochure of this kind. The book is exactly what its name implies. It is a group of hurried glimpses rendered by one who knew her well. It is neither a life of her nor a full study of her. I do not, however, say this by way of apologizing for the existence of the little book. For to say the truth, I have but little faith in the biographer of poets save those which they wrote themselves in their own poems. In Rossetti's case, who shall paint his portrait so truly, so vividly, as he has painted it in *The House of Life*, in *The Blessed Damozel*, in *Rose Mary*, in *Dante's Dream*, in *Pandora*, in *Proserpine*, and in many another wonderful poem and wonderful picture ? We verily believe, of all the characters that have appeared in recent times, Rossetti's was the most difficult to be adequately treated in a biography, however conscientious and exhaustive. It is not merely that the genius to be grasped was most rare, most subtle, most original, but the character to be painted was so indefinable, so complex, and even so self-contradictory, that the biographer who should give a portrait of him would be hard to discover.

" It was during Rossetti's illnesses that I was brought into closest relation with Christina and her mother. And I could fill a volume, and the book, on account of its subject-matter, would be one of the loveliest things in literature of reminiscences of these two in their relations to Gabriel and his illnesses. Yet I would not have touched upon these illnesses, not even to bring on the beauty of these relations, were I not driven to do so—driven, I mean, by the publicity that has been given to them already.

" While I ·am writing these lines a friend reminds me, with a sad smile, of certain words I wrote in a letter from Birchington on the day of Rossetti's funeral.

" All the disastrous chloral episode will now be sacred in the breasts of those who loved him.

" Sacred, indeed ! Why, in twenty-four hours the story of Rossetti and his drug was in every newspaper, and I was obliged to make reference to it in my obituary notice of him in the *Athenæum* in order to contradict certain wild versions of the story that were floating about.

" What a fantastic fate for him whose hatred of the tyranny of the Press was as great as Tennyson's ; so great that he never looked into a newspaper.

" It was through Rossetti's illnesses that the friendship of such a woman was given to me, at a time when her reclusiveness (even before the death of her sister Maria, upon whom she leaned) shut her in and away from so many people, more worthy, in a certain sense, of that friendship than I—people, I mean, who, by virtue of an entire sympathy with her in matters of special creed, might be supposed to touch her more nearly and dearly.

" A rare devotion to her brother, my friend, was the golden chain that enlinked so noble a soul to mine.

" It is now matter of only too familiar knowledge

that the curse of Rossetti's life was an insomnia, the origin of which is very obscure. It grew upon him year by year ; and in a fatal moment in the early spring of 1870 a friend, with the best intentions, suggested chloral, a comparatively new drug then, as a remedy. Being of a self-indulgent and impatient nature, Rossetti increased the doses of his drug as the power of the insomnia increased. And so far from the effects of chloral being harmless, as was then generally supposed, the mischief it insidiously works on the nervous system is appalling. No one who has not witnessed the agonies of a victim of insomnia can realize how irresistible is his yearning for chloral after he has once tasted the sweets of that fatal nepenthe. Periodical illnesses were the result of Rossetti's indulgence in the drug ; and it was when these illnesses took a particularly serious turn that Christina and her mother used to go to Cheyne Walk in order to relieve his few friends, as far as possible, from the anxiety and strain these illnesses caused. This it was that drew us so closely together, and no words of mine could convey to the reader the effect of having those two ladies moving about the house—a very dark house. They seemed to shed a new kind of light in every room and passage.

" On these occasions the only exercise that Christina took was a stroll around the great square garden which at that time spread out at the back of the two houses on each side of No. 16—the garden around which Rossetti himself (after he had ceased to go abroad at all) used to tramp every afternoon at the rate of five miles an hour. It was here that Gabriel's purchases from Jamrach's had used to dwell.

" Christina gave us great credit for the garden. She had no idea, she said, how beautiful fig trees looked when allowed to grow wild at their own sweet will. The jessamine, the roses and the marigolds mingled themselves with the thistles, Solomon's seals, daisies, blue irises, and rhubarb in æsthetic designs of Nature's own. The mulberry and cherry tree used to be a great joy to her.

" It was from her mother that Christina inherited that beautiful form of the Christian sentiment of which Maria knew but little, but which endeared Christina to so many who never knew her save through her work, but between whom and herself there was a bond of sympathy so sacred and so deep as to be something like a religion, making, indeed, the name of Christina Rossetti seem to throw upon every page where it appeared a blush of light as rare as the shadow of Israfeel's wing in the Arabian story. For if in the arena called the literary world, and in that other world where poetry is its own exceeding great reward, Christina was an acknowledged queen, she had other readers to whom she was much more than this—readers who, drawing the deepest delight from such poetry as specially appeals to them, never read any other, and have but small knowledge of poetry as a fine art ; readers who feel that at every page of her writing the beautiful poetry is only the outcome of a life whose unexampled beauty fascinates them.

" Although Christina Rossetti had more of what is called the unconsciousness of poetic inspiration than any other poet since Blake, whom in so many things she resembled, the writing of poetry was not by any means the chief business of her life. Not that she was indifferent about the prosperity of her verses among her readers. Yet no one felt so deeply as she that as the notes of the nightingale are but the involuntary expression of the bird's emotion, and again, as the perfume of the violet is but the flower's natural breath, so it is and must be with the song of the very poet, and that, therefore, to write beautifully is in a deep and true sense to live beautifully according to the sanctions of one's own creed, whatever that creed may be. Hence the nobility of temper exhibited by every line she has left us, for assuredly without nobility of temper no great literature was ever born.

" And especially may this be said of poetry, as she one day said to me.

" The language of all true poetry is what Gregory the Nazianzen calls ' the rhetoric of our lives,' and when M. de Pressensé, speaking of the Apostolic Fathers, said that they were ' not great writers but great characters,' he forgot, as I have on a former occasion endeavoured to show, that in the utterances of a great character there is a certain quality of greatness which is the very salt of literature— a salt which not the highest intellectual powers can give.

" And if in Christina's writings we see at its best what Christianity is as the motive power of poetry, her mother was to her, and, indeed, to all who knew her, the sweet embodiment of that power.

" The Christian idea is essentially feminine, and of this feminine quality Christina Rossetti's poetry is full. In motive power the difference between classic and Christian poetry must needs be very great. I am not one of those who think that modern poetry can hold its own against the poetry of Greece. But whatever may be said in favour of one as against the other, this at least cannot be controverted—that the history of literature shows no human development so beautiful as the ideal Christian woman of our own day, and the Christian idea is essentially feminine.

" Men of science tell us that among all the fossilized plants they find none of the lovely family of the rose ; and in the same way we should search in vain through the entire human record for anything so beautiful as that kind of Christian lady of whom Mrs. Rossetti was the type and her daughters two different kinds of ex-emplars—the Christian lady to whom self-abnegation is not only the first of duties but the first of joys.

" Nor is this all. The beautiful ' old-style courtesy ' which was so noticeable in Christina, and which has been so often commented upon—had not this also much to do with the Christianity that governed her life ?

" A religious system the heart-thought of which is self-abnegation—self-abnegation not as a means of self-

culture (as with the Stoics), not as a means of reaching
Nirvana (as with the Buddhists), but as a means towards
the ideal and universal benevolence which Christ taught
—how could it fail to surpass all other systems in beauty,
and especially in that quality of poetic courtesy which
in men goes to the fostering of such heroes as Sidney
and Bayard, and in women such characters as Christina
Rossetti and her mother ?

" For who has given us a definition of courtesy
which must last, one would think, as long as courtesy
itself lasts ?   It is he of whom Christina often talked—
St. Francis of Assisi : ' Know thou that courtesy is one
of God's own properties, who sendeth His rain and His
sunshine upon the just and upon the unjust, out of His
great courtesy.   And verily Courtesy is the sister of
Charity, who banishes hatred and cherishes love.'   Yet,
no doubt, the Christian idea must needs be more or
less flavoured by each personality through which it is
expressed.   The teaching of Scripture, and also, indeed,
the teaching of Nature and of man's life, is by symbol,
and depends, and must depend, upon the mind and the
temperament of him who reads.   And it is the expression of individuality breaking through ' the nets of
dogma,' yet partly conditioned by dogma, which gives
vitality—which alone *can* give vitality—to any religious
poetry.

" Powerful as is dogma over the instinctive expression of each individual soul, it is not omnipotent.   The
action of environment upon original character and of

character upon environment, comprehending as it does the entire human drama, is not to be quelled by systems, or dogmas, or schools. Hence the special interest of the study of devotional literature lies in observing in the case of each writer what kind of intellectual and emotional product is the result of the same creed, the same Scripture, acting upon various kinds of temperaments and natural characters.

" Christina Rossetti was much more conscious of this than was her sister Maria. There was no human saying that gave her so much pleasure as a beautiful saying of Origen about the countenance of Christ which I introduced to her—the passage, I mean, where, alluding to the well-known passage in the Apocrypha, *Wisdom* xvi. 20, 21, where the mystic virtues of manna are described, he says, ' Christ appeared to each according as he was worthy . . . like as it is written of manna when God sent bread from heaven to the children of Israel, which adapted itself to every taste.'

" With regard to Christina Rossetti, while upon herself Christian dogma imposed infinite obligations—obligations which could never be evaded by her without the risk of all the penalties fulminated by all believers —there was, in the order of things, a sort of ether of universal charity for all others. She would lament, of course, the lapses of every soul ; but for these there was a forgiveness which her own lapses could never claim. There was, to be sure, a sweet egotism in this. It was very fascinating, however.

" And was there not also an egotism of another kind in the saner serenity of Manes' system—an egotism which, perhaps, is not so fascinating ?

" No one, I think, could spend an hour in friendly converse with Christina Rossetti and her mother without feeling his moral nature braced up, so to speak, by a spiritual tonic. And this simply arose from the fact that while she seemed to breathe a sainthood that must needs express itself in poetry, all the charm of the mere woman remained in her—remained, and coloured her life with those riches of earth without which woman may be worshipped, but never loved as Christina Rossetti was loved by us all."

" My First Meeting with Christina.

" How well I remember my first introduction to Mrs. Rossetti and Christina !

" Not long after my friendship with Gabriel had ripened into intimacy, I was staying with him at Kelmscott Manor. One afternoon at Kelmscott he said to me, while we paused in the meadow to see with what gusto the poet of *The Earthly Paradise* could kill the Thames bream, ' The time has now come for you to know *all* my family—my mother and my sisters, I mean. You are the only man, I think, who saw on first meeting him what a good and lovable fellow William is underneath, and I know that you and my mother and sisters must get on together well.'

" Maria I had already met ; but I rather shrank from meeting Christina, and need I say why ?

" Many important people had I met in my somewhat various walks through the world, from the proud magnates who flourish in what we call society, to the still prouder magnates among the Romanies to whom Borrow introduced me at Wandsworth and elsewhere. I cannot say that any one of them abashed me much. I shrank somewhat, however, from the idea of meeting Christina Rossetti.

" Of all contemporary poets, she had seemed to me the most indubitably inspired. I had made a lifelong study of poetic art, yet Christina's art-secret had baffled me. Her very uncertainty of touch, as regarded execution, seemed somehow to add to the impression she made upon me of inspiration. She never made up her mind that she would write something, and then proceeded to write it. She always wrote just as the impulse and the form of expression came to her, and if these did not come, she wrote not at all. But it was not her inspiration which overawed me at the idea of meeting her. It was the feeling that her inspiration was not that of the artist at all, and not that of such dramatic passion as in other poets I had been accustomed to, but the inspiration of the religious devotee. It answered a chord within me, but a chord that no poet had theretofore touched. It seemed to me to come from a power which my soul remembered in some ante-natal existence, and had not even yet wholly forgotten. As to meeting Christina as an earthly woman, that had never till now occurred to me as a possibility, notwithstanding my relations with Gabriel.

" On the third or fourth day after the return to Cheyne Walk, having let myself in the house with my latchkey, I opened the studio door without dreaming that any one besides Gabriel was there. This was during the time that he saw no one but myself, his family, Madox Brown, Shields, and another or two. The canvases, pictures, and easels, of which the studio was full, were always so thickly scattered round about the doorway that one could hear the voices of those who were conversing before either seeing their faces or being seen oneself. I heard a voice, precise, formal, yet as sweet as a silver bell, say,—

" ' Yes, Gabriel, they are the loveliest apple-blossoms I have ever seen in a picture—quite perfect.'

" There was a something in the tone of the voice that banished all my awe of the saint, and I entered the room.

" I have not space, if I had the time, to describe here the mother and daughter. And yet, what a lovely picture of all that is sweetest in the gentle life of a Christian country they made, as they sat looking at Gabriel at work before his easel !

" After he had introduced me, he said, ' I want you to tell me what you think of these apple-blossoms.'

" ' My opinion is superfluous,' I said, ' for I heard as I entered the studio how they were characterized by the writer of *An Apple Gathering.*' I then repeated the most perfect parable-poem in the English language.

" ' But do you quite agree with what I said about these blossoms ? ' asked Christina. ' Remember that I am an ignorant Londoner, with an ill-educated eye, even for familiar apple-blossoms, while you are——'

" ' A yokel of the East Midlands,' 1 said, ' who has been surrounded by apple-blossoms and pear-blossoms, and all other blossoms from childhood. As you are so very kind, however, I will venture to say that the single little cluster of blossoms on the left side of the figure is just a little too white—wants more pink. And besides,' I said, turning to Gabriel, ' is not the shape of those petals—— ? ' '

" ' Just a little like those of pear-blossom ? ' said Christina, with a laugh.

" Whether it turned out that the bunch of bloom under discussion was bloom of pear meant for apple I do not remember. But I do remember saying to myself, ' A very saint, no doubt, but a playful one.'

" At this point Gabriel insisted on her reciting certain lines that she had written upon the wombat, in which she implored the pet not on any account to indulge in that habit of burrowing to which he was given, and not to turn up on the other side of the globe—lines which ran thus :—

"'O Uommibatte
 Agil, giocondo,
 Che ti sei fatto
 Liscio e rotondo!'

Christina here laughingly insisted on her brother giving an improved reading of this last line, occasioned by the wombat having proved a rough customer :—

"'Irsuto e tondo.

"'Deh non fuggire
 Qual vagabondo,
 Non disparire
 Forando il mondo.
 Pesa davvero
 D' un emisfero
 Non lieve il pondo.'

"Before the ladies left the house that day I had struck up a friendship with them which was one of the most beautiful influences of my life—a life which has since then been, I must think, unusually rich in such beautiful influences. And when they were invited to Cheyne Walk I was generally invited to meet them.

"The readers of Christina's poems need not be told that her leaning towards the allegorical view of nature and human life were, even at a time when allegory had taken for a time a place in poetic art such as would have astonished writers like Wordsworth, Scott, and Byron, a striking and distinguishing characteristic of her poetry. Yet while her poetical work may be described as being all symbolical, she was not much given to read symbols into the everyday incidents of life.

" All that is noblest in Christina's poetry—an ever-present sense of the beauty and power of goodness—must surely have come from the mother, from whom also came that other charm of Christina's, to which Gabriel was peculiarly sensitive—her youthfulness of temperament ; a youthfulness that showed itself underneath a certain rigidity of style in a remarkable way.

" Christina—as all who studied her character and can understand her reverential nature could not fail to discover—lived solely for the service of God and for the love of her art. She was the impassioned lyrical poet with the devout temperament of a nun."

As a sign of her religious tendency, the following, written to Watts-Dunton, November 22, 1886, is a touching example :—

" All I am doing is reading and thinking over part of the New Testament, writing down what I can as I go along. I work at prose, and help myself forward with little bits of verse. What I am doing is (I hope) not for my own profit, nor do I in the least know that it will ever become an available ' book.' At present, as you may divine, I am not likely to draw much upon the simply imaginative."

In her later years, growing each day more feeble in health, she led a semi-cloistral life in her peaceful house in Bloomsbury, where she died, December 29, 1894.

Swinburne's verses to her at the time of her death, on New Year's Day, 1895, are a superb tribute to her memory :—

"A soul more sweet than the morning of new-born May
Has passed with the year that has passed from the world away,
A song more sweet than the morning's firstborn song
Again will hymn not among us a new year's day."

"It was while staying at Bognor that I had the best opportunity of observing the kindred traits and sympathies that enlinked together Christina Rossetti and her brother.

"It was here that I first had an opportunity of observing that strange kind of sympathy between Christina Rossetti and the lower animals, especially birds, and it was in this attitude towards the lower animals that was most strongly seen between brother and sister. Christina had not been at Bognor more than twenty-four hours when the birds, especially the robins and blackbirds, seemed to know her. She said she would coax the birds to join the festival, and so she did. When she fed them, they approached the open window much nearer than they ventured to come when I fed them. One robin, after the morning meal, used to sing to her, and when she left us she sang no more.

"And here I cannot help recalling a pathetic incident which occurred at her funeral, where the only two intimate friends who (besides her brother and his children) followed the coffin in the mourning coaches were Miss Lisa Wilson and myself. Just before the coffin was lowered the golden rays of the winter sun fell upon it, and that moment there leapt from a tree beside the grave the joyful song of a bird that the sudden sunshine had reminded of summer, and to me it seemed the voice of that Christmas robin who had greeted her with his song in 1875."

The sonnets, *Two Christmastides*, that Watts-Dunton wrote at the time of her decease, may be appropriately given here as an additional page in this unfinished sketch of Christina Rossetti's poetic gift and singular personality.*

> " On Winter's woof, which scarcely seems of snow,
>   But hangs translucent, like a virgin's veil,
>   O'er headstone, monument, and guardian-rail,
> The New Year's sun shines golden—seems to throw
> Upon her coffin-flowers a greeting glow
>   From lands she loved to think on—seems to trail
>   Love's holy radiance from the very Grail
> O'er those white flowers before they sink below.
> Is that a spirit or bird whose sudden song
>   From yonder sunlit tree beside the grave
> Recalls a robin's warble, sweet yet strong,
>   Upon a lawn beloved of wind and wave—
>   Recalls her ' Christmas Robin,' ruddy, brave,
> Winning the crumbs she throws where blackbirds throng?"

>   *   *   *   *   *

> " In Christmastide of heaven does *she* recall
>   Those happy days with Gabriel by the sea,
>   Who gathered round him those he loved, when she
> ' Must coax the birds to join the festival,'
> And said, ' The sea-sweet winds are musical
>   With carols from the billows singing free
>   Around the groynes, and every shrub and tree

---

* Vide *The Coming of Love.* (John Lane, 1897.)

Seems conscious of the Channel's rise and fall ' ?
The coffin lowers, and I can see her now—
    See the loved kindred standing by her side,
As once I saw them 'neath our Christmas bough—
    And her, that dearer one, who sanctified
    With halo of mother's love our Christmastide—
And Gabriel too—with peace upon his brow."

XVIII.

MID-VICTORIAN FRIENDSHIPS.—III.

XVIII.

MID-VICTORIAN FRIENDSHIPS (III.)—TENNYSON.

IT has been well said by a modern critic * that " whatever we may think about the Victorian Age, from its literature at least we should conclude that it was an age when men valued friendship." Did they not write critiques about each other, and dedicate their volumes of poems to each other, and when one of them died was not some tribute to his memory sure to find utterance, usually in the form of a sonnet ? Who has not read these tributes in Swinburne's works—in Rossetti's ? Nor did they fail to remember each other's birthdays. Watts-Dunton's *Birthday Sonnets* to Meredith, and also to Tennyson, were fully appreciated. When the sonnet on Tennyson's eighty-second birthday appeared, the poet's son expressed to Watts-Dunton his father's thanks for the poem, adding, moreover, that he was proud to have seen it in the *Athenæum*.

Watts-Dunton's articles in the *Athenæum* had attracted Tennyson from the first, yet it was not until the Laureate was seventy-three years of age (1883) that he and his admirer met by chance at a garden party.

* Mr. R. A. Scott-James.

At Aldworth, near Haslemere in Surrey, where, as Tennyson told his friends, he "had passed his happiest days," Watts-Dunton went on frequent visits. He always spoke of Tennyson's picturesque Gothic mansion with enthusiasm as an ideal residence for a poet, overlooking, as every tourist knows—especially the American tourist—a lovely valley, far away on Blackdown Heath.

It was generally for the week-end that Watts-Dunton went to stay there, and on one occasion—in July 1884—he was invited to Aldworth expressly to meet that once enormously popular verse writer, Lewis Morris.

The prospect from the terrace at Aldworth is one of the finest to be met with in the county. Tennyson, who lived at this summer home for more than twenty years, has described the scene in all its autumn loveliness :—

> " Our birches yellowing and from each
>   The light leaf falling fast,
> While squirrels from our fiery beech
>   Were bearing off the mast,
> You came, and looked, and loved the view
>   Long known and loved by me,
> Green Sussex fading into blue,
>   With one gray glimpse of sea."

In one of the shady little bowers in the grounds at Aldworth, Watts-Dunton's pathetic essay on little children, called *The New Hero,** was read aloud to Tennyson, the proof sheets having been forwarded to the

* *The English Illustrated Magazine,* December 1883.

writer while there on one of his visits. This essay contains two sonnets, one of them being rich in sibilants. Tennyson disliked especially what he was fond of calling the " hissing line," and after ridding a line of its sibilants, he would often speak jocularly of " kicking the geese out of the boat." On this occasion he challenged one of the lines :—

" And scents of flowers and shadow of wavering trees."

Tennyson declared that although " scents " might be more accurate than " scent," this was a case where " the claims of music ought to be dominant over other claims." Watts-Dunton, after giving consideration to Tennyson's criticism, adopted " scent " in place of " scents."

Tennyson, occasionally, at Aldworth took Watts-Dunton into one of those leafy summer-houses and read *Becket* to him while this poetic play was still in proof.* The whole morning was occupied in the reading. The remarks upon poetic and dramatic art that came from the Poet Laureate would, as Watts-Dunton affirmed, " have made the fortune of any critic."

On another occasion Watts-Dunton spoke to the Laureate about the *Lotus Eaters*, a poem for which he had the warmest admiration. " I have been expatiating to some of my friends," he said, " on the

* *Becket* was published in 1884. Two years later (July 1886) scenes from *Becket* were given at the Open Air Plays, in wooded grounds at Coombe, and Tennyson was among the audience.

extreme felicity of your repetition of the word 'land' in the opening stanza :—

> " ' " Courage," he said, and pointed toward the land ;
> " This mounting wave will wave us shoreward soon."
> In the afternoon they came unto a *land*
> In which it seemed always afternoon.' "

Tennyson nodded. " Didn't it strike you as a bit lame ? "

" Certainly not," said the critic emphatically. " I felt that a second-rate poet would not have dared to repeat the word in the third line ; he would have written ' strand,' or some word that rhymed to land . . . but he would certainly shrink from repeating ' land.' "

" Then you think the repetition effective ? "

" Extremely so. The deliberate repetition there is infinitely more effective than a rhyming synonym. In fact, to me it seems just one of those points that differentiate a poet of the front rank from a second-rate verse writer."

Tennyson grunted, and then burst into one of his hearty guttural laughs. " Very gratifying what you say, 'pon my word, for to tell you the truth—the use of the repetition was quite accidental—*I never knew I had repeated it !* "

This frank avowal appealed to Watts-Dunton's sense of humour, and he would quote it against himself with much relish. " That's an illustration of how the enthusiastic critic sometimes overreaches himself ! "

It was shortly before Tennyson's death that the editor of the *Magazine of Art* invited Watts-Dunton to write an article upon the portraits of Tennyson. Two articles were written, and a special value is attached to them, inasmuch as Watts-Dunton had the advantage of consulting the poet upon the project, and succeeded in obtaining his aid in making the selection. Tennyson died, however, before these articles appeared. In speaking of the portrait painted by G. F. Watts (in 1859), Watts-Dunton says: " There is a mystery about it, a certain dreaminess which suggests the poetic glamour of moonlight." And in his mention of the Mayall photograph, he remarks : " The further any portrait departs from that type, the further it departs from the truth. Therein ' Nature's idea ' in Tennyson's face must be sought."

Shortly after Tennyson's death Watts-Dunton wrote the *Aspects of Tennyson* in the *Nineteenth Century*, in two articles—one principally reminiscent, describing the poet and the man, and the other, in which he speaks of him as a nature-poet, has a special interest on account of its reference to evolution.

" It was," he says, " the ignorance of Nature, in the naturalist's sense, displayed by many poets that caused Darwin, a man of rare imagination and of true poetic instinct, to turn away from poetry ; for, of course, no poet, in Darwin's view, could have real knowledge of Nature who was ignorant of the new cosmogony of growth. To the poet who believes, and rightly believes, as Wordsworth did, that ' every flower enjoys the air it breathes,' a flower is a fascinating object, to be sure ; but what is it to the poet who, thanks to the revelations of the naturalist, can spend an entire morning over a single blossom, as the poet of the future will do, tracing its ancestry step by step, while the surrounding floras and faunas pass before his imagination, lapping his soul in a poetic dream such as was withheld from all English poets before Tennyson ? " *

He wrote various notices in the *Athenæum* of Tennyson's poetic volumes as they appeared, the one on *The Lover's Tale* being the first published, early in 1879. Among other reviews of Tennyson in this journal may be mentioned those on *Ballads and Other Poems* in 1880, *Locksley Hall* in 1887, and *The Foresters* in 1892, a few months before the Laureate's death.

His poems to the Laureate, those which he named *Tributes to Tennyson*, consist of four sonnets that appeared in the *Athenæum*. The first sonnet is one having reference to the publication of *Ballads and Other Poems*, when Tennyson was in his seventy-first year, " the most richly various volume of English verse,"

---

* Watts-Dunton regarded a flower as an object in nature so fascinating, and, as he expressed it, so " dreamily conscious of life," that he never approved of " cut flowers." He loved to see them " enjoying the air they breathe," as he would often remark when glancing meditatively at a vase of flowers on a dinner table

to quote Watts-Dunton's own words, " that has appeared in his own country." This sonnet opens with the lines :—

> " Beyond the peaks of Kàf a rivulet springs,
> Whose magic waters to a flood expand,
> Distilling, for all drinkers on each hand,
> The immortal sweets enveiled in mortal things." *

The next sonnet he wrote upon Tennyson was on the occasion of his eightieth birthday, and is dated from " Gypsy Hill at Sunrise, August 6, 1889," describing—

> " . . . Heathery Aldworth, rich and ripe
> With greetings of a world his song hath won."

And the third sonnet, already referred to, was written two years later, on his eighty-second birthday, while the fourth, *In Westminster Abbey*, is descriptive of the emotion he experienced while standing beside the poet's bier on October 12, 1892. It appeared in the *Nineteenth Century* :—

> " I saw no crowd : yet did these eyes behold
> What others saw not—his lov'd face sublime
> Beneath that pall of death in deathless prime
> Of Tennyson's long day that grows not old ;
> And, as I gazed, my grief seemed over-bold ;
> And, ' who art thou,' the music seemed to chime,
> ' To mourn that King of song whose throne is time ? '—
> Who loves a god should be of godlike mould.

---

* The mountains of Kàf, mentioned in this poem, are, according to a Mohammedan tradition, entirely composed of gems, whose reflected splendours colour the sky.

" Then spake my heart rebuking sorrow's shame :
   ' So great he was, striving in simple strife
   With Art alone to lend all beauty life—
So true to Truth he was, whatever came—
   So fierce against the false when lies were rife—
That Love o'erleapt the golden fence of Fame.' "

XIX.

MID-VICTORIAN FRIENDSHIPS.—IV.

MID-VICTORIAN FRIENDSHIPS (IV.)—GEORGE MEREDITH,
W. E. HENLEY, F. H. GROOME, GEORGE BORROW.

GEORGE MEREDITH, though seldom a visitor at
The Pines, saw Watts-Dunton frequently after
their meeting at the Omar Khayyám Club, at the time
of Watts-Dunton's election, and they became very
intimate. Always regarded as a welcome guest at the
" Cottage," Meredith would write to his friend, " Any
day you please to name—and certainly you will sleep
here. Your coming will rejoice me. State the hour
of your train, and you shall be met. Give my warm
love to Swinburne."

Whenever he went down to Box Hill, Watts-Dunton
usually stayed two or three days at that cosy home
amid the Surrey hills. And in those first days of
Watts-Dunton's visits Meredith would saunter out
to meet his friend at the station, his favourite little
dachshund at his side, walking with a firm, buoyant
stride and swinging a short stick in his hand. He
usually dressed in a light-coloured walking suit, with
a touch of red in his necktie, the iron-gray hair visible
beneath the round " wideawake." The house in which

he lived is a small one—a six-roomed cottage; but Meredith spent most of his time in his little chalet— consisting of a single sleeping room and study—to which guests were seldom invited. Watts-Dunton often remarked after a visit to Box Hill upon Meredith's exhaustless eloquence, his capacious memory, and his wonderful flow of ideas. But what struck him more than anything else was an irresistible love of chaff, which Meredith sometimes indulged in rather inordinately. In one of his chaffy moods he wrote to Watts-Dunton, following immediately on a certain visit :—

> " Au voleur, au voleur, au voleur !—

> " All day I've been thinking upon it,
> And cannot devise what to say.
> Oronte comes to me with a sonnet,
> And carries my penknife away.

Such is the tale here—the maid declaring that she saw the gentleman with the missing instrument in hand. So the suggestion is, that to make humble restitution for what is both complimentarily and indulgently, and at the same time fitly, called his fit of abstraction, he should journey hither again on a morning, and lunch, and acquit himself by leaving the damnatory thing on my table—whereupon no remark will be made. Consider this.—My love to Swinburne."

At the time of Groome's death (1902) Watts-Dunton wrote a poem, called *The Spectre in Gypsy Dell*, as a tribute to his friend's memory. It appeared in the

Athenæum, and he sent a copy of it to the author of *Harry Richmond*, who had a great admiration for Groome as a writer on gypsy folk-lore.

" I should be divided between admiration of your Sonnet and the feeling that inspired it," Meredith writes, " were they not so interwoven. My thanks are offered to our beloved Swinburne for urging you to send it. The death of Groome saddened me. For me it is time to go. But I am affected by the loss of younger men still good for work. His *Kriegspiel* had a memorable gypsy heroine, a fitting sister to Rhona ; and one cannot say more. I hope you are in labour. When the weather is humane I shall expect to see you some afternoon as promised."

At the time of Swinburne's first serious attack of pneumonia, in 1903, Meredith wrote to Watts-Dunton :—

" The papers tell me of Swinburne's illness and that the crisis is over. I can feel for you and all about him. I have myself just come from a point where, as the doctor said, the end could be seen ; they pulled me back, and thereby did a man of seventy-five small service. But I am older and less capable than Swinburne ; he can work and sing still, and the loss of him would be a calamity for the country. Pray spare a few minutes to let me know of his present condition, and also tell me something of yourself. The *Athenæum* misses you, but I trust the cause of it is productive work soon to be given to the world."

In reply to this letter Watts-Dunton wrote to Meredith from The Pines (November 30, 1903) :—

" Swinburne was deeply touched and so was I by your solicitude. I am thankful to say that his recovery has been as swift as was the invasion of the pneumonia germ, and that he is now apparently out of all danger. As to your saying that the loss of you would not be a calamity to the country, Swinburne and I take a very different view of that matter. It is very gratifying to us, who love you and your work, to see the immense place that you hold in the imagination of your country. It is singular that shortly before Swinburne was taken ill we were discussing over the little dinner table the question as to which is the happier fate for the writing man—to get an immense fame at starting, as Swinburne did, and then to be confronted by the spectre of that fame whenever a new book issues from the press. I can imagine nothing more vexing than to be told by every critic and paragraphist that one's best work was all done when one was young, and I said the most fortunate of all the poets and imaginative writers of our time is George Meredith. He did superb work from the first—miles above that of any of his contemporaries. It was greeted with rapture by the few people whose opinion is of worth, and comparatively ignored by the

great mass of readers ; but after a while a great light
was shed upon this mass of readers, and now, when
he has time to rest upon his oars a bit and see what he
has achieved, his fame is in everybody's mouth. No
one has ever said that *The Amazing Marriage* or *Lord
Ormont and his Aminta* ' suffered by comparison '
even with *The Ordeal of Richard Feverel.* No one
ever thinks that you are superannuated or ever will be
superannuated. That swimming scene between the
two lovers is the most delightfully youthful piece of
romance in our literature, and everybody says so. I
write this because I think that when you say that the
doctor ' pulled you back, and thereby did a man of
seventy-five small service,' you say what you ought not
to say, and I feel quite angry with you on account of it.

" With affectionate and admiring regards,

" Dear Master,

" Yours as ever,

" T. WATTS-DUNTON.

" *P.S.*—Please, when you see your son, thank him
from Swinburne and me for his most kind and sympathetic letter."

Just before the time of writing this letter to Meredith,
telling that no one could ever regard him as an old
man, Watts-Dunton's sonnet, *To George Meredith, on
his Seventy-fourth Birthday*, appeared in the *Saturday
Review* (February 15, 1902) :—

" This time, dear friend—this time my birthday greeting
   Comes heavy of funeral tears—I think of you,
   And say, ' 'Tis evening with him—that is true—
But evening bright as noon, if faster fleeting ;
Still he is spared—while Spring and Winter, meeting,
   Clasp hands around the roots 'neath frozen dew—
   To see the " Joy of Earth " break forth anew,
And hear it on the hillside warbling, bleating.'

"Love's remnant melts and melts ; but if our days
   Are swifter than a weaver's shuttle, still,
Still Winter has a sun—a sun whose rays
   Can set the young lamb dancing on the hill,
And set the daisy bud in woodland ways
   Dreaming of her who brings the daffodil."

The expression in this sonnet, " heavy of funeral
tears," has reference to the recent loss of their friend
F. H. Groome.

When acknowledging a copy of *Aylwin* from Watts-
Dunton, Meredith wrote (December 19, 1898) :—

" I must thank you for the full pleasure I have had
in *Aylwin*—and only these later days, for I have been
at work, and dared not let a magician interpose. I am
in love with Sinfi. Nowhere can fiction give us one
to match her, not even the *Kriegspiel* heroine, who
touched me to the deeps. Winifred's infancy has infancy's charm ; the young woman is taking ; but all
my heart has gone to Sinfi. Of course it is part of her
character that her destiny should point to the glooms.
She soon comes to me again in her conquering presence. I could talk of her for hours. The book has

this defect—on the mind it leaves a cry for a successor. I have noted minor bits of criticism, which we will discuss when we meet. My love to Swinburne. It is brave news in these days of the trickling or bounding verse that he has volumes in the press."

On the title-page of *Aylwin* was inscribed a motto which ever since the novel appeared has given pause to a number of Watts-Dunton's admirers—Meredith among others :—

" Quoth Ja'afar, bowing low his head : ' Bold is the donkey-driver, O Ka'dee ! and bold the ka'dee who dares say what he will believe, what disbelieve— not knowing in any wise the mind of Allah—not know-ing in any wise his own heart, and what it shall some day suffer.' "

Many a letter was addressed to the author, asking him in what book of the East the quotation could be found. He would ponder seriously, though with a half-concealed twinkle in his eye, over these letters ; but though he seldom omitted to acknowledge them with his usual courtesy, his legal apprenticeship had left him such a master of the art of never committing himself to an opinion, that his replies soon made it evident that he had no intention of satisfying the curiosity he had so artfully aroused. Even a powerful appeal from *Notes and Queries* failed to elicit any satisfactory re-

sponse. On his return from one of his visits to Box
Hill he spoke to a friend of George Meredith's enthusiasm over the motto. " I can't help envying you ; to
have hit upon such an apt quotation was a stroke of
genius ! " Meredith had exclaimed. " Didn't Meredith
ask you where you picked it up ? " his friend inquired.
" Not he ! " was the reply ; " the author of *The Shaving
of Shagpat* is far too knowing a fellow to expose his
ignorance. He clearly wished me to infer that he was
familiar with the quotation." " I've long suspected,"
said the friend, " that you yourself are the author."
" You're quite right," said he with a hearty laugh—
" I'm the author. But you're the first man to whom
I've ever made the admission."

Meredith's volume, *Poems and Lyrics of the Joy of
Earth*, was reviewed by Watts-Dunton in the *Athenæum* in 1883, and doubtless this critique was one of
the first to introduce a wider circle of readers to his
work ; and W. E. Henley, by his appreciative articles
on Meredith's prose fiction, a few years later, helped
still further to establish the fame that the author of
The Ordeal of Richard Feverel so richly merited, but
which he so tardily won.

Henley was frequently at The Pines before he
went to Edinburgh. At the time when the *Scots
Observer* was started he was anxious to get Watts-
Dunton to contribute to his paper, and wrote to him
(December 6, 1889) from the office of the *Scots Observer*,
9 Thistle Street, Edinburgh :—

" I have added your name to my list of contributors, and I should like you to honour your signature soon. Why not write *The Three Fausts ?* *

" I hear of a certain piece of prose which I should love to have ; being a man who lives to dare, and having a very hearty contempt for the libellous on the other side—the New Democrats, whose best weapon is slander.

" I thought I explained that the reason I didn't come was that my hours were counted, and that every one of them was already bestowed elsewhere. If I didn't, I do now ; and next time I am in town I will give you an opportunity of forgiveness.

" I am glad you like the journal. I confess I look upon it with a certain pride. It costs me much time, pains, and invention ; but it's worth it, I think. At all events it is a pleasure to me to make a good number, and I imagine it must be a pleasure to others to read the results. Of course it ought to be in London ; with a good publisher it would, I am pretty sure, go as it deserves to go. Here the beginnings have for various reasons been harder than they need have been. But —*Enfin !* We are as full of heart as may be.

" We have been demonstrating to Arthur James, or I should have writ before. It was a sight worth see-ing. It atones for much.

" Ever yours sincerely,
" W. E. H."

---

* The poem, *The Three Fausts,* has reference to his sonnets on Berlioz, Gounod, and Schumann. Vide *The Coming of Love.*

A very frequent visitor at The Pines was that remarkable gypsologist Francis Hindes Groome. It was shortly after George Borrow's death that he and Watts-Dunton came together, and if the author of *Aylwin* set great value on " Lavengro's " insight and erudition in matters associated with gypsy lore, there is no doubt that the " Tarno Rye " was a man whose opinion on everything connected with gypsology he valued most.* By a strange and fortunate chance Groome came into Watts-Dunton's life at a moment when he was in the midst of his gypsy romance—at a moment when he most needed the friendly aid of that gypsy scholar. The great bond of sympathy between them was, it need hardly be said, George Borrow ; and in their walks together over Wimbledon Common — strolls in the footsteps of " Lavengro "—the sayings and doings of the " walking lord of gypsy lore " were naturally a favourite topic of conversation between them.

Groome was never tired of hearing Watts-Dunton relate, as they passed by Gordon Hake's house on the Kingston Road on their way to Richmond Park, how it was there that he first came to make Borrow's acquaintance. That incident has been so frequently recorded in books on Borrow, since Watts-Dunton first told it in the *Athenæum*, that every Borrovian must by this time know it by heart.† But there were a

* Francis Hindes Groome ("Tarno Rye")—vide *Old Familiar Faces*, by T. Watts-Dunton (Herbert Jenkins, Ltd., 1915).

† Vide *Old Familiar Faces* (George Borrow), by T. Watts-Dunton.

hundred and one other episodes in connection with
Watts-Dunton's personal recollections of " Lavengro,"
many of which have never yet been published, that
were poured into the only too ready ear of the " Tarno
Rye." The much-debated question of the " veiled
period " (1825–32) was often discussed. As a matter
of fact, there was nothing to unveil. It was a period
of impecuniosity, partly spent at his mother's home in
Norfolk—a period during which he experienced a
fierce struggle for existence that conquered his spirit of
independence, as it will do in the proudest man. He
kept out of sight ; that was all. It was a period of
mystery without which the mysterious life of " Lavengro," with his perplexing personality, would have been
stripped of one of its most characteristic phases. No
man ever lived who took a greater delight in the fascinating art of mystification. One might as well attempt
to locate the various places described in Borrow's narrative of his wanderings over England to be found in
The Romany Rye, or, indeed, most of his works ; one
might as well attempt to locate the places mentioned
in *Gulliver's Travels*, as to solve such questions. Who
has ever located Mumper's Dingle, or the famous
church Borrow attended with the gypsies ? It was
never his intention that any one ever should do so. He
never revealed the goal or the purpose of his travel.
Delighting in peregrination and the impressive atmosphere of mystery all his life, the name given to him
by one who knew him well, and who admired him

greatly—the name of the "Unknown"—summed up George Borrow's personality in a single word.

Although Borrow walked over many a time from Hereford Square to the Sunday midday dinner at Gordon Hake's house without waiting for an invitation, Hake would sometimes send a line to "Lavengro" when he let weeks go by without putting in an appearance, expressing a hope that he would "soon be coming that way." In those days Borrow never replied to a letter of this description, but he seldom failed to answer the appeal in person.

On these occasions he would invariably leave Hereford Square, partaking of an early breakfast, and step out with vigorous strides by Hammersmith and Barnes in the direction of Richmond. Having reached the gates facing the "Star and Garter," he would turn into the Park, taking the pathway between the Pen Ponds, and make for the Robin Hood gate.

He was never known to pass the "Bald-faced Stag" without stopping to drink "a glass of swipes"—his favourite term for mild ale—never failing to indulge in that grimace of his after swallowing it. The great Grimaldi never could have excelled "Lavengro" in facial expression when a sense of humour of this sort came upon him. It was inimitable.

Watts-Dunton would tell the "Tarno Rye" of his many rambles with Borrow through Richmond Park, calling on the way at the "Bald-faced Stag" in Kingston Vale, in order that "Lavengro" might introduce him to Jerry Abershaw's sword, which was one of the special glories of that once famous hostelry. And then how, one summer day—" a day whose heat would have been oppressive had it not been tempered every now and then by a playful silvery shower falling from an occasional wandering cloud, whose slate-coloured body thinned at the edges to a fringe of lace brighter than any silver "—Borrow remarked with a genial smile, " These showers seem merely to give a rich colour to the sunshine, and to make the wild flowers in the meadows breathe more freely." In a word, it was one of those uncertain summer days whose peculiarly English charm was Borrow's special delight. He liked rain, but " he liked it falling on the green umbrella (enormous, shaggy, like a gypsy tent after a summer storm) that he generally carried."

" No one ever loved Richmond Park," Watts-Dunton would say, " more than Borrow, and he seemed to know every tree. And how often have I seen him stop on a day in midsummer, and, glancing about him, exclaim, ' This is England ! '

" And now," added Watts-Dunton, pausing in front of a huge oak near the Pen Ponds—" and now, Groome, I'll show you something which I've never yet pointed out to any one. If you look closely at the bark on the trunk of that big oak tree you'll discover the initials ' G. B.,' carved out by ' Lavengro ' himself, and, underneath, ' T. W.,' carved out by your humble servant."

Watts-Dunton, in speaking to an intimate friend about the " Tarno Rye," remarked that of all the friends that he had made in later years (this was in 1889) Groome was the man who had the most entirely won his heart. The charm of his society, he readily admitted, partly arose from the life he had led among the gypsies (having, in fact, married a gypsy), and partly from his freedom from a writing man's vanity, which, as Watts-Dunton declared, " came upon him like the scent from new-mown hay."

" I shall often look back," Groome once wrote to Watts-Dunton, " to the pleasant days I spent with you at Putney, and our walks over the Common and in Richmond Park." Moreover, it must be remembered, Groome was an East Anglian, and his father and Fitz-Gerald were friends of long standing. " A great writer, old Fitz," Borrow used to say in the days when he and FitzGerald saw so much of each other. " Ah ! that man has only to die in order to be recognized. He lent me the manuscript of *Omar Khayyám* long before it was published. Ah ! what glorious talks we had together at Oulton and at Yarmouth."

Groome—a man who knew more about FitzGerald than any other member of the " Omar Club," as his book, *Two Suffolk Friends*, clearly shows—wrote to Watts-Dunton on May 12, 1895 : " Your *Omar* poem in yesterday's *Athenæum* moves me to write you a line,

for its melody is running in my head. I like it greatly.
. . . The book on my father and FitzGerald will be
out, I hope, in June." *

Watts-Dunton's poem, *Toast to Omar Khayyám*,
which he called an East Anglian echo-chorus, and inscribed to " Old Omarian Friends in memory of happy
days by Ouse and Cam," is included in Miscellaneous
Poems in *The Coming of Love.*

When Groome published his *Two Suffolk Friends*,
Swinburne wrote to him in his most characteristic
style :—

" THE PINES, PUTNEY HILL, S.W.,

" July 15, '95.

" MY DEAR MR. GROOME,

" How to begin thanking you for the gift of
your most delightful book is my first difficulty ; how
to end without wearying you with more expressions of
gratitude than I could expect you to have the patience
to read is the second. I only wish (as I have just been
saying to Mr. Watts) that I could tell you what I cannot undertake to write—that is, how much and how
many things I enjoy in reading it. So I must begin,
and end, my remarks at random, on the off-chance that
they may not bore you. My father told me many years
since that, when he was a midshipman under Lord
Collingwood, an old sailor taught him the *Ballad of
Captain Ward*, and asked if I knew any more of the
words than just the opening. When I was able (long

* *Two Suffolk Friends* was published by T. C. and E. C. Jack
(1895).

afterwards) to send him a correct copy from the British Museum he was much pleased. Do you know the three glorious folios of the *Roxburgh Ballads*—street songs, with engravings, inlaid in fine thick paper? I took D. G. Rossetti once to see them—having discovered them by a mere fluke—and he made pencil copies of some of the rough headings, which are as full of character as the text. But the original black-letter *Ward Ballad* is to the version given at page 46 of your book what Shakespeare's *Lear* is to Tate's. It begins like this (I don't know what sailors have to do with ' tuck of drum '—perhaps it's metaphorical) :—

> " ' Strike up, you gallant sailors,
> With music. and tuck of drum :
> I will you tell of a rank rover
> That on the seas is come.

> " ' His name is Captain Ward,
> As plainly doth appear ;
> There has not been such a rover
> This thrice three hundred year.'

I can't swear, but I think that is pretty exactly accurate. And isn't it Homeric? I'd do it into Greek hexameters if it wasn't too much trouble. (On second or third thoughts I can't remember whether the word is ' robber ' or ' rover '—but it's all one.)

" As to the story of Master Charley, I can only say I had to put the book down and wink—hard—to keep the tears back. One doesn't want to ' blub ' (as schoolboys say).

" But ' Posh ' is my delight, and FitzGerald must
have been a beast if ever he was too hard on him.   One
of my earliest friends was just such another fellow—a
fisherman whose cottage was on (or just beyond) my
father's property.   His wife was a favourite of my
mother's, and she used to go with me on a visit to their
cottage half-way down the ' chine ' (*need* I add that I
always wished to stay and live there ?) when I was too
small a boy to understand what was the matter, or how
anybody could look unhappy whose house was built in
a cleft of the cliff overhanging the sea.   But when I
was of Etonian age, of course I had to be told that my
old friend ' Charley ' used to drink rather excessively
by fits and starts : for I had seen him, when sent for,
enter my father's study with exactly the look and bearing of a schoolboy entering the flogging room, and
found that he took my eagerly offered hand in a shame-
faced sort of way.   My father persuaded him to take
the pledge for a time (he had more sense and more
good feeling than to ask him to do it for good and all).
Now, Charley had a brother of the same trade as himself ; John was his respectable name.   John was the
pink of propriety and sobriety.   But Charley thought
that what was good for him must be good for John.
So, when he went to take the pledge, he took it for John
as well as himself.   And the delicious thing is that poor,
good John felt himself bound to observe his brother's
pledge—which he had never heard of till after it had
been taken for him without a word of warning on the

part of my friend Charley. It set a schoolboy off laughing ; but don't you think your father and Mr. FitzGerald would rather have admired it ? I must add that poor old Charley was the most faithful, loyal, grateful, and affectionate of men. But all the fisher-folk who could, I think, came up from miles off to my father's funeral, though he had sold the property and left the neighbourhood (to my lifelong sorrow) for years before.

" I fell in with Major Moor's delicious *Suffolk Dictionary* years ago, and, when hardly of age, had the sense to see what a wonderfully and uniquely good book it was. If only there were such a vocabulary for every English district ! And if only E. F. G. had carried out his intention of editing and enlarging it, instead of treating Æschylus as Ducis treated Shakespeare ! He and Browning both sent me their damnable travesties of the *Agamemnon*, and I knew not how to acknowledge either.

" Yours sincerely and gratefully,

" A. C. SWINBURNE."

Watts-Dunton, in writing of *Kriegspiel* in the *Athenæum*,* says :—

" But whatever may be the temporary success of any work of fiction, the quality by which it really passes into literature is that of truth of organic detail. The

* *Kriegspiel*, by F. H. Groome. Vide *Athenæum*, Vol. I., 1896.

incidents, the manners, and the scenery must be so true that they seem to be a natural growth. Here is Mr. Groome's strength. His pictures of East Anglia and the lights and shades of East Anglian character and manners are worthy of the writer of *Two Suffolk Friends;* and as regards the pictures of gypsy life, the book is full of touches which could only have come from a writer who has had intimate personal contact with the Romanies, and who was at the same time deeply versed in their traditional lore. This enables him to introduce touches that seem to spring up as naturally as flowers from the soil. . . . As a gypsy novel, as a novel depicting gypsy life, *Kriegspiel* is unrivalled."

In a long letter to the " Tarno Rye," Watts-Dunton opens his heart to him on the subject of his passion for the open air :—

" I hope I may not have misled you into thinking that I am a Romany scholar. I only wish I were. My sympathy with the gypsies is based mainly upon three facts : *First*, a long course of ill-usage from every kind of European people ; *secondly*, the mystery connected with their history ; and *thirdly*, the fact of their leading an open-air life—a life for which I have always had a passionate love. Most of my reading—and I have read a good deal more than a man ought to read, considering the brevity of our life and the infinite riches of Nature—has been out in the fields, under hedges and trees in all kinds of weather. . . . I dare say that (as in my own case) the Nature passion prevents you from doing much work. Alas! that is the worst of it! Nature is a siren whose wiles are fatal indeed. To be chewing the cud under an elm, to enjoy the delicious struggle with the wind and rain, or to stroll along the sands in a half-dreamy consciousness of the wide sparkle of the sea, is not to *work*, and (if we are to believe the Carlyleans) not 'to pray.' Still, are not our rewards —yours and mine—all sufficing? While the poets, for instance, are grinding away at their rhymes in hermetic-ally-sealed rooms, spinning descriptions of Nature out of their brains as the industrious spider spins his web out of his bowels, we are enjoying poetry worth all that they can write, and a good deal more. Not that I despise poetry; on the contrary, I love it; but how few poets have the genuine Nature instinct! Their instinct is to *express*, not to enjoy.

" Your anecdote about Boswell is delicious. Would to God I had that dear creature's self-esteem! I can imagine the coolness with which such temperate praises as yours were received by our beloved grammarian of Codling Gap. I envy you in that you know him personally; indeed there are, I fear, many matters as to which I envy you. I should so like to send him my two Borrow articles, wherein I kneel to his greatness as poet, philosopher, and scholar. Could you not give me his address? I would then send him the two numbers of the journal. And might I use your name as an introduction if I wrote to him? Who knows but that I might get a letter from him. I should prize it almost as much as a letter from the Ghost of Shakespeare. I was showing that part of your letter to Swinburne the other day, who agreed with me that you were far too moderate in your eulogies, having ignored Boswell's claims *as a poet-philosopher.* This is where he is so great, though, to be sure, his science, philanthropy, thrift, and self-help do not lag far behind."

In his writings on Thoreau, Watts-Dunton shows more clearly than anything else that his pet subject was " the children of the open air." His first essay on the " hermit of Walden wood " appeared in the *Athenæum,* November 3, 1877, being a critique of H. A. Page's book, *Thoreau : his Life and Aims.* Many years later— 1906—Watts-Dunton wrote the Preface to the World's Classics edition of Thoreau's *Walden,* originally published in 1884 ; and in this Preface he exploits his theory that the truly happy part of a nature-worshipper's existence comes after the age that Thoreau had reached when he died—namely, forty-five. " It is impossible," he says, " for a man who has not passed the meridian to know what a glorious thing it is to live." About Thoreau, as Watts-Dunton has related, he had many interesting talks with George Borrow, who always spoke of him rather contemptuously as the " Yankee Hermit ; " and Watts-Dunton himself had his doubts as to whether Thoreau was a veritable " child of the open air."

When talking of Borrow, Watts-Dunton would often remark, " No man's writing can take you into the country as Borrow's can ; it makes you feel the sunshine, see the meadows, smell the flowers, hear the skylark sing and the grasshopper chirp."

Speaking once of Bret Harte, he said, " A sense of the open air second only to Borrow is awakened in Bret Harte's stories. I believe I am right in thinking that the love of Nature and the love of open-air life are growing ; this will secure a place in the future for Bret Harte." *

Among the " sonnets of friendship," as they might be called, contained in *The Coming of Love*, there is one entitled *A Talk on Waterloo Bridge :* " the last sight of George Borrow," beginning with the lines—

> " We talked of ' Children of the Open Air,'
>   Who once on hill and valley lived aloof,
>   Loving the sun, the wind, the sweet reproof
> Of storms . . .' "

so often quoted by writers on " Lavengro."

Not long before his decease, in one of his letters to Mr. Clement Shorter, having reference to Borrow and East Anglian connections, Watts-Dunton wrote : " Owing to my own early associations with the Norfolk coast (to us in the East Midlands the ' sea ' always meant the North

* See obituary notice of Bret Harte in *Athenæum*, by Watts-Dunton, Vol. I., 1902.

Sea that washes Yarmouth, Lowestoft, and Cromer),
I am naturally drawn to that birthplace of great men,
at the head of whom is Nelson. Moreover, my own
mother's family, like yours, is pure East Anglian. But
you will be interested to know that owing to the fact
that Swinburne's late mother, Lady Jane H. Swinburne (*née* Lady Jane H. Ashburnham), was born at
Barking Hall, the poet shares your enthusiasm and mine
for the neighbourhood. Shortly before that dear lady
died she took Barking Hall as a temporary residence,
and the poet and I visited her there, and she showed us
the very bedroom in which she was born.

" Nelson is, of all heroes, Swinburne's favourite,
and one of the most cherished of his possessions is a
lock of Nelson's hair, given to him not very long ago.

" Swinburne and I have made several visits to the
coast near Cromer, and the scene of the early part of
my story, *Aylwin*, as you know, is laid there. So,
altogether, we at The Pines claim to be as thoroughly
East Anglian in sympathy as yourself.

" It is very kind of you to suggest that I ought to
write a Life of Borrow. But there is a great difference
between recording reminiscences of a man and writing
his life.

" After all that I have written about ' Lavengro,'
if the scraps were put together they would make a fairly
good-sized book. Yet I feel that I have not said a tithe
of what I have to say concerning that remarkable personality. I have seen him, as you know, with the gypsies ;

and it was only with them that the real man seemed to express himself."

That Swinburne loved the East Anglian coast as fervently as his mother loved it, or even Watts-Dunton himself, his poem, *By the North Sea*, alone would testify. But he was more than that ; he was by nature one of the open-air fraternity if ever there was one—more of a child of the open air than George Borrow, for he was never known to carry an umbrella ; he loved the wind—a storm was his greatest delight. He once wrote to Watts-Dunton from Leigh House, Bradford-on-Avon, where he was staying with his mother, in a letter dated October 31, 1882 : " I need not say how much I like your article on Thoreau. I didn't know you thought so highly of any part of his work as the last paragraph seems to intimate that you do."

The truth is that Swinburne, as Watts-Dunton has remarked, who " had at one time been so Gallic in his tastes, had got to know England with an intensity such as I have never seen equalled, except perhaps in the case of George Borrow."

XX.

A DAY WITH "LAVENGRO."

XX.

A Day with " Lavengro."

ON one occasion Watts-Dunton, while touring the East Coast with a friend, came unexpectedly, during a stroll along the shore near Dunwich, upon Borrow. The following extract from a description of a " day with ' Lavengro ' " (hitherto unpublished) was written by him with a view to its insertion in one of his works of fiction. It is such a characteristic sketch that we have ventured to give it here.

" When we got nearer to Borrow we stopped, for he was standing stock-still, and gazing before him like a man in a trance.

" ' I have often seen him in this condition,' I said *sotto voce*, turning to my fellow-tourist. ' He is subject to a singular metaphysical trance in which the world to him seems a delusion—a lying dream. But I have also known him to sham this possession for the sake of effect ; or, at least, l have thought he was shamming. He's a tremendous *poseur*. Whether his vision is really upon him now, or whether he has already seen us, and is " playing the showman," I'll be hanged if I can say. Mystification is the very breath of his nostrils. It's possible that he may have caught sight of us, and instinctively put himself into pose.'

" ' But he wouldn't pose to you, his intimate friend, would he ? ' said my companion.

" ' Oh, wouldn't he ? You show great ignorance of the born mystifier, or you wouldn't say that. Let us stop here for a moment and watch him.'

" Between the fingers of Borrow's left hand I saw a little white flower. I recognized the flower as being like some that had on the previous day attracted my admiration on the common, and which I had been told was called the ' Dunwich rose.' We then approached him, and I touched him on the shoulder. Borrow gave a violent start, like a man suddenly awakened.

" I could not resist breaking into a smile, for at first I thought the vision was a sham. But as I gazed more closely in Borrow's rich brown eyes they certainly looked to me like the eyes of a man possessed of a dream.

" ' The vision was upon you, Borrow,' said I.

" ' Yes, and you have dispersed it ! But I am none the less delighted to see you after this long while.'

" And he shook my hand with great cordiality.

" He then told us of the remarkable psychological effect produced upon him by the sight of the ruins of a city that was once so famous. He had passed, he said, into a kind of trance, in which the old city of Dunwich in its glorious days appeared before him. The streets were full of bustle, and the sea in front full of ships.

" ' I wish I had your visionary power, Borrow, and could see the city of Dunwich of old times,' I said.

" ' I never come to this spot without seeing the same vision,' said Borrow.

" ' I begin to envy you these visions of yours ; but I suppose I must be content with seeing things as they are, Borrow, as ordinary mortals see them,' I said, in a vein of irony which did not escape Borrow, as I saw.

" ' Then do *you* never see visions ? ' said he. ' I quite thought you did. When I am in England I come here every year expressly to experience it. A great city to a man like me has a ghost of itself. Old Rome has a ghost of itself, Athens has a ghost of itself, but nothing like Dunwich.'

" ' To a man like you, Borrow,' said I, with a smile.

" Borrow made no answer.

" Presently he said in a semi-jocose manner, ' Have you yet discovered the meaning of the word " cockle " ? You boggled over the phrase " the cockles of the heart " when we last met.'

" ' No,' I said ; ' but I've no doubt you are per-fectly right. If ever there was a born " word-master," it's my dear old friend Borrow.'

" Borrow looked pleased and flattered, and his quiz-zing mood for the moment vanished, but it soon returned.

" ' There you are wrong, according to the critics. They give me credit for possessing Mezzofanti's parrot-like memory for words. And it is a fact that I rarely hear any word in any language that I don't seize it as an Oulton hernshaw seizes upon an eel, and it is not often that it manages to wriggle out of my beak ! But the critics have all decided that if you want a scholarly knowledge of languages you must not come to me.'

" ' I know how heartily you despise the critics, Borrow,' I said.

" ' No one can despise them so heartily.'

" ' But that white flower between your fingers—that's the Dunwich rose, I see.'

" ' Yes, the famous Dunwich rose,' said he. ' I am half inclined to believe that it was by holding that rose between my fingers that the Dunwich vision came. The flower flourishes here among the ruins, as well as farther away on the common.'

" ' It's said to have been a favourite with the old monks,' said I.

" Borrow snorted, and said, ' It's the most harmless thing they ever did if they cultivated this little flower.' He raised his hand to look at it. ' It seems Purity itself.'

" ' I see that you are still as fervid a no-Popery man as ever,' I said ; ' as fervid as Fitz's brother John *ever was.*' *

" ' I am still as good a Protestant as ever, Watts ; as good a Church of England man as ever, and shall wage war against the abominations of Rome as long as I breathe ! The only quarrel I ever had with Fitz's

* This scene with George Borrow is supposed to have taken place many years ago.

brother John was when he spoke slightingly of Norfolk
ale. No good Protestant ought to say a word against
Norfolk ale or good red wine. Fitz says " John was
as mad as a March hare," but the only thing mad that
I could ever see about him was his disparagement of
ale.'

" ' Then you think,' I said laughingly, ' that his
sanity was shown by his attacks upon the arch-enemy ?
But surely,' I went on in a more serious tone, ' surely
you will admit that Romanism had its function once ?
During the Dark Ages, for instance.'

" ' It was Romanism's special function to make the
Dark Ages dark,' said he.

" ' I hope that the shades of the vanished Fran-
ciscans in these ruins don't hear you, Borrow. Surely
the Roman Catholics were not all bad ? '

" ' *All !* Monasteries and nunneries are the black
spots upon the face of the earth which God made so
fair.'

" ' Not all, not *all*, Borrow.'

" ' Name one—name one that's not black.'

" ' Well, such good religious houses as the East
Anglian Crabhouse Nunnery, that struggled so nobly
for very existence in the mud and marshes near Lynn,
don't deserve John FitzGerald's lash or yours.'

" ' Crabhouse Nunnery ! ' said Borrow, with a scorn-
ful sniff. ' A disgrace to Norfolk ! '

" ' A disgrace to Norfolk, Borrow ? How's that ?
Don't let our sound Protestantism lead us into bigotry.'

" ' I don't deny that at one time—at the time when William de Dunton sent his daughter Philippa, with a good slice of land at her back, to live a saintly life at Crabhouse—things were tolerable—just tolerable—at Crabhouse Nunnery. But how did it end—how did it end ? '

" ' Ah ! I begin to see,' I said, ' that I have opened up a subject on which I am no match for the great champion of no-Popery. I know that Crabhouse Nunnery came to an end somehow ; but I own I don't in the least know what the end was.'

" ' Then I do. It ended in the disgraceful scandals about the foul nun, Agnes Smith.'

" ' I'm afraid,' I said, with a smile, ' that Agnes Smith and her naughty story, whatever it was, are beyond my ken. So, including even Crabhouse Nunnery, you think that nothing good ever can come out of Romanism ? '

" ' Nothing ! '

" ' Well, well,' I said, gazing meditatively at the monastic ruins, from the ivy of which a blackbird sang joyously, until, as we approached, it bustled out with a warning shriek of alarm and flew away. ' Anyhow, the sight of these crumbling cliffs on which these ruins stand affects me more than any other sight in East Anglia, the last remnant of the old city now at the bottom of the sea. What a sign of man's impotence, when confronting the stupendous forces of Nature, is afforded by all this East Anglian coast ! '

" ' Man's impotence when confronting the God of Nature and His mysterious ways,' said he in a solemn voice.

" ' You hadn't used to talk in this fashion once,' I said.

" Borrow responded rather angrily.

" ' That was before the Bible had saved me from the horrors. These ruins,' said he, ' which in a little while will follow what was the centre of a mighty city, were once the cradle of the Christian religion in East Anglia.'

" ' Ah ! then Romanism is the Christian religion after all,' I said in a low voice.

" Borrow, evidently in a fix now, turned a deaf ear on this remark, and we began to walk along over the heather. And presently ' Lavengro ' began to talk in a somewhat formal, not to say pedantic, manner of the past glories of Dunwich and East Anglia. His pedantry would have been disagreeable in any other man. But it was accompanied by a simplicity that was really charming.

" ' The difference between East Anglia and other parts of England,' said he, ' is that to this very day it retains its old name, while the other Saxon divisions of England—Mercia, Wessex, and the rest—are forgotten.'

" ' Then you consider,' I said, ' Norfolk and Suffolk to be properly one county ? '

" ' Certainly,' said he, ' although there are differences between the North folk and the South folk ; but

the two folks have features that set them apart from
the shires. Where is Mercia now ? Where is Wessex
now ? Where are the other Anglo-Saxon divisions of
the country ? The great counties of Norfolk and Suffolk, that gave birth to Nelson, and Ket the Tanner, and
Margaret Catchpole, and Giant Hales and the rest, are
one and the same.'

" ' A quaint association of celebrities ! ' I said.

" He then began to talk eloquently about Hales,
the famous giant.

" ' He was a great friend of mine,' said Borrow.
' After he left Yarmouth he lived at the " Craven Head "
in Long Acre. I have many a time drunk swipes there.
He used to show us the watch and chain our Queen
gave him, and he was honoured by half the crowned
heads of Europe. He stood eight feet in his stockings,
and had a countenance as noble as Shakespeare's. A
celebrity if ever there was one ! '

" On parting from Borrow I said, ' Won't you come
to luncheon to-morrow at the apartments we have taken
at Dunwich ? ' and I told him the address. ' Where
are you staying ? '

" ' At the " Swan," Southwold,' said he. ' But I shall
enjoy the four-mile walk. I am as much a tramp as
ever.'

" After he was gone I turned to my companion and
said, ' He used to be as fine a platter-man as you'd find
in England, and I daresay he is now. His favourite meal,
I remember, is a one-joint meal—a boiled leg of mutton

and turnips. And, by-the-bye, there is one thing I ought to tell you, as he is coming to luncheon with us to-morrow. Unless you wish to rouse his ire, you must be careful to make no allusion to his published writings. That would be a mortal offence ! It is one of his affectations to ignore everything that he has published.' "

XXI.

AT THE PINES.

Algernon Charles Swinburne (æt. 65)

XXI.

At The Pines.

IN the autumn of 1879 Swinburne began his new
life on Putney Hill. Before he took up his permanent abode there, however, he went on a visit to
Watts-Dunton at Ivy Lodge, in the Werter Road, off
the Putney High Street, where his friend had been residing, with his sister, Mrs. Charles Mason, since he left
Danes Inn. It was that memorable visit to Ivy Lodge
that directly led to the two poets becoming house-mates
at The Pines. The event was brought about more by
accident than by any design or even forethought on
Watts-Dunton's part. It never entered into his calcula-
tions as to what might flow out of the very natural circumstance of Swinburne becoming a guest at Ivy Lodge.

At this time (1879), as Watts-Dunton has recorded,
" Swinburne's energy was at fever heat ; " he was not
only at work upon his eloquent *Study of Shakespeare*,
but he was engaged upon three other volumes—*The
Modern Heptalogia*, a brilliant anonymous essay in
parody ; *Songs of the Springtide*, and *Studies in Song*.
Such a tremendous output of activity could scarcely fail
to prove a drain upon the physical system. As a matter
of fact, Swinburne was in a very grave and distressing

state of physical health during these months of profuse composition. At this time he was residing in rooms at Guilford Street, and Watts-Dunton had suggested a " run down " to Putney for a week or two ; for, as he assured him, " the salubrious air of Wimbledon Common would invigorate and soon restore him to health." The expectation of getting so many hours of Watts-Dunton's companionship, without any other inducement, was prospect enough for Swinburne, and he eagerly accepted the invitation.

So feeble was Swinburne's condition when he arrived at the Putney villa in the Werter Road that he needed the support of Watts-Dunton's arm when stepping out of the carriage. His recuperation, however, was surprisingly rapid. From the day he became a guest at Ivy Lodge his health began to improve. After a few morning drives out to the Windmill—so famous a landmark to Swinburne in after years—the poet could dispense with the cab ; he could walk without difficulty up Putney Hill, across the Common, and even back again.

Now it chanced that Watts-Dunton was at this very time contemplating a change of residence, and was, indeed, only waiting until the builders had completed the construction of those semi-detached houses at the foot of Putney Hill, for one of which he was negotiating with the landlord for a lease of twenty-one years.

When it reached Swinburne's ears that Watts-Dunton contemplated becoming the tenant of No. 2, The Pines—a much larger house than Ivy Lodge—

he expressed an eager wish to live there with his genial and devoted friend as a sub-tenant, as he had lived with Rossetti at 16 Cheyne Walk seventeen years before. In the first instance he broached the subject of this ardent desire on his part in a letter to his mother. Lady Jane Swinburne wrote to Watts-Dunton as soon as her son's letter reached her, urging Watts-Dunton to allow " Algernon " to join him, declaring that such an arrangement would not merely be beneficial to his health, but remove him completely from his bohemian surroundings. She regarded the project as an ideal one. Her son, whose irregular life gave her deep anxiety, would be enabled to follow his poetic pursuits without a single distraction—without a single care in life, and in the sympathetic and intellectual society of his chosen friend.

Lady Jane Swinburne had indeed for a long time been greatly concerned about her son's health, and when staying in town at No. 11 Lowndes Square, in April 1879, had frequent visits from Watts-Dunton.

On October 9, 1879, " one van of furniture, as per estimate and contract "—to adopt the carter's own phraseology on this memorable occasion—was removed from 25 Guilford Street, Russell Square, where Swinburne lodged, to The Pines, Putney Hill. This van contained Swinburne's worldly effects. They filled two rooms—one room on the first floor, looking out upon the beautiful back garden, and still known as " Swinburne's library," and a bedroom on the floor above, with a " commanding view " of Putney Hill from the top window in front of the house.

Yet none the less sufficiently reckless to cause his best friends grave concern, the interposition of Watts-Dunton at this critical period proved a godsend to Swinburne, and the poet's connection with bohemian life ceased entirely. The acquiescence of Swinburne in this revolutionary change of his whole mode of living was so remarkable that one cannot help regarding many of the " man-about-town " habits as assumed more from thoughtlessness and the imitativeness generated by living among a loose set, for Swinburne was always exceedingly responsive to his environment. Watts-Dunton had shrewdly divined this long ago, and felt that by wholly changing the environment he might save both the poet's health and reputation.

Within a few days of his having settled down on Putney Hill, the report got noised abroad that Swinburne had been placed at The Pines by his family under Watts-Dunton's supervision. This report was, of course, instantly contradicted by all the friends of the two poets who heard it ; but those bohemian acquaintances of the bard's, whose visits to The Pines were necessarily interdicted, never ceased to give publicity to this ill-founded gossip, whenever any reference to the author of *Atalanta* afforded them the chance.

Soon after he had settled down at The Pines under the friendly surveillance of Watts-Dunton, one of his former bohemian cronies came to see him. As a rule,

companions of this type never got any farther than
the front door—the customary " Mr. Swinburne is not
at home " being sufficient to deter them. But this
gentleman, who had dined generously, brushed aside
lightly the usual formula. " You have another look, me
dear," he adjured the indignant parlourmaid. Mean-
while he waited with alcoholic confidence the arrival of
his former friend, whom he had felt sure was indoors.

Watts-Dunton's sister, Mrs. Mason, was the first
to appear, and soon realized the condition of the caller.
In a minute or so Swinburne appeared at the doorway,
bristling with indignation, when he espied the condition
of his visitor.

" Hullo, Algernon, ole buck ! " said the visitor,
holding firmly on to the table with one hand, while he
held out the other to Swinburne.

The " ole buck " glared at him for a moment, speechless with rage, the new-born fire of ascetic disapproba-
tion in his blue eyes. Then, refusing the outstretched
hand, he said curtly, " Come upstairs." The visitor,
however, was physically incapable of accepting the invitation, and speedily found himself outside the front
door, in place of being in Swinburne's sanctum.

It was Saul among the prophets with a vengeance !

Swinburne now renewed that acquaintance with
Wimbledon Common which had begun during his
sojourn at Ivy Lodge. With the simple enthusiasm
of his boyish nature he started off every morning upon
his walk—sometimes with Watts-Dunton and some-

times alone—never giving a thought to " climatic conditions," never consenting to be burdened with umbrella or overcoat, but facing rain, hail, or snow with
all the stolid indifference of a well-seasoned, weather-
beaten, seafaring man. And so it came about that
Wimbledon Common grew to be an earthly Paradise
in his regard. It was impossible to mistake his somewhat eccentric-looking figure, even at a distance. He
invariably went the same walk at the same time morning after morning, and, consequently, inquisitive strangers sought to strike up an acquaintance with him.
This was often done on the pretext of drawing attention to some colour effect in the scenery—which it was
fondly hoped would draw the poet. Swinburne invariably discouraged all these familiarities. Drawing
himself stiffly up, he would growl in a deep voice, " I
can't hear what you say," then hasten on his steps.
On more than one occasion, however, some unusually
persevering and thick-skinned person would walk and
talk at his side for some considerable portion of the
way, despite all discouragement. When Watts-Dunton
could trace the whereabouts of the intrusive stranger,
he would communicate with him and tactfully suggest
that the poet regarded his attentions as undesirable.

Swinburne had a special inside pocket made in
his coat for books and papers—a " poacher's pocket."
On coming in from a walk across the Common his
coat bulged in the most extraordinary way with papers
and books that he had purchased at a bookseller's in

Wimbledon. Often he would bring in presentation copies of books for Watts-Dunton, and he would produce these from his pocket with the air of a conjurer flourishing rabbits from a silk hat.

From the period of *Songs of the Springtide*—the period when he settled down at The Pines—Swinburne's inborn passion for writing about the sea grew keener ; even more pronounced than in the " old Étretat days." Indeed, there was no seaside resort in the world in which he took a deeper interest than he took in Étretat. That never-to-be-forgotten swimming incident off the Normandy coast was a favourite subject of talk with him whenever friends came to see him.

He now began to be widely regarded as the " laureate of the sea " ; and he was soon to become still more familiar with the sea in his annual swimming excursions in the company of Watts-Dunton ; * the sea in the neighbourhood of Guernsey and Sark, the romantic coast of Cornwall, and the Isle of Wight, the breezy downs of Sussex, the crumbling cliffs of Norfolk and Suffolk—these resorts he and Watts-Dunton combined to make famous. The two poets, in truth, grew so thoroughly attached, as the years went on, to the English coast, that with the exception of their brief visit to Paris to assist at the jubilee of *Le Roi s'amuse*, they never again went beyond the British Isles.

" As for the sea," as this famous son of Admiral Swinburne had frequently reiterated when speaking of

* Vide *A Midsummer Holiday* (1884).

swimming excursions, " its salt must have been in my blood before 1 was born." And again, in that autobiographical poem, *Thelassius*, this sentiment is still more emphatically expressed in the three famous lines :—

> " Love of the wind and sea
> That bred him fearless, like a sea-mew reared
> In rocks of man's foot feared."

Living as Swinburne now began to live (1879) with Watts-Dunton and his sister, Mrs. Charles Mason, and a boy for whom he developed a deep affection, he never ceased to speak of this change from bohemian freedom to suburban respectability and restraint as " the happiest event that had occurred in his life since his earliest days in the bosom of his own family." And in his dedication of *Tristram of Lyonesse*, written soon after he had settled down at The Pines, Swinburne expressed his appreciation of all that he had gained through his meeting with Watts-Dunton.

> " This is a friend that, as the wise man saith,
> Cleaves closer than a brother ; nor to me
> Hath time not shown, through rays like waves of strife,
> This truth more sure than all things else but Death.
> This pearl most perfect found in all the sea
> That washes toward your feet these waifs of life."

About this time, while staying at Leigh House, Bradford-on-Avon, with his mother, he wrote a letter to Watts-Dunton, which is interesting as showing three sides to his many-sided character—his love of literary research, his sense of humour, and his genuine affection for children :—

" On Friday *week* I shall hope to find you at home at The Pines. A thousand thanks for all your good offices about the book. I am very sorry you have to give up your intention of visiting these parts—but I congratulate you on your three days of communistic piscatorial society—as Thomas Cloacinus might have expressed it with his usual terse and unaffected elegance.

" Give Bertie my love, and tell him he can't want to see me again more than I want to see him.

" On the Monday after I leave, my mother and sisters and Edward are coming to town. My mother is still (as for many days back) confined to her room with periodically recurring attacks of a feverish kind, but I hope she may be getting a little better.

" I am working myself out to the verge of sickness and delirium over the confused tangle of Lamb-Gutch and Nott MSS. Never have I undergone such a course of grinding toil over such bewildering trivialities. But if I can succeed, by verifying every line from his hand, in the extraction of Lamb (without distraction to myself) from the chaos of cobwebs in which the dunces have involved his jewels of commentary, I shall be rewarded, though I feel vividly that ' *non sum*,' my dear sir, ' *qualis eram* ' in the days of my youthful toil over the text of Blake.

" You may be interested as a friend—perhaps Mrs. Mason also may be interested—to hear that I have lost my heart to a young lady. Do not tell Bertie, who is too old to care for a love tale ; but it is no more than the truth to assert that nothing can excel the rosy contour of her cheeks, the azure radiance of her eyes, or the sweet half-humorous kindness of her cordial though condescending smile. Her name is Miss Rosa Giles. Flowing tresses and pearly teeth are not among the charms which have subdued me ; for I will not conceal from you that she has not a tooth in her head, nor a hair (to speak of) upon it. Her age (I am told) is exactly four months ; she is daughter to the family washerwoman, and empress of the heart of

"Yours ever affectionately,

"A. C. SWINBURNE."

"Bertie," the son of Mrs. Charles Mason, was a little child when Swinburne went to live on Putney Hill. It was about this boy that the poet wrote his child verses. Concerning "Bertie," Mrs. Lynn Lynton once remarked to Watts-Dunton, having heard of Swinburne's devotion to his little nephew at The Pines, that "a man who really loves a child knows a great happiness ; " and she added, "Loving all children is pleasant, but loving one specially, and doing what we can to mould the character and enrich the intellect, is the greatest joy of middle life. All epochs have their natural instincts, their natural joys ; and this belongs to us when the passionate personality of our fervid youth has passed."

XXII.

THE MIDSUMMER HOLIDAY.

Swinburne's Room at "The Pines"

XXII.

THE MIDSUMMER HOLIDAY.

MEANTIME Swinburne had joined Watts-Dunton
as house-mate at The Pines. His new life on
Putney Hill began, as we have stated, in the autumn
of 1879.

After the death of Rossetti in the spring of 1882,
the intimacy between the two poets at The Pines
became much closer. There was less intellectual
affinity, less artistic affinity also, between Watts-
Dunton and Swinburne than had existed between the
author of *Aylwin* and the author of *Sister Helen*. But
the attractive simplicity of Swinburne the man, and it
may be added his essential lovableness, enlisted very
warmly Watts-Dunton's sympathies, whilst on Swinburne's side the charm and tenderness of Watts-Dunton
inspired an even warmer personal affection. However,
widely as Watts-Dunton differed from Swinburne in
certain artistic tendencies, they had one potent inclina-
tion in common—a passion for the sea. In a passage
from his Preface to Coleridge's *Lyrical Poems*, speaking
of the *Ancient Mariner*, Swinburne expressed regret
that " this great sea-piece has not more in it of the air

and savour of the sea "; and when in the summer of the same year (1882) he and Watts-Dunton went together to the Channel Islands, staying at St. Peter's Port, Guernsey, for some little time, and then at Petit Bot Bay, he sang :—

" My heart springs first and plunges, ere my hand
   Strikes out from shore : more close it brings to me,
More near and dear than seems my fatherland,
   My mother sea." *

And then Watts-Dunton, no less inspired by the sight of the " mother sea," while on this visit with Swinburne to the Channel Islands, chancing to hear the story of the " storm child " who lived in the Casket Lighthouse, instantly set to work to record this real incident in verse. It will be found in the opening sonnet of *The Coming of Love*, where it is told how :—

" Amid the Channel's wiles and deep decoys,
   Where yonder Beacons watch the siren-sea,
   A girl was reared who knew not flower nor tree
Nor breath of grass at dawn, yet had high joys.
     *   *   *   *   *
The cold bright sea was hers for universe
Till o'er the waves Love flew and fanned them warm.

" But love brings fear with eyes of augury :
   Her lover's boat was out ; her ears were dinned
   With sea-sobs warning of the awakened wind
That shook the troubled sun's red canopy.
Even while she prayed the storm's high revelry
   Woke petrel, gull—all revellers winged and finned—
   And clutched a sail brown-patched and weather thinned,
And then a swimmer fought a white, wild sea.

* *In Guernsey.* Vide *A Midsummer Holiday* (1884).

' My songs are louder, child, than prayers of thine,'
The Mother sang. ' Thy sea-boy waged no strife
With Hatred's poison, gangrened Envy's knife ;
With me he strove, in deadly sport divine,
Who lend to men, to gods, an hour of life,
Then give them sleep within these arms of mine.' "

While at Guernsey they went to Hauteville to pay a visit to Victor Hugo, but were disappointed to find that he was away. Hauteville failed to please Watts-Dunton, for he describes the interior decorations of that " tall unpicturesque house where the French poet lived and wrote " as a " ridiculous attempt at romanticism." . . . " All the materials for an antique interior of a modern house are there," he writes, " but they had better have been left with the curiosity dealers. No doubt the panels are of genuine black oak ; no doubt the carvings are as grotesque and antique as need be ; no doubt the tapestry and the dishes and plates are all that could be desired. But if, as here at Hauteville, these carvings are in the wrong place (some of them nailed upside down), if the plates are sunk in the tiles over the grates, if the tapestry (which is evidently meant to be hung on walls) is stretched along the ceiling, why the less said about such antiquities the better."

Although the two poets missed the chance of seeing Victor Hugo while on their visit to Guernsey, they met the " master " in Paris two months later.

This visit to Paris—the only visit they made to the Continent during their residence together at The Pines, as already mentioned—came about in this wise.

Vacquerie, the editor of *Le Rappel*, a relative of Hugo's and a great friend of Swinburne and Watts-Dunton, together with other important members of the Hugo *cénacle*, determined to get up a representation of *Le Roi s'amuse* on the jubilee of its first representation, since when it had never been acted. Vacquerie sent two stalls, one for Swinburne and one for Watts-Dunton, and the two friends were present at that memorable representation.* Long before the appointed day there was on the Continent, from Paris to Petrograd, an unprecedented demand for seats, for it was felt that this was the most interesting dramatic event that had occurred for fifty years.

Writing to Watts-Dunton from Leigh House, Bradford-on-Avon, October 8, 1882, Swinburne says :—

" You will have seen by Vacquerie's note that we need not be in Paris till the 20th of next month, when we shall have our seats for the 22nd, and be able also to see the rehearsal, which, as he says, will be no less interesting than the second representation of the play just fifty years after the first. So, as I think of staying here till the week for our departure, will you send me *Le Rappel* (and *Pall Mall*) as before, beginning with the numbers that have come since my departure ? I want all the occupation I can get, having hitherto been

---

* Watts-Dunton's sonnet, *At the Théâtre Français*, on the revival, after fifty years, of *Le Roi s'amuse* (November 22, 1882), is to be found among the Miscellaneous Poems in *The Coming of Love*.

unable to do a single satisfactory stroke of work, and having nothing else to fill up the solitary hours with. I really believe the stimulus of your criticism and encouragement has come to be—in the all but inspired language of the Church Catechism—' generally necessary to salvation ' if not to creation in my case ; for if I do write a few lines I am immediately impelled to scratch them out. . . .

> " ' Peace for her was the dower as a guerdon
>   Given of the storms to their cradle-child ;
> Peace the note of the sea's chant's burden
>   For leagues of triumph that flamed and smiled
> From dawn thro' noon to the sunset season,
>   A watchword whispered of dawn to noon
> For all the dark deep's trouble and treason,
>   And sealed by light of the moon.'

" It is all I have done since I came—I do feel most awfully torpid, tho', of course, I am cordially enjoying my stay here — only my working faculty seems actually benumbed. I have not spirit even to turn a sentence of Chesterfieldian Johnsonese, attributing this paralysis to the withdrawal of the daily influence of what I might perhaps be allowed to term the Beams —the solar refraction, so to speak, of a superior intelligence by whose vivifying medium the, *etc.* ' Seriatim,' I fear this stanza is hardly up to the mark, and I know you will tell me if you think so." *

* " Seriatim " was used by an illiterate friend of the poet's as meaning " seriously," and so the word became a standing joke between Watts-Dunton and Swinburne.

On the 8th November, about a fortnight before the date of the famous revival at the Théâtre Français, Swinburne wrote : " Let me have a word to say when I must be at Putney in good time for our punctual appearance in Paris on the 21st. I suppose about a week from to-day will do."

While still at Bradford-on-Avon, waiting patiently for the " great event," he corresponded frequently with Watts-Dunton.

" Did you get my account of the scriptural studies in which I am still engaged, finding real interest in the comparison of versions ? . . . Delight is the only word for my feeling about your last sonnets. I think—but then I am an interested party—they are about your very best, or, more properly, among those which are to be so counted. Isabel [Swinburne's sister] puts them side by side with that other splendid pair of Arab subjects. I have just written three which I rather like, in a very different but very serious line of thought or feeling."

Writing at this time about *Locrine*, having taken the manuscript to Bradford-on-Avon with him, Swinburne says :—

" Alice has had a very bad cold, lasting longer than mine, if less complicated ; but it is on the mend. . . . I have read out to her the two first acts of *Locrine*, with most favourable results. My voice is coming back, though the exertion has left it rather hoarse, and I am still now and then reminded of my cold by sneezing and coughing."

Alice Swinburne, in many respects the most intelligent of Swinburne's sisters, always took a keen pleasure in listening to her brother's readings from his works, and in the correspondence with him about them she was the one who showed the most marked sign of interest in literature ; all the poetic genius in the family —the passionate love of literature—would seem to have descended upon Algernon. *Locrine* did not appear until 1887, when the author dedicated it " To Alice Swinburne," this favourite sister of his.

Again Swinburne writes at this period, his mind engrossed in thoughts of Victor Hugo and his work :—

" I want to ask if you can find in either of my rooms the little Elzevirean edition of *L'Art d'être Grandpère*, which I did not, as I meant to, bring with me as a present for my mother. I thought it had been put up with my other things, but it has been left behind. I need not say how much obliged and how glad I shall be if you can send it carefully packed. I would not have it soiled or crumpled on any account, having kept it ' clean and uncut ' on purpose for a gift-book. . . . I find among my coats one which I seem to recognize as yours, a thin, loose, blue coat, with broad black bands on the sleeves ; so if you miss the article you will know where it is. Shall I send it, or bring it when I return ?—which will be before long. Alice and Isabel leave for Chelsea in two days' time, to stay with my aunt, Lady Mary Gordon, on a visit of some undetermined time—of which you shall have due notice ; afterwards I shall accompany my mother and Charlotte to London. We have good accounts of my sister-in-law.

" I am well into the second book or canto of *your Tristram*, containing the adventure illustrated by Morris on the walls of the Oxford Union in the sunflowery style which you may remember.* The only person to whom I have shown it is my revered friend the Primate,† whose too flattering and characteristic comment I cannot forbear to send you. . . . ' Seriatim,' I hope you will like the fight. I don't say Morris couldn't and wouldn't have done it better ; but I do *not* think any other of us all could. . . . Best regards from all."

On another occasion, while at Bradford-on-Avon, he wrote, in reference to Victor Hugo, for his interest in the " master's " work increased with the years :—

" Could you send me (carefully packed) the four volumes of the *Légende des Siècles*, the second volume of the *Contemplations*, and the *Théâtre en Liberté* (which I want particularly) ? My mother was asking me to read to her yesterday, and I could think of nothing.

* *Tristram of Lyonesse* (published in 1882) was dedicated " To my best friend, Theodore Watts."

† Dr. Stubbs, at one time Swinburne's tutor.

" *P.S.*—I cannot find the new tie which came in at the last moment. ' Ye would not see your natural friend ane scrub,' as King Jamie said, and unless you send it I shall make but a frowsy appearance."

Again, he writes in another postscript :—

" After my letter to-day was gone, I remembered a slip of the pen in my sonnet to Bright—' The *lion* England '—' sees yet beside *her.*' When (if ever) you send it anywhere, please substitute ' lioness ' for ' lion.' "

And then, three weeks later, comes another letter from Bradford-on-Avon, expressing that yearning for " wide sands where wave draws breath," which at this time of the year recurred to the author of *By the North Sea* with almost magnetic force.

" I suppose you are now nearly ready for the seaside. I begin to get impatient for it, and feel the want of bathing before summer is out. My mother is writing to you to explain how Aunt Ju's having postponed her visit till now has made it impossible to invite another guest at the same time ; so she hopes to see us later after our seaside holiday—for which I am ready whenever you are—some day, I suppose, next week, unless you are otherwise engaged or oppressed by work. When you settle a time I will be at Putney a day or two before, so as to have time to unpack and repack, as of course I shall not want to carry about the country all the books, etc., that I brought down."

After the visit to the Channel Islands, so closely associated in Swinburne's mind with the year of the Hugo " revival," the trips to the seaside were repeated every autumn, the two friends always choosing some resort on the south or east coast. These annual " swimming excursions " went on for twenty-three consecutive years, though frequently causing Watts-Dunton considerable inconvenience in the midst of his endless literary engagements. Swinburne, on the contrary, always began to exhibit an almost feverish yearning for a plunge into the sea at the first sign on Wimbledon Common that " the bees were stirring— birds were on the wing."

Cromer was the resort first chosen, after the visit to Guernsey. This was, perhaps, their favourite watering-place, for here they spent many an autumn holiday after this visit in 1883. Indeed it was at Cromer, in 1904, that Swinburne saw his beloved " mother sea " for the last time.

At this time (August 1884) Watts-Dunton's father died suddenly of heart failure. He was out for a walk near St. Ives after a visit to a friend. He fell in a fainting fit by the roadside, close to a cottage in the village through which he was passing, and was carried into the house, where he soon succumbed to this attack. It happened on a warm summer afternoon, and it is supposed that the walk, in spite of his vigorous constitution, had proved beyond his strength, for he was over seventy years of age.

After their two first seasons at Cromer they went to Seaford. This was in October 1885. And here an incident occurred which may be touched upon as an interesting instance among many of Swinburne's remarkable pluck, and at a moment when his presence of mind was put to the test even more severely, perhaps, than on the occasion of his famous adventure off the coast of Étretat, when borne out to sea by a strong ebbing tide. He went one morning for a long walk along the Seaford shore with Miss Theresa Watts, who was staying at the time in the Church Road with her brother and Swinburne. Suddenly Swinburne came to realize that they were in imminent peril of having their retreat cut off by the tide. The situation caused the poet no alarm whatever on his own account: it was this kind of episode that inspired him to write—

> " Yours was I born, and ye,
> The sea-wind and the sea,
> Made all my soul in me
> A song for ever."

He had no dread of the sea, as he has often reiterated in many such a verse as well as in conversation. But he felt the greatest concern for the safety of his companion. With frequent words of encouragement, and with the skilful support of his arm, as they hastened at the top of their speed over the rough shingles and slippery rocks, he contrived at last to reach a place of safety, though, as Miss Watts has good reason to remember to this day, not a moment too soon, for they were not merely drenched from head to foot by the blinding spray cast upon them by the incoming tide, but anticipated, with the approach of every recurring wave, to be lifted off their feet and swept out to sea.

While at Seaford that year Watts-Dunton—busy over the proofs of *Aylwin*, which many of his more intimate friends were reading with great interest—received a letter from Madox Brown with valuable hints regarding the painters and their models in the novel, embracing many technical points connected with an artist's studio.

" I have very carefully read all you have sent me," Madox Brown writes, in a letter dated Manchester, October 13, 1883, " and perhaps twice over all that relates to painters ; but so careful a writer are you that I cannot put finger on any passage that can be called incorrect or inartistic. You will perceive, if you take the trouble, that I have made two small marginal addenda to your text of about four words each ; but even of these I do not feel sure—as improvements. It seems to me that the fact of Cyril using models for his caricatures requires *emphasizing*, because, though quite correct with such advanced men as this artist represents, yet to most readers it would not appear so, caricatures being formerly always drawn without models. But then, as the words proceed from Lord Sleaford, *he* would not be likely to emphasize the fact—and, therefore, the emendation is questionable. The second addenda I think you will see is rather more important, because Cyril's observation that the composition represents a figure behind a veil rather savours of that sort of composition which *writers* are apt to invent for painters. You cannot paint a figure hidden by a veil. It is true that later on you explain that the veil is gauzy or transparent ; but for a short time Cyril's speech is misleading, and injurious to the writer, because so many writers compose *impossible* pictures, and readers, therefore—artistic ones especially—are always on the look-out for those sort of touches. The description of the gypsy model's eyes is peculiar ; but I dare say you got it from Rossetti, as it reads as if you had, and I should leave it. Perhaps they all discourse a trifle too glibly about ' predellas,' as D. G. R. was perhaps the only man in England who ever painted one ; also it seems to me that Madame Aylwin is somewhat over-acute in mediæval and Oriental types for a lady from the provinces whose husband never purchased pictures ; but it is what some ladies, no doubt, might say, and is the only slight little passage I can at all find to carp at in all the sections I have read.

" The artistic part somehow strikes me as more commonplace than the rest—perhaps because to *me* it *is* more common ; but certainly Wilderspin is a quite original character. Is he not intentionally compounded out of Rossetti and Shields ? The pictures are Rossetti's and the clothes Shields'. Cyril is very lifelike,

and like many a member of the ' Arts ' Club. But
Sinfi Lovell is my heroine—always interesting and
always grand, and the way she (of her own strong will)
takes herself off is very pathetic. One can't help hoping it *is* the last of her—at least the last time she crosses
Aylwin's path—for her own peace of mind. It is very
late, and I cannot be of the least use to you in it, you
see, for I can find no lapses in it."

Next year Watts-Dunton and Swinburne engaged
apartments near the Seaside Road at Eastbourne, the
chief recommendation being—to Swinburne, at least—
the excellent supply of boats at this end of the town.
For what " the bard," as Watts-Dunton loved to call
him, most yearned for was a leap from the stern of a
rowing boat, unencumbered by the " regulation bathing costume," head foremost into the waves. For the
three successive years following upon this visit to Eastbourne, they went to Lancing-on-Sea, usually about
September, their apartments being at No. 2 The Terrace ; and there they remained for five or six weeks
on each occasion, " weather permitting."

The proofs of *Aylwin* were, of course, still having
" consideration." He was too much occupied on the
Athenæum and elsewhere to complete the revisions and
bring out the novel.

The letters that he wrote almost daily from Lancing, or wherever he chanced to be, to his sister, Miss
Theresa Watts, who resided permanently with him

on Putney Hill, illustrate his intellectual restlessness.

Before going with Swinburne to Lancing in the following autumn, Watts-Dunton wrote to him at his mother's house (August 4, 1887), on the subject of *Locrine*, which the poet was correcting for the press :—

" I hope that by this time you will have received the proof of the dedication.* The manuscript was so unusually clean, even for your manuscripts, that as the book cannot possibly come out till October, I went to the expense of having a copy of it made for the printers, so that it should be unsoiled of their dirty fingers. Hence some little further delay. But the entire poem is in Chatto's hands.

" Remember, however, that the poem should not appear before the autumn season. A new edition of the *Selections* will, I hope, be needed very soon.† What changes would you like besides removing the two last of the Guernsey poems ? I saw William Rossetti, and entirely made peace with him anent Whitmania. . . . Kindest remembrances to all at Leigh House."

While staying at Lancing there came the request from Watts-Dunton, as on all previous and subsequent occasions up to the very last, for books to be sent him or some other material for literary work. When away

---

* *Locrine* (published in 1887) was dedicated " To Alice Swinburne," his favourite sister, as mentioned already.

† *Selections from Swinburne.* (Chatto and Windus.)

from The Pines, even on these midsummer holidays, his craze for work increased :—

" In the large bookcase in the front room is a book (in two volumes, I think) called *The Frontier Land of the Christian and the Turk*. It is bound, I think, in green cloth. The volumes are about the size of Robinson's *In Bad Hands* and other three-volume novels. I wish you could send it at once. Also please see if there is a copy of Sharp's new novel from Hurst and Blackett. Open all parcels of *books*, and tell me what they contain. Thanks for *Peveril of the Peak*."

Another instance of how immersed he was in work when on visits to friends, is seen in a letter which he wrote to Messrs. Hurst and Blackett about *Aylwin*, while staying at Lady Mary Gordon's at Northcourt, with Swinburne—for they went in each other's company to country seats as well as to the seaside :—

" Dear Sirs,—*Aylwin*, Volume 2.—My address from to-day till next Tuesday will be as under. Please send proofs there. . . ."

In the following autumn they were again at Lady Mary Gordon's. On July 6, 1891, Lady Jane Swinburne wrote to Watts-Dunton from Northcourt, telling him that her sister, Lady Mary Gordon, looked forward to a visit from him and Swinburne early in the following month at The Orchard, and there they went on the 4th of September. Meantime they visited Brock-hampton Park, Andoversford, in Gloucestershire.

A letter from Professor Jowett, Master of Balliol, dated Boar's Hill, April 18, 1884, contained a cordial invitation to Watts-Dunton and Swinburne to visit him at Oxford. That visit inspired the following reminiscence :—

> " We walk through flowery ways
> From Boar's Hill down to Oxford, fain to know
> What nugget-gold, in drift of Time's long flow,
> The Bodleian mine hath stored from richer days ;
> He, fresh as on that morn, with sparkling gaze,
> Hair bright as sunshine, white as moonlit snow,
> Still talks of Plato, while the scene below
> Breaks gleaming through the veil of sunlit haze."

They also frequently went to stay with Lady Jane Swinburne and other members of the Swinburne family. When, however, Watts-Dunton found himself too full of engagements to leave The Pines, as sometimes happened, Swinburne would go alone, and on these occasions he never failed to write at frequent intervals to his friend.

While Watts-Dunton was staying with the Swinburne family at Dursley, in September 1894, he and Swinburne took the opportunity of making some inquiries into Shakespeare's connection with Gloucestershire, and they soon satisfied themselves as to the poet's familiarity with that county. He had evidently stayed at Dursley with one of the Shakespeares who was living there during the poet's lifetime. They also found that the Gloucestershire names of people mentioned by Shakespeare were still largely represented at Dursley, and the description of the neighbourhood easily identified.

In a letter from Frank Hindes Groome to Watts-Dunton dated October 23, 1894, he says : " I read of your Shakespeare researches at Dursley ; they sound most interesting."

And in another letter—one from Mr. Coulson Kernahan—to whom Watts-Dunton also wrote about the pilgrimage to Dursley—" I am very interested," says Mr. Kernahan, " in what you tell me about Shakespeare and Gloucestershire. Will you not write a paper on the subject for one of the reviews ? It would be deeply interesting. . . ."

While at Chestal with his family, Swinburne described the scenery, in a letter to Watts-Dunton which his friend always regarded as one of the best prose delineations of nature he ever read, and he preserved it with special care among the thousand and one letters from literary friends :—

" CHESTAL,
" *August* 14, 1894.

" MY DEAR WALTER.

" I am almost glad that you could not get a copy of the Kelmscott *Atalanta,* as it gives me the pleasure of sending you one of my two extra copies, which I hope will reach you with this letter, and in which I have written your name. The other, of course, is my mother's, who is delighted with the book. I wrote my acknowledgments yesterday to dear old Topsy for the books and the cheque—actually specifying the amount as enclosed, which was more than you told me to do."

In an answer to this letter, Watts-Dunton wrote from The Pines, August 16, 1894 :—

" It is simply characteristic of your generosity to send me so priceless a present as the Morris edition of *Atalanta*, with your autograph set therein. It will be among the chief of my treasures.

" With regard to Sir John Swinburne, I cannot but think that the proper thing to do, notwithstanding everything, is to send him the manuscript for the Copheaton library. I will give you my reasons when we meet. So shall I tell Chatto to send you a copy of the book for you to send on, if you agree with my views ? Chatto has the list of articles for the forthcoming prose book, and I will get it for you, and we will have everything arranged as we wish.

" Your description of that aerial castle and of the Cotswolds is really admirable. I shall specially preserve the letter containing it (of course, however, I do keep your few letters to me)—as a specimen of your best descriptive power in prose."

XXIII.

LAST DAYS.

XXIII.

LAST DAYS.

THAT the death of Swinburne should leave a great void in Watts-Dunton's declining days, goes without saying. A prominent landmark in his life —more prominent even than the Rossetti landmark— had been removed. Swinburne and his welfare, from the hour the poet put foot inside The Pines until the end came, had been first and foremost in Watts-Dunton's thoughts. Watts-Dunton's profound sense of responsibility is in no instance more forcibly illustrated than in regard to the Swinburne fosterage. It has no parallel in the divers records of modern literary friendships. In a semi-detached suburban villa, clad with ivy to hide its prosaic face, these two poetic friends lived together in wonderful harmony for thirty years; and if the atmosphere of romance with which they surrounded their lives ever showed signs of rarefaction, the " midsummer holiday " furnished a fresh supply.

Despite Swinburne's amazing vitality, it was clear for some time before the end that his health had begun to fail. Signs of weariness, never before apparent, were

becoming every day more perceptible when he reached
home from his morning peregrinations.

The shock sustained by the poet's decease was
greater than Watts-Dunton ever fully realized. Whether
he retained the exceptional health and buoyant spirits
that he had experienced before his bereavement is very
doubtful. He showed signs of nervous irritability in a
marked degree. He was not only sole legatee; he was
appointed Swinburne's sole literary executor, and he
began to imagine himself overburdened with literary
and business affairs.

The labour involved in scrutinizing the Swinburne
manuscripts and letters, the papers connected with the
Swinburne estate, and other documents relating to the
Swinburne family, which through the poet's death
came to be exhumed from legal strong-rooms, caused
Watts-Dunton, in his weak state of health, to shrink
with dismay from the thought of tackling the onerous
task. And yet he felt, with his innate sense of responsibility, that as a man of affairs, if not out of regard for
his dead friend, the task was one which it was his bounden
duty to confront. In fact, his legal experience soon
led him to realize that to procrastinate in this instance
was obviously impracticable, and although considerably
exhausted by the effort, he gave to these business
matters all needful attention. But with a satisfactory
adjustment of the Swinburne affairs, Watts-Dunton's
sense of responsibility was only partially set at rest.
He began to be haunted by the thought that there was

Drawing-room at "The Pines," showing the sofa where Watts-Dunton used to receive visitors, and on which he died

(*Photo by Poole, Putney*)

another task in store for him—a task far more onerous than these matters of business—the writing of the Swinburne biography. A biography must be undertaken ; friends expected it ; and they did more than tacitly regard him as the man best qualified for the work : many of them were responsible for paragraphs that appeared in the literary journals announcing that he was projecting an " official Life." For a time he hesitated to contradict the assertion. It was impossible to hide the fact, so well known to every one, that he possessed practically all the material required for such a Life—not merely in regard to manuscripts, letters, and, above all, personal reminiscences extending over a period of more than thirty years—but also in regard to family letters and papers touching upon the poet's early life, mostly in the hands of Miss Isabel Swinburne, who was eager to assist her brother's friend as far as lay in her power. But, in spite of these exceptional opportunities, Watts-Dunton achieved absolutely nothing in the shape of a Swinburne biography, beyond a page in the poet's life—if it may be called even that—prefacing the latest edition of *Selections from Swinburne*.

The first among the very few letters that Watts-Dunton wrote, breaking the sad tidings of Swinburne's death, was the one to the poet's sister, Miss Isabel Swinburne. It is dated The Pines, April 10, 1909.

" The end was certain this morning . . ." he tells her, " but it came much more rapidly than anybody expected. My telegram to you was scarcely gone when he passed away, peacefully and with a happy smile upon his lips. The last I saw of him was last night, when I thought I never saw a man more happy and cheerful; and he might very well be so, for never was there a better man. His passing away should be taken as a tremendous lesson to the Pharisees who spoke ill of him."

At that trying moment Watts-Dunton received a large number of letters of condolence from friends of his late house-mate who were friends of his own, expressing appreciation of the poet's genius and of his fine nature. Among those letters there was one that he greatly prized :—

"Box Hill, Dorking,
"*April* 13, 1909.

" My dear Theodore,

"The blow was heavy on me. I had such confidence in his powers of recovery. The end has come! That brain of the vivid illumination is extinct. I can hardly realize it when I revolve the many times when at the starting of an idea the whole town was instantly ablaze with electric light. Song was his natural voice. He was the greatest of our lyrical poets—of the world's, I could say, considering what a language he had to wield. But if I feel the loss of him as a poet of our life torn away, how keenly must the stroke fall on you, and at a time of prostration from illness! Happily, you have a wife for support and consolation. That helps

to comfort me in my dire distress of mind on behalf
of your stricken household, which I see beneath the
shadow.   I will hire a motor and be with you when
I know that you are in better health, and we can talk.
My respects to your wife.

"GEORGE MEREDITH."

Within five weeks of writing this letter the famous
novelist was also dead.

In the early autumn of this year (1909), still in feeble
health, Watts-Dunton rented a bungalow near the sea-
front at Margate, where he sojourned with Mrs. Watts-
Dunton for some weeks.   The old manifestations of
excessive mental activity, so apparent during the holiday trips with Swinburne to East Anglia or the south
coast, still prevailed.   Indeed, that ingrained habit of
colossal unrest seemed even more persistent.   That
" literary portmanteau," containing the manuscripts of
long-projected publications packed amidst a heap of
reference books, was in evidence as before.   It held the
manuscript of his long-promised novel, *Carniola*, the
end of which was in sight.   His intention was to devote
each morning during his stay at Margate to reading the
work through from the first chapter to the last.   With
the aid of his secretary, considerable headway was made :
the early hours after breakfast were devoted to the reading, during the first three or four weeks.   But owing to
a sudden turn of inclement weather, he contracted a
slight catarrh.   All work, as a consequence, was aban-

doned, and by the doctor's advice he went home to Putney Hill.

His last two autumns were spent at Eastbourne. Here his habit of getting to work betimes still clung to him. But towards noon he would stroll down to the " front " with Mrs. Watts-Dunton, whose readings from some one of his favourite works of fiction in a cosy shelter never failed to afford him keen enjoyment.

Only a few weeks before his death he took great care in preparing the latest edition of *Aylwin*. He corresponded with his publishers frequently upon the subject. " I originally intended," he wrote in one of his last letters to them, " to preface this edition with new and interesting matter about characters in the book. But I found that this new material would be too long for a preface, and, besides, would disturb the arrangement of the book too much ; so I have incorporated in two Appendices—one by myself, quite recently written, and the other consisting of a reprint of some articles which appeared soon after the publication of *Aylwin*." *

Mental occupation in some shape or another, as has been made evident, was the ruling passion from first to last. But it was only to be expected that during spells of senile indisposition, that naturally increased with advancing years, a break would occur in the requisite energy for taking up imaginative work. At these

* " A Key to the Characters in *Aylwin*." by Thomas Hake.
Vide *Notes and Queries* (1902).

times, however, there were no actual signs of mental stagnation : he would fall back upon the lighter efforts of thought happily found in dictating letters. And these letters were frequently revised with the same ungrudging toil that he was wont to bestow upon his journalistic compositions. He would in some cases linger over the business of revising a single letter during the greater part of two or three mornings, failing at times even then to be fully satisfied with the result. One letter out of a thousand may be quoted, which, though somewhat brief, was written at a moment when he was in no mood for mental exertion of an exacting nature. It had reference to a dinner given to W. D. Howells in New York (March 2, 1912) on his seventy-fifth birthday. It was read at the banquet, among other letters from a number of Howells's admirers across the Atlantic—letters from Thomas Hardy, Arnold Bennett, W. J. Locke, J. M. Barrie, Arthur Pinero. The epistolary tribute from Watts-Dunton to the famous American novelist is dated from The Pines, February 20, 1912 :—

" The dinner in celebration of Mr. Howells's birthday will be looked upon as one of the great literary events of this eventful year. And is it not piquant as coming in the midst of the avalanche of talk—good, bad, and indifferent—about the Dickens Centenary ?

" Dickens and Howells ! Nobody loves Dickens ' this side idolatry ' more than I do, but that does not blind me to the surpassing quality of Howells's work in the very opposite kind of fiction. His place is as distinct and assured in one form of the novelist's art as Dickens's is in the other. I think these two great men represent the very opposite poles of prose fiction. While one finds everlasting delight in observing and depicting the striking, the odd, the grotesque, the other finds as deep a joy—a deeper joy, perhaps—in observing and depicting the ordinary, the familiar. Howells realizes that in this universe there is nothing that is not wonderful, and that the ' ordinary ' is the most wonderful of all. In this regard one is the exact complement of the other.

" And then look at the enormous array of Howells's output and its variety. No doubt there are in these marvellous and bewildering days novelists and poets whose output is even vaster in quantity than his, but there are none, I think, whose quality is so great in style and in matter.

" When does he write his ' pot-boilers ' ? Sometimes, I suppose ; but I can never recognize the culinary quality.

" As to his style, it is in my judgment as near perfection as any style in our language—lucid, and exact to a degree, easy, masterful, never exaggerated, and has a movement which, I think, I could discern anywhere."

He was constantly being asked to write on Dickens, Thackeray, and every other novelist of note.

" If my hands were more free," he said, in answer to a letter from Mr. Spielmann, " I should like to write upon Thackeray, and, on the whole, I think I might have selected *The Newcomes* as being to me one of the most interesting and suggestive of his stories. But besides some practical work that I want to finish, I have already undertaken to write as much criticism as I shall care to write for some time to come.

" I may say, however, that although I agreed to write an article upon *Oliver Twist* for Mr. Sproul, the New York publisher, upon terms such as I do not generally accept, 1 should not care to write upon those terms in future."

This article on *Oliver Twist* was subsequently undertaken by Swinburne, and afterwards incorporated in his volume, *Charles Dickens*, edited by Watts-Dunton.*

Watts-Dunton did write an article on *A Tale of Two Cities*, however, for Mr. Sproul's *édition de luxe* of Dickens's works ; but, although completed, it did not appear in that series or in any other edition of Dickens—so far, indeed, it has never been printed ; the only one he did print about the author of *Pickwick* was the article *Dickens and Christmas* in the *Nineteenth Century ;* and in a letter to a lady, dated Eastbourne, July 26, 1913, who has written copiously on Watts-Dunton's work, he says : " My article upon Dickens and Christmas in the *Nineteenth Century* is, I think, the one I like best."

* Chatto and Windus (1913).

His article on *David Copperfield* was only partially written at the time of his decease. It was his intention to produce a book of critical essays on Dickens, and include *A Tale of Two Cities* and *Dickens and Christmas* in the volume. And still another volume—a book upon the *Comedy of Humour* and the *Comedy of Repartee* —was projected, consisting of, or rather based on, his articles in the *Encyclopædia Britannica* on Wycherley and Vanbrugh ; an article in *Chambers's Encyclopædia* on Congreve ; a long study on Etheredge, and two long articles on Ben Jonson.

He was also frequently asked in these days by journalistic strangers, no less than by journalistic friends, to furnish them with details about his own life and work. Madame Galemberti, a lady of rank, well known in literary circles as a contributor to Italian journals, while engaged upon a pen portrait of him, corresponded with Watts-Dunton with regard to his career. In one of his letters to this lady, dated a little more than a year before he died (April 22, 1913), Watts-Dunton says :—

" My first and only love was literature, more especially metre. I believe I am a good lawyer, or at least a fair lawyer ; but law makes no demand whatever upon the higher faculties of man, and is very unsatisfying. I have abandoned it for years.*

" Latterly I have interested myself deeply in science,

---

* He retired from the legal profession in 1900.

whose recent revelations are overwhelming, bewildering, and almost out-dazzle poetry.

" I am afraid I cannot interest you by discussing the latest school of poetry. The realistic effects which it aims to produce have hitherto been supposed to be the work of prose ; but they are, no doubt, powerful young men and powerful young writers, and see what they see. . . . I have just been reading William Watson's latest volume. Watson's sonorous and artistic lines always give me pleasure, but his poems to his beautiful young wife in his latest volume are especially delightful."

At this very time, as it chanced, Mr. Watson was staying in the vicinity of Watts-Dunton's native town, and some correspondence took place between them about Swinburne and others. In a letter addressed from Old Hollies, Buckden, Huntingdon (May 24, 1913), Mr. Watson writes :—

" My dear Watts-Dunton,—Your very kind and very interesting letter of yesterday reaches me here to-day, together with those fine book-gifts. How am I to thank you for these generous gifts of noble volumes— chief of all, the lovely copy of *Aylwin*, for which my wife sends her grateful thanks, coupled with the reproaches that you did not centuple its value by autographing it for her! She has the great advantage over me of not having read a word of it—an advantage which she is hastening to forfeit ; but both of us had already wondered where you got *your* Rhona.   My wife when a girl knew a Rhona in her County Tyrone, who must now be over forty-five, and I am interested to hear of *your* Rhona in the Tollemache family.   At any rate this beautiful copy of *Aylwin* shall be kept for our own Rhona, who grows in all desirable qualities day by day.

" For my part, I am glad to have these Swinburne volumes—even though they do lack your autograph— *Tristram* and the *Songs before Sunrise.*   I remember first reading the *Sailing of the Swallow* on its original appearance in, I think, the *Gentleman's Magazine,* which must have been a good while ago.   I must say, however, that to my mind the richness and exuberance of Swinburne's imagination and diction were rather a barrier than an aid to his mastery of narrative art.   The *Songs before Sunrise,* of course, I have known from long, long ago. By the way, I had an idea that Swinburne never altered his text ; but in the noble concluding stanzas of *An Appeal,* in this new edition, I find an alteration which I cannot think an improvement.   The line which I used to know as ' Asks for counsel of blood ' has become ' Cries for surety of blood,' which seems to me both far inferior to the earlier reading, and also to lead up much less naturally to the succeeding line.

" You may not agree with me, but I have always thought the choruses of *Atalanta* and *Erechtheus* the very summits of Swinburne's genius.   I rate them much higher than the choruses and dramatic lyrics of Shelley's *Prometheus* and *Hellas,* except that I should put ' The world's great age begins anew ' as high as Swinburne's lyrics and choruses, but all the rest of Shelley's, including ' Light of light, thy lips enkindle,' on a far lower plane than the finest of A. C. S.'s. Of the two great choruses of *Atalanta*, I, unlike most people, should place ' When the hounds of Spring' even higher than the sublime ' In the beginning of years.' I think the first line of the *Artemis* chorus the most splendid first line in the language, and what follows is little if anything below it. In the *Poems and Ballads* themselves are, of course, some glorious things, such as *Felice*, with its wonderful terseness—not a usual trait with Swinburne ; the beautiful *Triumph of Time ;* and, whatever one may think of its subject, the superb *Anactoria*, in which I think the rhymed heroic measure is used with an individuality and a masterliness not equalled elsewhere, even by Chaucer or Dryden. Of the poems of Swinburne's later or middle period I should rank *Ave Atque Vale* as one of the most perfect in form and expression ; and to my mind the very last poem in which he sang with all his original fire was the magnificent " Down the Way of Czars." I don't remember its title, but I can never forget such lines as

"' Night hath one red star—Tyrannicide.'

No poem of my time thrilled me more, and it showed the man in his noblest light, as a great and fiery hater of oppression—the light in which I shall choose to think of him to the last.

"It is most pleasant to hear of Mrs. Watts-Dunton as reading my new little volume aloud to you, and of her fondness for the lyrics addressed to my wife ; nor need I say how proud I am of your own generous words about them. It is distressing to hear that the effects of the accident to your eye still remain ; I had hoped they had passed away.

"I do not know whether you remember this village. The present name of our house was given it by ourselves; before that it had no distinctive name, I think. It is a roomy old cottage with some seven bedrooms and four sitting-rooms, of which we use three. But we live out of doors more than within, and such work as I do is mostly done in the garden, where our lovely little girl also spends most of her time.

"Yours most sincerely,

"WILLIAM WATSON."

The latest piece of literary work Watts-Dunton ever wrote was his Foreword to *The Keats Letters, Papers, and other Relics*, published by Mr. John Lane, forming the Dilke bequest to the Hampstead Public Library. He dictated the essay to his secretary one morning in a couple of hours, while resting on a seat near Swinburne's favourite spot under the hawthorns on Wimbledon Common. It was in the early spring of 1914 ; a soft south wind was blowing, and a skylark sang blithely overhead ; a more genial morning could not well be imagined. The Foreword finished, he looked round him at the budding hawthorns on all sides, and then began to recite *Work without Hope*, in those deep, rapturous tones in which he had recited the selfsame poem many a time before on many a similar spring morning :—

> " All Nature seems at work. Slugs leave their lair—
> The bees are stirring—birds are on the wing."

It was at the suggestion of Miss Isabel Swinburne that Dr. Williamson, the editor of the Keats volume, approached Watts-Dunton with regard to the writing of this Foreword.

In a letter agreeing to the project, Watts-Dunton writes to Dr. Williamson from The Pines :—

" I dare say you are aware that to a critic so possessed by the poetry of Keats as I am, while it is easy to write at some length upon him and his poetry, it is almost impossible to say anything worthy of the subject in a few lines. I shall, I hope, however, be able to send you what I want to say upon the subject by to-morrow night's post. No doubt you remember that on the occasion of the inauguration of the American memorial bust of Keats in Hampstead Parish Church, on July 16, 1894, a sonnet of mine was read and published, called *To a Sleeper at Rome*. I shall probably quote part of this sonnet. I hope that before long I shall have the pleasure of making your personal acquaintance, if you can, without inconvenience, come out to see me. A friend of my dear friend, Miss Isabel

Swinburne, must needs be a friend of mine. By-the-bye, are you aware that Keats is her favourite poet of the past, as well as my own ? "

Those who knew Watts-Dunton, however slightly, need scarcely even read his essay in the *Athenæum* of August 20, 1887, on Sir Sidney Colvin's *Keats* in the English Men of Letters series, in order to realize the deep delight he took in studying every line of poetry the author of *Hyperion* ever wrote.

Comparisons have occasionally been made, not without warrant, to Watts-Dunton's affinity with Leigh Hunt, in his leniency as a critic, no less than in the interest he took in other men's work. As Leigh Hunt encouraged Keats in those early " half-fledged " days, so it may be surmised that Watts-Dunton, quick to recognize merit in " youthful aspirants " wherever the faintest sign of talent could be detected, would have been among the first to discover that Keats's early poems gave promise of work of a high order of merit, had he lived in the Leigh Hunt days.

In a letter to the *Times* (April 18, 1914), soon after writing his Foreword for the Keats volume, Watts-Dunton says, in reference to *Endymion* :—

" I heartily join Mr. Arthur Lynch in thanking you for your article upon Keats, and for all that you, with Sir Sidney Colvin, are just now doing in honour of the beloved poet's fame.

" By-the-bye, Mr. Lynch is the very first man that I have found who is in entire sympathy with myself as to the amazing poetical genius seen at work in *Endymion*.

" To a precious and beautiful but necessarily expensive book, immediately to be published by Mr. John Lane, *The Keats Letters, Papers, and other Relics*, forming the Dilke bequest in the Hampstead Public Library (edited by Dr. George C. Williamson, with an Introduction by Mr. Buxton Forman), I have contributed certain Forewords from which I hope you will let me quote a sentence or two concerning *Endymion*.

" ' The conventional talk about the futility of *Endymion* has come down to us from the unfair criticism of Keats's own time. It is full of poetry. When it descends into prattle, which it sometimes assuredly does, it is always the prattle of a baby Olympian.'

" In *Endymion*, Keats, in his determined revolt against 18th-century canons and 18th-century movements, does certainly perpetrate some inharmonious lines. But these occasional blemishes were owing mainly to the influence of Leigh Hunt's exaggerated theory about the rhyme-pause and enjambment."

He was also engaged during these last days in revising his two most ambitious essays—one in the *Encyclopædia Britannica* and the other in *Chambers's Cyclopædia of English Literature*—with a view to their publication in book form. He gave to the volume the title, *Poetry and the Renascence of Wonder*.

One morning, while conning over the pages of the manuscript heaped up on the table at his side, he turned to his secretary with a look of sudden elation. " This book," said he, placing his hand upon the pile—" this book is going to be my *magnum opus*."

The manuscript was placed by him for publication, during the last week of his life, in the hands of his friend, Mr. Herbert Jenkins, who has recently published Watts-Dunton's volume of reminiscences of famous friends, *Old Familiar Faces*.

Mrs. Watts-Dunton's Sunday " At Homes " at The Pines included most of the best known among literary and artistic circles of these latter days. And there was one thing above all others that gave these gatherings a peculiar interest. There were some few among the guests whose recollections carried them back to the days of the mid-Victorian period : it formed a link with the dim, half-forgotten past. The fact that Watts-Dunton, through his friend Trelawney, connected this circle with the period of the " Renascence of Wonder," was in itself interesting.

Literary folk, however interesting, are rarely at their best on social occasions, and it is therefore no slight tribute to Mrs. Watts-Dunton's personality that she was able to impart life and " go " to functions that are too often stiff and uninteresting. Everything depends on the woman who directs at such times, and gracious as Watts-Dunton was to his guests, his growing infirmities prevented him necessarily from taking a very active part in social converse. But he always greatly admired the skill and tact which his wife displayed in arranging these functions.

Among the visitors at these gatherings, Mr. and Mrs. Walter Jerrold were frequently to be 'seen, and, as Mr. Jerrold well knew, his talk about his famous relative always gave Watts-Dunton great pleasure, for no man ever appreciated the genius of Douglas Jerrold more than he did.* Every one who came to these receptions, indeed, seemed to interest Watts-Dunton in some special way. He delighted in a long discussion with Mr. Ernest Law about his Shakespeare researches ; and to compare notes with Mr. George Dewar, the brilliant author of *The Leaning Spire* and many other " Nature " books, about their individual experience by mead and stream, was a diversion of which he never grew tired. But Mr. James Douglas, often accompanied by Mrs. Douglas, came perhaps more frequently to The Pines than most of the visitors. With this original and brilliantly equipped friend, Watts-Dunton's talk ranged from the lightest town chatter to subjects philosophic and profound. It was a matter of constant surprise to Mr. Douglas, during these talks, how Watts-Dunton's omnivorous mind was keenly alert in all current events ; no affair of public interest, from the last phase of " labour unrest " to the racing of aero-

---

* Douglas Jerrold's tomb is close beside Watts-Dunton's grave in Norwood Cemetery.

planes, seemed to escape his attention. " When we want to be up to date all round," Mr. Douglas once said to him, " we *pay you* a visit."

Mr. T. J. Wise, the famous bibliographer, was an always welcome friend, for although Watts-Dunton was never in any sense a bibliographer, Mr. Wise was of great assistance in supplying information regarding the titles of contributions to magazines of some of Watts-Dunton's favourite authors, as well as the dates of publications, in connection with literature on Borrow, Coleridge, Keats, and more especially Swinburne.

" I must not delay to thank you for the Coleridge Bibliography. It is amazingly full and complete," he wrote to Mr. Wise (January 1, 1914), " and is a source of continual delight to me. It is really most generous of you to send me such a book. Don't forget your promise to come and see me early in the new year, for there are many things I want to talk to you about."

And then would frequently come to The Pines Mr. Ernest Rhys, to whom Watts-Dunton always felt deeply indebted for the valuable aid he gave in reading the Welsh portion of *Aylwin* at the time the proof sheets of the novel were being finally revised.* Mrs. Rhys, too, was a friend of whose novels Watts-Dunton often spoke and fully appreciated, and what perhaps gave

* The " Arvon " edition of *Aylwin* was dedicated by Watts-Dunton to his Welsh friend, Mr. Ernest Rhys.

still greater zest to his sense of friendship was the thought that Swinburne had always expressed pleasure when she came with Mr. Rhys to luncheon with them. The most constant visitor at The Pines, however, was Mr. Mackenzie Bell, a friend of thirty years' standing, whose interests in literature were similar in some measure to those of the author of *The Coming of Love*.

Mr. Clement Shorter was another visitor with whom Watts-Dunton had certain literary interests in common. Besides, Watts-Dunton was a genuine admirer of Mrs. Shorter's poetry.

"It was most kind of you to send me Mrs. Shorter's new volume of poems," he wrote to Mr. Clement Shorter (November 17, 1912). "Anything from her has an especial attraction for me and my wife. These poems have all the charm of her previous poetry. They have all the *naïveté* which so few modern poets can achieve. For the moment that a modern poet tries to be *naïf*, he egregiously fails. It is an endowment of the very few. I have been greatly struck by the ballad, *The Guardian Angels*. It is an old story, and, for aught I know, based upon fact ; anyhow, Mrs. Shorter has immortalized it. No one can, I think, treat the subject again. . . . Another poem in the book that has attracted me very much is the last—*When I shall Rise*. The love of Ireland reminds me of Emily Brontë's love of the Haworth Moors (pointed out by Swinburne), where she makes a character thrown out of Heaven upon the beloved heather that she knew so well and that was Heaven to her. . . . I was much delighted with your remarks about poor Gissing. They were sorely needed at this very moment."

Another among his friends was Mrs. John Lane, whose works he highly appreciated, and whose society always pleased him ; he was a frequent guest at Mr. John Lane's house.

Mr. W. H. Chesson, one of the younger generation among Watts-Dunton's literary friends, was during the last years a welcome visitor. " Such a lover of Swinburne," Watts-Dunton wrote to him in one of his letters (March 7, 1914), " and such an able champion of him and his work, is necessarily dear to me. . . . Name a day soon for coming."

Another literary friend sometimes to be seen at The Pines, whose critical essays never failed to attract his attention, was Mr. George Sampson. " I have of late been reading, and reading with true admiration," he wrote to Mr. Sampson (March 20, 1914), " a lot of your articles in the *Daily Chronicle*—among them articles upon such divers subjects as Charlotte Brontë and Lord Wellesley. Your portrait of Wellesley as the antithesis of his younger brother ' in his sublimity ridiculous,' while the great duke was, in Tennysonean phrase, ' in his simplicity sublime,' is a splendid epigram."

Mr. Coulson Kernahan, a less frequent visitor in the

later days than in earlier times, always cheered him
greatly with his sympathetic comradeship and abound-
ing vitality. His reiterated inquiries, such as, "Where
is the Life of George Borrow?" "Where is the Life of
Rossetti?" "Where are the Reminiscences of Tennyson,
Browning, Lowell, Morris, and others with whom you
were on such intimate terms?" would at times somewhat disconcert Watts-Dunton, although Mr. Kernahan
was by no means the only literary friend who ventured
to put these awkward questions.

Nor were there any among his visitors for whom he
had a more truly sincere admiration than that which he
felt for Mr. and Mrs. Wilfrid Meynell. He once wrote
to Mr. Meynell :—

"THE PINES,
"28 September 1908.

"DEAR MR. MEYNELL,

"It was very kind of you to send me the
Selections from Francis Thompson's Poems, which I appreciate greatly. There is no doubt whatever that this
remarkable man was a true poet. He had the veritable
ecstasy. His career is astounding. I have gathered
together every scrap relating to him, with the purpose
of pondering over so extraordinary a life, and if I may
say so, for pondering over the unequalled kindness of
yourself and the fine poet, your wife. I do not know
anything in the annals of letters nobler and more self-
sacrificing. I love to think of noble conduct. It gives
me intense pleasure, and consequently I love to think
of you and poor Thompson. It will be a pity if it is

not recorded more fully than you two can record it. I know much more about it through Thomas Hake than you think ; but let it pass. Perhaps I have already said too much about it to please you. I was aware that Thompson had written about the last essay on Shelley in the language. I fully intended to get the *Dublin Review* in order to read it, but I have not done so, and perhaps I should never have got it, for ' Time driveth onward fast,' and ' in a little while our lips are dumb.' Swinburne is not much in accord with Thompson's poetry. Its eccentricities shock him, as indeed they shock me. I did not know that Thompson reviewed Swinburne's *Collected Poems* in the *Athenæum*. I don't think I read it, and I am sure that Swinburne didn't, but I shall get the number containing the article and read it. Of course you are aware that I haven't written much for the *Athenæum* for ten years, although I feel a warm interest in the paper, and look upon the brilliant young editor as one of my friends. My wife is an enthusiast about your wife's poetry. She will not hear that there is any living poetess to be compared with her, and, on the whole, I am inclined to agree with her.

> " Believe me to be,
> " My dear Mr. Meynell,
> " Yours ever,
> " T. WATTS-DUNTON."

He read Mr. Wilfrid Meynell's Life of Disraeli with peculiar interest ; and it was through perusing this biography that he became inspired with the idea of making a special study of Beaconsfield's character—a personality that had always fascinated him, and which resulted in his producing a pen-picture of this famous statesman in his novel, *Carniola*.

An eye trouble during the last few years of his life necessitated the use of a green shade. He could see to read, though not without difficulty, and occasionally not without pain. He admitted that he acted in opposition to the advice of his oculist every time he looked into a book ; that he ran the risk by so doing of losing his sight entirely ; but, as he declared, to so confirmed a bookworm the temptation was irresistible. He never used a pen, however, except to sign his name, after his eye trouble became apparent. It is somewhat remarkable that after middle life his personal appearance underwent no very marked change. He had grown old at forty, and his hair only began to turn gray after he had passed his three score and ten years. His forehead remained unwrinkled to the last. This feature, as he affirmed, was a racial peculiarity which he inherited from both parents ; and his eyes, concealed behind that disfiguring green shade, were still bright under thick dark-brown eyebrows. He lived in constant dread, though never taking all the precaution that he was urged to take, that he would some morning open his eyes to find himself blind. His old friend, Mr. Frank Taylor, a near neighbour, whom he appointed one of his executors, gave him invaluable assistance in legal affairs of a

confidential nature during these last days, when he most
needed the advice of a man of tact and exceptional
capacity in adjusting intricate matters of business.

He suffered throughout his life from insomnia, and
yet in his face there were seldom any signs of weariness ; his eyes were almost always bright and wakeful,
and yet he would declare that he considered himself
fortunate if he slept for four consecutive hours during
the night.

Although endowed with a strong sense of humour, he
was never witty and rarely humorous in his talk (though
he had plenty of fun, which is another matter), and the
humour in his novels is certainly not their strongest point.
But he was quick to appreciate humour in others, whether
in life or letters, and his essay on Sterne's humour is
one of his most masterly pieces of analysis. One day
shortly before he died, a friend chanced to relate an
incident that took his fancy, and he laughed until the
tears rolled down his cheeks. No one ever appreciated
a humorous story—not even Rossetti—more thoroughly
than he did. His genial nature, that rapid flash which
still brought the bluish light into his eyes, his round,
rosy face, his strong, deep-toned voice, made it difficult to realize that he was over eighty years of age.
Even at the closing hour of his busy life the mental
vigour was undiminished. He was seated on the sofa
in the drawing-room over a cup of tea scarcely an hour
before he died, ready to dictate letters that needed
attention, having just had his favourite literary column,

contributed to the *Star* by Mr. James Douglas, read to him.

At that closing hour, as it chanced, his secretary had gone upstairs to the library to look for some manuscript, and on re-entering the drawing-room found Miss Theresa Watts seated near the sofa, believing her brother to be dozing. The secretary, however, bending closely over him—for the expression on his face gave cause for alarm—quickly realized the truth. He had died in his sleep from heart failure without a movement, resting with the cushion supporting his head, as he often rested of an afternoon for a short siesta prior to giving attention to literary work.

XXIV.

"WALTER THEODORE WATTS-DUNTON AND I."

BY CLARA WATTS-DUNTON.

Mrs. Watts-Dunton

XXIV.

" Walter Theodore Watts-Dunton and I."

BY CLARA WATTS-DUNTON.

I HAVE been asked by the authors of this biography to contribute a chapter about my marriage with Walter Theodore Watts-Dunton. In complying with their request, I know it is impossible to do much more than give in outline the story of a heavenly relationship. Part of what I must write even in so doing may seem to some people more appropriate to other pens than mine, for there are those who regard the reticence of the bereaved as if it were a tribute beautiful as flowers to " days that are no more." But I hold that it is well to transmit to the living one's bright and lovely memories, and in performing this task I remember that my husband was always pleased when I told a new friend, as I sometimes did, the romantic story of our love. As to the kindly pressure applied to my pen by those of the public who are interested in the makers of literature, I may remark that, shortly after my husband's death, I received from Mr. Stringer Bateman, a sympathetic stranger, a sonnet in acrostic form, the initials

spelling MRS. WATTS-DUNTON, and the contents en-
deavouring to persuade me to write memories of my
husband and Swinburne.

I was a schoolgirl of sixteen—in matters essentially
worldly a mere child—when I first saw Walter, as I
shall henceforth call the subject of this narrative.

One Monday—a day when, after a week-end of
liberty, I was wont to resume the thraldom of a weekly
boarder—my mother (Mrs. Reich) said to me, " You
can return to school by a later train than usual. I am
going to take you this afternoon to see a friend of mine
—Mr. Watts."

From her point of view the visit was, doubtless, so
far as it concerned me, simply a girl's accepted opportunity for seeing a distinguished poet and critic, and
for adding to my stock of artistic *personalia*. As for
me, I was pleased at the idea of seeing one of whom
I had heard much. I had all the self-possession needed
for meeting a celebrity, and did not feel at all shy.
I already knew and admired one of his works—the
sonnet sequence on the *Fausts* of Berlioz, Gounod,
and Schumann.

It would be difficult to make a materialist understand what strange event happened in our minds when
Walter and I first saw each other. The scene was the
dining room at The Pines, Putney Hill, and the formula
of introduction and salutation was conventionally cordial
—no more ; and yet at the first glance, and on the mere

sound of the words, " How do you do ? " a magnetic
arrow invisibly thrilled us both—a sympathy radiant
from him to me and from me to him ; and I was profoundly conscious of the fact that I would never be
quite the same again.

Of the conversation that ensued nothing need be
recorded but this. Walter asked me if I was interested
in pictures, and on my saying I was he showed me Rossetti's imaginative chalk drawing of Mrs. Morris as
Pandora. He asked me if I could see the evil spirits
escaping from the box despite Pandora's effort to shut
it, and I looked at the agonized faces of the vices and
diseases that curiosity let loose upon the world. This
picture by the painter-poet, who was Walter's greatest
friend till death divided them, made a deep impression
on me. I was struck by the skill with which the living
miseries afloat on the air are differentiated and presented processionally in what I may call a diminuendo
of distinctness, so that the spectator realizes that Pandora's box was a populous world. It was strange to
be near Pandora at that moment.

I wish I could describe the quality of the voice in
which Walter expounded this picture to me. I thought
I had never heard a voice so resonant and rich in tone.
It thrilled me ; and in this connection I may say that
years afterwards, when we were at private views of
picture exhibitions together, and happened to be separated by the diversity of our casual interests, I could
always distinguish his clear, deep voice amid the rook-

like din of the chattering crowd, even if the voice of his interlocutor was inaudible to me.

This first visit over, I returned to school, and confided to a friend the memory of " my wonderful meeting," and because Walter was a poet, I met him again in that region of lessons, larks, and dreams. There was a girl who kept a rack for literature above her bed, and here one day I found a *Pall Mall Magazine* containing Walter's poem on Miss Ellen Terry's representation of Queen Katharine in *King Henry VIII.* I do not know how to analyse my pleasure in this production ; part of it was undoubtedly the pleasure of seeing his name in print, of feeling that he was, as it were, alive and accessible in this popular periodical, which anybody could easily buy. I know that I insisted on its remaining in my friend's rack long after the magazine was out of date and she was fretful to replace it.

The first letter containing direct mention of me written by Walter to my mother had a peculiar fascination for me. It was a letter proposing that I should dine with Swinburne and himself. Regarded as an invitation it was ineffective, owing to my shyness of Swinburne ; from another point of view it was a wonderful success. Thrown carelessly by my mother into a dressing-table drawer, it was there so often examined by me that it wore out.

An invitation from Walter for a *matinée* performance of Ibsen's *Hedda Gabler* on the Wednesday following our first meeting was powerless to release me from scholastic thraldom ; but on the Saturday after that unprosperous Wednesday, I, being again at large, took him some French beans which I had grown in my garden. The beans were magic beans. They were the cause of a delightful talk in his garden at The Pines. I felt I had always known him, though there could be no end to what we had to say to each other. We discussed poetry, music, etc., so long that my mother anxiously sent a servant to claim me.

After this garden talk our friendship rapidly grew into a habit, or—if you like to believe in reincarnation —into a resumed habit. He would say, " I wonder where and by what wonderful accident I first met the one girl who could suit me—was it in some isle in the Ægean Sea ? " Innumerable *matinées* and private views gave him occasions for securing my society with my mother's sanction ; but he showed his wish to be with me in ways more subtle than the sharing of tickets for entertainments. I remember that once, when I was about to take an early train with the object of attending a Monday morning session of my school, I found him on the railway platform awaiting me, not wholly with the view of expediting my departure. He had been there since 8.30 a.m.

My school has but a humorous connection with my romance as seen in the above anecdote ; but I must give it the credit for deliberately providing me an opportunity for shining artistically in the presence of Walter, who thus expresses himself in Mr. James Douglas's admirable monograph :—

"Some years ago I was invited to go to see the performance of a French play given by the pupils of a fashionable school in the West End of London. Apart from the admirable French accent of the girls, I was struck by the acting of two or three performers who showed some latent dramatic talent. I have always taken an interest in amateur dramatic performances, for a reason that Lady Archibald Campbell in one of her writings has well discussed—namely, that what the amateur actor or actress may lack in knowledge of stage traditions he or she will sometimes more than make up for by the sweet flexibility and abandon of nature. The amateur will often achieve that rarest of all artistic excellencies, whether in poetry, painting, sculpture, music, or histrionics—*naïveté*. . . . Now, on the occasion to which I refer, one of these school-girl actresses achieved, as I thought, and as others thought with me, this rare and perfect flower of histrionics ; and when I came to know her I found that she joined wide culture and an immense knowledge of Shakespeare, Corneille, Racine, and Molière with an innate gift for rendering them."

One trivial incident always recurs to my mind when I think of the dawn of my love for Walter. I longed to reciprocate his innumerable kindnesses by some acceptable gift. What could I give him ? He seemed utterly without material wants that I could supply, and in any case my pocket-money was insufficient for

the purchase of expensive presents. I consulted my
mother, and asked her to sound him. " Do, mother,
ask him," I entreated, " if he would like my tortoise.
You see, I have nothing to give him, and he might
like it."

My mother told me that the pathos of my projected
offering brought the tears into Walter's eyes.

The tortoise proved, however, a rank individualist.
He had buried or otherwise hidden himself in a garden
which was too large to dig up in its entirety for the
purpose of recapturing him.

It was very soon after the youthful interpreter of
French drama had been met on the railway platform,
to the detriment of her scholastic punctuality, that Walter
said to me, " You know unless I marry you I shall never
marry—I shall die a bachelor."

The idea of marriage I had at the time was of companionship heavily weighted by undesired responsibility ;
yet I was sure that if ever I did marry somebody, that
somebody could only be Walter. This certainty on my
part was the more deserving of credence because the
school which I attended (a school which taught the
technique of society manners, " presentations," etc.)
provided opportunities for the growth of romantic ideas,
not only in theatricals, but in dancing lessons attended
by a variety of men young or mature, often handsome,
and always well polished. But the charm of mere
youth and comeliness was nothing to me compared
with that inner correspondence of heart and mind which

I had with Walter, and after his open avowal of what he regarded as the summit of earthly happiness, I permitted him to consider himself prospectively accepted and engaged, though he volunteered to wait till I was twenty-one before asking me to be definitely betrothed.

The reader will already perceive that my marriage was not one of those unions between May and December which satirists contemplate with malicious enjoyment, though a candid friend has regaled me with a legend of myself as an amanuensis seeking a sort of emancipation by a marriage of convenience. The prosaic is not always true ; in this case it is merely a bad fairy tale.

Poverty was never one of the spectres of my spinsterhood ; and even if I had been the Grethel of nursery fame, I should have known how to make the stage yield me the bread which was beyond the reach of the woodcutter and his unmotherly wife.

My marriage was, in fact, a triumph over materialistic prejudice, and a proof of the supertemporal power of love ; and it is only fair to Walter to say that he used his pen as forcibly as he knew how to emphasize the reasons why we should not be united.

In 1902—three years before I changed my surname—he wrote me a long letter, in which occur the words, " I love you too much to accept without long and painful hesitation the sacrifice you are willing to make for me." He represents the whole world as my field of choice ; he calls himself not only old, but " poor." He tells me that I am " too young and inex-

perienced to know my own mind," and he says that if
" after our marriage I saw in those dear eyes a shadow
of regret—a consciousness that you had made a mistake
—I couldn't live another hour.". He adjures me to
consider " for God's sake " ; he directs me to think
of the cynical and meddlesome, so volubly censorious
of disparate marriages. He exaggerates my youth till
it becomes babyhood, and he pitilessly distinguishes
between his buoyancy of temperament and the fact of
his septuagenarianism. Finally, he bids me wait for
six months ere our private understanding become a
" formal engagement."

Walter was too busy to write long letters often, and
the large number of letters which he wrote me during
our periods of separation are, as a rule, very brief and
usually dateless. They are the perfectly spontaneous
expression of his feelings, and are only casually or accidentally " felicitous " from a literary point of view.
The " Express " messenger was his favourite postman,
and in theatre attendances which I could not share with
him he would give to his absence some of the charm
of presence by telegraphing to me between the acts. In
the reverse case I would do likewise.

His special name for me comes from the gypsy
tongue—" Minaw " (my beloved one)—the word which
our friend Francis Hindes Groome described as " the
softest, tenderest vocative of any language."

" Minaw " is inscribed on the watch which Walter
gave me on the last birthday of my maidenhood, Sep-

tember 14, 1905. He would also call me his " young rascal," and define himself as a " gone coon." When I asked him if he would like my company on certain occasions, his reply was, " Ask a donkey if he would like beans ! " and in humorous homeliness of expression he was an adept.

I, for my part, owed my name for him (" Gualtiero ") to the playfulness of Dante Gabriel Rossetti, who Italianized Walter's name in an inscription which he wrote in a seventeenth-century copy of *The Decameron*.

I have gone through piles of Walter's letters to me in order to recapture the sound of his voice—the idiom of his humour, the accent of his affection. It is not his fault that the following excerpts from his correspondence are more like footlines to unpublished pictures or gleanings of a listener than an orderly arrangement of life in letters. I give them because, such as they are, they bear the stamp of his individuality. They convey him to the reader in something like the way that the whortleberry conveys the heath to the townsman : the townsman expects the heath to yield heather ; he does not expect it to yield " whorts." At least one can say of Walter's letters that they fulfilled the promise of the last words which his friend, Mr. Douglas S. S. Steuart, heard him say : " What from the heart doth spring, the heart doth reach."

[May 1903.]

" Minaw, I am so very glad that your mother and you can go. The train leaves Putney Bridge at 12.30

sharp. However, your mother will see that you don't miss it. She will also see that you don't bewitch the waiters, and make them give us double the quantity of good things for the money—in order to ' hoodoo ' (lovely, elegant Yankeeism !) your confiding guests.'

[*May* 1903.]

" I am looking impatiently forward to 12 o'clock in the Park ; I am always looking forward to 12."

[*June* 1903.]

" I should like to see the good lady who so trusted the bright eyes of a stranger (the darling's bright eyes !) as to lend the owner of them a ' quid.' I wish Groome were alive to hear me tell him of this." [Many more would like to have seen my trustful helper in the shop where I was accidentally unprovided with money than would have been good for her. The case referred to was literally one of trusting at sight.]

[*No date.*]

" Minaw, it is *the* ' buffday '—the only one that is interesting to me—and, alas ! where is my present ? Well, dear, we will keep the ' buffday ' at the end of the week."

[PUTNEY, *November* 17. 1903.]

" What you said about my being like a new six months' lover was most true, though you said it half in jest. Those few minutes in that shivery waiting-room were Paradise."

[No date.]

" Oh, you d-e-e-e-e-e-e-e-e-r child ! " [The long-drawn-out substitute for " dear " imitates the ecstatic pronunciation of this adjective by the charming poet, Mrs. Louise Chandler Moulton.]

{PUTNEY, *September 2,* 1905.]

" I have had such a fright, such a horror ! The first intimation I got of the accident was the announcement, ' Terrible Railway Accident. Cromer Express Smashed. 10 killed, 46 injured.' I was too dazed to read that it was [the] 9.15 train. I have never, I think, had such a shock. I have been able to do no work at all to-day."

In concluding these quotations I recall that the title of Walter's book of poems was an allusion to our love. I wanted to know what the title was to be before the book was named. " Wait till I name it in the publisher's room," he said to me, as we were on the way to Mr. John Lane's. When I heard the words, " The Coming of Love," pronounced, they sounded like a complete love-letter to me.

No two children could be happier in an unexplored labyrinthine garden than were Walter and I from the moment that we knew each other's heart. When I look into his *Aylwin* I see his heroine, Winifred, listening to her lover saying at parting, " Oh, what a lovely day we have had, Winifred ! " and I hear her murmur en-

couragingly, " And—and . . ." till from his lips comes
the prophecy, " And shall have many more such days."
It was I who originated this mode of farewell ; Winifred was happy in her copying, and there is more than
the compliment of a pretty dedication to connect me
with the novel called *Aylwin*. Saying this reminds me
that Walter signs himself " Aylwin " in a letter written
to William Sharp, October 19, 1898, where he informs
his friend that the novel is " intended to be the pro-
nouncement of something like a new gospel—the gospel
of love as the great power which stands up and con-
fronts a materialistic cosmogony, and challenges it and
conquers it."

Author and worker to the last days of his earthly
life, Walter was often very preoccupied by literary tasks
when our daily meetings took place ; but he could
never resist what he described as my " holiday face."
He would almost resolve that he was too busy to turn
the day into one of our "lovely days," and then he
would say, " But let me look at your face. Is it a holiday face ? Yes, it is almost a holiday face," and he
would resign himself to the happy inevitable.

One particular incident seemed a landmark in our
progress towards perfect harmony. The scene was a
hansom cab conveying my mother, Walter, and me
down the Haymarket. Suddenly I saw on the hoarding of the Carlton Hotel an advertisement of the advertising agent, Walter Hill. " I have just seen your
name on a hoarding," I said to my *fiancé* (not then fully

known as such). " What name was it ? " he asked eagerly. " Walter," I replied. This was the first time that I uttered those syllables to him, and he trembled all over.

I noticed once that the dinner-table at The Pines supported a particularly cumbrous and (in my opinion) ugly cruet-stand. In May 1904 I said, " Walter, you will have to choose between me and that cruet. I will never condemn myself to sit in front of that object every day." Afterwards I referred in a letter apologetically to my criticism, with the result that I received the following reply and verses :—

" No ; I liked that about the ' crime of the cruet.' It's such a delight to be with you that, even when you scold me, it's pleasant."

" CLARA v. CRUET.

" (A short ' ode ' on the Japanese model.)

" Get rid of that cruet !
 How dare you to palter ?
For, if you but knew it,
 I'm ' It,' my dear Walter.

" You say that, as poet,
 You mean to be ' It ' ;
But not if I know it !—
 No, devil a bit !

" The crime of that cruet
 What virtues can heal ?
Oh, Walter, you'll rue it
 Unless you're genteel."

In 1902 an event occurred which brought home to me very clearly the depth of Walter's affection for me. I had a severe illness, in which the exhausted brain refused to be cumbered with even the memory of a host of useful English words. I had to describe the things I wanted and could not name, and life was piteous and ludicrous. But every day, during my long and wearying invalidism, Walter was as a ministering angel. He sent me eau-de-Cologne by the gallon to drench the place of my unhappiness with pleasant odour, and cried like a child at sight of my wasted body. To him I wrote the first words returning strength permitted to come from my hand. The little note is before me now. " Minaw . . ." I begin, " I am so stupid. I hope I shall be better in a day." It appears I was able to keep the little gypsy love-word in my heart, whatever else my brain was relinquishing.

Walter and I were married, November 29, 1905, at St. James's Church, Piccadilly. The Church service was kindly abridged, in compliance with our views. Our honeymoon was spent in London. The magical change in our lives was achieved, I may say, in a mood resembling that of Wemmick in *Great Expectations*, who said, " Halloa ! here's a church. Let's go in ! "

I had only been married two hours when my husband asked me to find in his bag a book entitled *Philosophers and Actresses*. At his request I read from this amusing work an anecdote about the marriage of Scarron which struck me as peculiarly appropriate. The notary in-

quired of Scarron what dowry he gave his bride. " Im-
mortality," he replied. " The names of kings' wives
die with them ; that of the wife of Scarron will live
for ever." I have been told that irony decreed that
Scarron's wife should be remembered by the majority,
not as the spouse of a great writer, but as the wife of
a king ; but as on the day when I read his boast to
my husband I still feel that the life and fame which
belong to fine literature have not less than the power
which Scarron believed them to have.

The hotel where Walter and I lived during our
honeymoon looks on to a route of motor-buses which
run to Putney.   On the day after our marriage I watched
him from the balcony of the hotel set forth for The
Pines, and I well remember a new and tender concern
for his welfare holding me in a sort of enjoyable anxiety
as I saw him cross a road and enter a bus ; he was
my man at last, and with the sense of possession came
a new capacity for fear.

My memories of Swinburne are too numerous for
importation in anything like their entirety to this essay
in autobiography. Fully to present that dear and
familiar figure as I knew him would be to " side-track "
the main subject of my narrative.   I reserve, therefore,
much of my " Swinburniana " for another literary
adventure.

It was in November 1903 that Swinburne first
became a vividly interesting theme in correspondence

between Walter and me — witness these epistolary
snatches :—

[*November* 18, 1903.]

" Mr. Swinburne is dangerously ill of pneumonia.
A physician from London came last evening, and a nurse
has come. I have telegraphed to his sister at Lyme
Regis, and I expect her this afternoon."

[*Later than above.*]

" It [Swinburne's illness] is double pneumonia like
yours ; but he is not unconscious or delirious as you
were, darling. But it does so bring back that frightful
time to me. . . . The night nurse says that he is in
the same state as yesterday. . . ."

[*Later than above.*]

" He is very ill—dangerously ill. But the crisis has
not been reached. Two nurses and doctor in attend-
ance. . . . Don't tell anybody about illness, lest it
should get into papers."

[*November* 21, 1903.]

" There is no change for good or for ill. The nurses
are not very sanguine, but I am hopeful."

[*Later than above.*]

" You will be pleased to learn that the patient is
passing through the crisis favourably."

And so the great lyrist lived to see me reign domestic-
ally at The Pines, to share our home, and to write at
seventy *The Duke of Gandia.* It is an amusing circum-

stance that Swinburne's portrait appeared as a sort of substitute for my own, side by side with my husband's, in the *Daily Mirror* of December 12, 1905, which chronicled my marriage. On this occasion the news editor particularly wanted my portrait, but I was unable to provide one, and at the last moment the vacant place allotted me was filled by the most appropriate countenance he could think of.

Perfectly charming was the grace with which Swinburne welcomed the change in his home life made by my marriage with Walter. He took an early opportunity to say to me, " You must not call me ' Mr. Swinburne ' now, remember, but ' Algernon.' I hope you will look upon me as a brother-in-law." So I did, and when, after a tactfully audible descent of stairs, followed by a second warning of approach in a slow and rattling revolution of the door handle, he would cross the threshold of our sitting room, I would fairly take him by the hand and drag him in. It was after such preliminaries that he came to us one Sunday evening with one of those enormously circulated budgets of horror called Sunday newspapers in his hand. " I hope I don't interrupt," he said, " but I have something here which I feel sure will appeal very much to Clara." He then read us some lurid account of a conjugal fight, and wound up by saying, " You haven't, I notice, started doing this yet."

Swinburne told me that he considered my husband the greatest man he had ever known, and though I am well aware that his reverence for Hugo and Mazzini, and the superlative eulogies which other objects of his admiration received from him may be advanced to diminish the weight of this utterance, I yet feel that it was a deeply sincere one.

Thanks to Walter's vigilance and his interposition between this superb poet and the interfering prose of business and social relations, Swinburne was able to give all his working hours to art. Swinburne's gratitude is divinely manifest in his dedications ; but I have seen sometimes in Swinburne's eyes when they were directed to my husband an expression more wonderful than those dedications—an adoring look.

This look haunts me the more because Swinburne was one of those who could joyously front the " cauld blast." Well I remember one winter day when he had been for a long walk, and we were waiting lunch for him. He burst all glowing into the dining room, stamping the snow from his boots, and I can still hear the voice, loud and challenging, in which he said, " I'm sorry I'm late ; but I had such a glorious time out to-day. The snow was lovely ; it reminds me of the days when I was a kid. I didn't want to come away from it."

In 1906, while I was on a visit to Cromer, I received this letter from my husband, dated from The Pines on the 25th of August of that year :—

" . . . Swinburne was delighted with your post-

card, and asked me several times whether I had thanked
you for it, as I promised to do.   I want you to get me
a *lot* of them before they are out of print.   *Aylwin* was
written, and S.'s *Midsummer Holiday* in part at Cromer.
Don't forget this. . . ."

The death of Swinburne was the greatest blow
experienced by my husband during the years when I
knew him.   True, in 1904 he wrote to me: "I am in
deep distress.   One of the most loyal friends left to
me in the world, Professor Arthur Strong, is dead.
You knew him.   The loss to me is very great."   The
loss of this acute critic, who, with no uncertain hand,
pointed to Walter's triumphant craftsmanship in poetry,
cannot be belittled by me of all persons.   But the loss
he suffered in the passing of Swinburne was immeas-
urable.

Walter was himself invalided on that lamentable
April 10, 1909, when his friend died, and I shall never
forget that same day the sight of my husband sitting
up in bed (to which he was still confined) gazing steadily
at a photograph of Rossetti's picture called "The
Sphinx" or "The Question."   I knew what question
he was asking and of whom.

At Swinburne's funeral I was the representative of
my husband, who was prohibited by illness from at-
tendance thereat, though it sorely vexed him to be
unable to pay the last mournful homage to the body of
one whom, to quote his own written words, he "loved

so dearly." I may as well here repeat what my friend, Mr. Edward Clodd, has already affirmed in print, that my husband was not responsible for the incongruity of a Christian form of burial in the case of his dead friend.

Next from the crowd of human memories which surround my mental image of Walter, I summon my memory of Mrs. William Morris. It was in the summer of 1905 that he took me to call on her at her temporary home in Kensington.

I was much impressed by her beauty, which was not the characteristic beauty of old age. I took special notice of her beautiful lines—the perfection of the modelling of her face, neck, and figure—and realized how fortunate Rossetti was in having had such an original to work from. Walter thought her the most beautiful woman he had known, and I can believe she was in youth the loveliest woman of her time.

To one who had not charm or power to draw her out she must have been freezing in her statuesque quietness and incommunicativeness, but to Walter she unbent, and when I ventured to ask her if Rossetti in his art had not exaggerated her throat she vivaciously replied, " He always did ; it was a mania with him."

I may here remark that Mrs. Morris gave to us, in token of esteem and friendship, Rossetti's beautiful drawing of her reclining full length on a sofa.

As, in departing, I was going down the stairs of

her home, my husband saw her look at me approvingly, and in an expressive and charming way she nodded to him as though to say, " You have chosen well."

About eight months before her death I saw her again. Her beauty was as striking as ever. She wore on that occasion a dress of amethyst coloured velvet, most simply made and hanging in folds, the bodice cut rather low at the neck and outlined by beautiful lace.

The graceful poet, Louise Chandler Moulton, was a friend whom I owed to my husband ; her understanding of the spiritual ideality of my marriage was perfect. The letter by her which follows was postmarked February 27, 1906.

> " 28 RUTLAND SQUARE,
> " BOSTON, MASS., U.S.A.

" DEAREST MRS. WATTS-DUNTON,

" Your letter and your lovely, *lovely* picture have just reached me—and I make haste to thank you for both. The picture is such a dear. It is standing beside me on my writing-table, and to look at it makes the world seem better and brighter. I think it must make *both* your poet housemates happier to see your face. . . .

" I feel so lame from this wretched rheumatoid arthritis, that sometimes I think I won't cross the sea at all—but I suppose I shall, though I've not yet taken my passage. But London always lures me as the spring comes on, and the swallows homeward fly.

" Did I not see somewhere that T. W.-D. was about to publish a new novel ? I wonder if you are its inspiration ? I can quite fancy you might be. My love to him, and remembrances to Mr. Swinburne. I hope I shall see you all, when summer comes, and I am always,

" Yours most warmly,

" LOUISE CHANDLER MOULTON."

The novel referred to was, of course, *Carniola*, a story which, existing partly in the plastic form of proof and MS., and partly in the brain of its author, was an intellectual treat which Walter allowed me in somewhat tantalizing fashion to enjoy. I may here remark that Treffy Dunn, Rossetti's assistant, painted my portrait as Rhona Boswell in *The Coming of Love*.

Francis Hindes Groome is a friend who deserves to occupy more space in this budget of memories than I can allot him. Critics both and lovers both of gypsies and gypsy lore, my husband and Groome were true *confrères*, and to Groome the secret of Walter's engagement was confided long before it was generally known. When Groome came to London I was sure to see him ; and we three—Walter, " Frank," and I— made many delightful expeditions together—" happy rambles " referred to by my husband in the Dedication of his *Coming of Love*. Groome gave me all his books. In *Kriegspiel* he has written, " To the most flat-

tering of critics from the most beflattered of authors,
13th April 1897."

Both Groome and Walter were much amused by my
misunderstanding of the nature of their gypsy enthusiasm. Having seen an advertisement of a caravan
for hire, I was on fire with desire to go on the road. I
wrote to a girl friend, and asked her to join the party,
in which I—false prophetess that I was !—included
Walter and his friend. I was careful to explain to both
Walter and Frank the literary advantages they might
obtain by a caravan tour. Groome's prospective duties
in washing up, etc., were clearly defined to him, and
there was much nudging of and winking at each other
on the part of both men as I grew warm in my little
oration. Imagine my disappointment when I found
that nothing would induce either the creator (in fiction)
of Sinfi or the creator (in fiction) of Saygul to live for
a time in a house on wheels.

When Groome died my husband was profoundly
unhappy, for he loved the man. Often after our marriage Walter would sigh to me, " Oh, if dear Groome
could see our happiness ! "

The artist Whistler was a favourite theme of my
husband. He used to describe to Mrs. Jopling Rowe
and me, when she was painting my portrait, Whistler's
manner of painting—how the somewhat short-sighted
genius would stand, armed with brush and palette,
about ten feet from the canvas, and suddenly rush to-

wards it and dab a blob of paint upon it, one eye shut the while.

He told us that Whistler enjoyed cooking little French dishes, and was a first-rate hand at an omelet. Leaving the painter's art out of the question, Whistler, it appears, was a born cook, and could have run a restaurant on French lines with huge success. Here is one of my husband's pet anecdotes about Whistler.

One day when Whistler and a fellow-artist were what is called " stoney broke " in Paris, they racked their brains to find something on which mine uncle would advance some money. Suddenly it occurred to Whistler or his pal that the mattress of his bed might be offered to the man of usury. Figure to yourself one of the artists walking into the muddy street with the mattress on his head, and plodding bravely along. He is well on his way when a hurrying step is heard. " There's no need to pawn it," gasps a voice. " Put the thing down." A remittance despaired of had arrived. Such is their insolent joy at this relief that the mattress is left in the muddy street for the *chiffonier* to appropriate.

When my husband hyphenated his patronymic Watts with his mother's maiden name, Dunton, Whistler sent him a postcard from France addressed " Theodore Watts Dun t'un ? " and signed by a butterfly as usual. This was not the most prosperous of puns, but in the circumstances it was perhaps the best possible.

Of the editorial magnates whom my husband knew, certainly none was nearer his heart than Sir William

Robertson Nicoll and the Rev. John Stuart Verschoyle, a former editor of the *Fortnightly Review*. Both these friends pleased Walter much by their intelligent sympathy with what he regarded as the most important event of his life—his marriage, the event that by his own intention begins his record in *Who's Who*."

The late Sir James Knowles, founder and editor of the *Nineteenth Century*, figures in an incident, or rather sequence of incidents, of some interest to me. Sir James having met me at a private view of the Royal Academy, he wrote to Walter and asked him to bring me to a party he was giving.

This was actually the first " grown up " party which I ever attended, and as a remarkable artistic compliment was paid me on my appearance thereat, I may be excused for describing the dress to which they who will may say I owe my thanks for this tribute. To begin with, it was the first rather long frock to replace in my case the juvenile short frocks which, ceasing at the knees, keep a child from thinking of womanhood and encourage her to romp and run. I was very sorry to leave off short frocks, as I was in no hurry to be " grown up," and with the *naïveté* of a child I induced Walter to intercede with my mother on my behalf. Certainly, if any long dress could console a girl who wanted to wear a sort of tunic, it would be the dress I wore at Sir James Knowles's party. It was a beautiful old rose velvet, hanging straight from a yoke in artistic folds and caught in at the waist by a silk girdle. With this I wore a

Vandyke collar and cuffs of Irish lace. Among Sir James Knowles's guests was Sir Edward Poynter, P.R.A. He not only asked me if he might paint my portrait, but offered to present me with it on its completion. Unfortunately, in my nervous inexperience, I imagined that the portrait contemplated by the distinguished artist was something in the fashion of Eve before she was convicted of fruit stealing, and much to my and Walter's regret I declined his offer. As I was leaving his house Sir James gave me a beautiful reproduction of the portrait of Tennyson by Millais. My husband, who had enjoyed Tennyson's friendship, had it framed for me, and it was given a place of honour in my boudoir at home.

The procession of interesting persons would be a long one could I bid all our notable friends pass across my reader's field of vision, but I must now return to the main subject of these memoirs.

When I was holidaying I received this letter among many others :—

" THE PINES . . .
[*No date.*]

" DARLING GIRL-WIFE,

" You are the delight of my whole being, my love, and when you come in upon me (as you came last evening) it seems as if

" ' A stream of attar and balm
Thro' a woof of Clara-music blown
Floats fused, a warbling rose,
Making all senses one.'

" WALTER."

By way of commentary on the above, I remark that the lines of verse are adapted from three which occur in my husband's *Athenæum* review of Browning's *Ferishtah's Fancies*. " Clara-music " is an allusion to an effect as of a vocal call in Rossini's overture to *Semiramide*. In the middle of this work all the instruments vibrate on three long accented notes which seemed to Walter's and my fancy to utter my name. When the first of them had begun to sound on our gramophone he would call me to him with " Clara, Clara, Clara."

[No date.]

" DARLING BRIGHT-EYES,

" I can't resist the impulse to write to you, altho' I have nothing to say except that I love you more and more every hour of every day. It's wuth a thousand fourpence ha'pennies to relieve myself by saying this, and sending it by the ' blarmed bor.' . . ."

" THE PINES,
" *August* 30, 1910.

" . . . I was dreaming about roses last night. *When shall it be roses ? "*

Above was addressed to me at Cromer. I had a dress suitable for a fairy, embroidered all over with pink roses. This my husband delighted in, and roses became a symbol between us—a symbol which I used when I decked his funeral with roses.

In the playfulness of poetic moods Walter was to me " my bird," and I was to him his " nimble elf."

He certainly deserved the epithet I bestowed on him, not only for his poetry, but also for his early rising. In a letter written to me before our marriage, when a cold rendered " breakfast in bed " desirable for him, he confesses : " In my eagerness to get a good long day's work yesterday . . . I got up at 5.30 and lit my fire as usual. It seems to have increased my cold a little."

He was entirely free from the lethargy of mental old age and its old-fogeyness, if I may be allowed the word.

Like Locker-Lampson, he could say, and often did say, " Whatever my mood is, I love Piccadilly ; " and nearly always we would lunch twice a week at some restaurant, and walk down that charming promenade. After such an outing he would return home, showing no signs of fatigue, and after tea would work for hours.

He was very fond of society—no one was less of a recluse. Whistler took note of this fact when he inscribed on the fly-leaf of a presentation copy of *The Gentle Art of Making Enemies*—" To Theodore Watts, the Worldling."

Walter retained, even physically, a real youthfulness. Time never parched his smooth skin, and his hand, which had often served Rossetti for a model, remained supple and comely. I used to say to him in fun, " It isn't a bit of good massaging your forehead ; you haven't a line in it." It was, doubtless, with consciousness of

his vigour that he would retort on me in parody when
I was cross :—

"Crabbed youth and age cannot live together."

In childhood he must have resembled, I think, the
portrait by Sir Thomas Lawrence of Master Lambton ;
and assuredly the child was never extinct in him, but
often peeped out at me.

As an illustration of Walter's extraordinary memory
I relate the following incident. At a party, where we both
happened to be, I said to a friend that I had been reading the wonderful chapter called " Vashti " in Charlotte Brontë's *Villette*. Having forgotten for a moment
the name of the actress (Rachel) personified by the
novelist as Vashti, I appealed to my husband, who
laughingly obliged ; and, the interest of the company
being attracted, he then and there reeled off whole
paragraphs of the chapter in question, with the effect
of thrilling those who heard him. This anecdote does
not, however, do justice to the richness and riches of
Walter's conversation. To be with him constantly was
to learn something fresh every day.

It was noticeable that Walter's power directly to
influence the creative art of others did not wane in
his last years. What it was in his earlier years I could
not but know, for in my drawing-room hangs the large
charcoal drawing (" The Spirit of the Rainbow ") which
Rossetti did in illustration of my husband's sonnet, *The
Wood Haunter's Dream*—a drawing which has been

described as Rossetti's " only successful attempt at the
wholly nude."

This beautiful sonnet by Mr. G. F. R. Anderson,
called *A Last Talk at The Pines*, shows the effect on a
younger man of one talk with my husband :—

" We talked of Clara, and the love that shines
    Sunlike and quenchless, and defies the tomb,
    Until it seemed to fill that magic room,
That sanctuary of song within The Pines,
Till that dream-haunted chamber which enshrines
    The names, whose scripture Love's own rays illume—
    Swinburne, Rossetti, Borrow, Hake, and Groome—
Seemed echoing song and Aylwin's golden lines.

" We talked of Life and Death—Life's ' Appian way '—
    And youth and age, and leaves that fade and fall,
    And I acclaimed him youngest of us all,
So bright his oceanic mind that day ;
' Not death, but youth and love,' I heard him say,
  ' Keep the bright kingdom of the stars in thrall.' "

Again, take the case of a talented dramatist, one at
least of whose published dramatic works my husband
wished to see staged. My husband was so fortunate as
to inspire him with the idea of writing a sonnet sequence,
with the happy result that any up-to-date anthologist
would hesitate to ignore Mr. John Lawrence Lambe.
I reprint one of them now, because the opening quatrain
of it seems to me, spiritually, to convey the charm of
The Pines (the outward appearance of which has, I
observe, been kindly testimonialized in answer to a
detractor by the poet, Mr. Samuel Waddington).

" Dear house, with door wide open, where of old
    I paused and pined to enter, radiant light
    Beams from thy window, this dark Christmas night,
In warmest welcome through the piercing cold.
How long the flame of genius and the gold
    Of purest friendship glowed, serene and bright,
    Within these walls, where yet, though years take flight,
They shine in beauty and splendour manifold.

" Dear friend, whose voice, amid the world's disdain
    And bleak indifference, thrilled my famished ears
With new and rapturous hope, when all in vain
    I reaped the stricken harvest of my years ;
Lingering I stand before the casement pane ;
    No voice have I to greet thee with—save tears."

Here I may say that Mrs. Holman-Hunt, after asserting in a letter to me that my husband had a " genius for friendship," continued : " I once asked him how he accounted for that rare influence he had exercised so notably, and he told me that since his schooldays he had had it. ' The boys said, " If you want a reform made popular in school, get Watts to support it." ' "

The story of my bereavement begins with my remembrance of the misery I experienced in imagining, as I sometimes did, what it would be like to be left alone without Walter. This feeling was at its acutest one evening when some perversity of anticipation caused me to figure the drawing-room—where, cheerily lit and expecting me, he would be working or conversing—as dark, dark because he had passed away. Oh, the joy of seeing the light as usual—the intense relief of knowing that he was still living ! In my emotion I went to

him and told him that I had been haunted by Rossetti's
terrible speculation :—

" O love, my love ! if I no more should see
Thyself, nor on the earth the shadow of thee."

Walter laughed, dismissed my fears, and gloom
ended in jollity.

In May 1914 I was at Margate, and there, on the
12th, I received the last note I had from him—a briefly
affectionate trifle in all but two words : in them no
trifle at all.

" Good-bye, dearest." Those were the words, and
they afterwards struck solemnly upon my ear, because
he had never hitherto written the word " good-bye "
in closing any letter or note. But at the time of
first reading this " good-bye " I was not impressed by
its singularity, though I now think it was significant to
him of more than he could say outright.

About a week after my return to London I found,
as it were, a shapeless gloom flitting from time to time
across my mental field of vision. I was uneasy. I
felt he knew that a time for uneasiness was at hand ;
but we did not express what we felt ; our uneasiness
was belied by his physical appearance : he looked fit
and well. In corroboration of the latter statement I
quote the words of his close friend, Mr. Thomas J.
Wise, the eminent bibliographer of Swinburne. " Only
a week ago," wrote Mr. Wise to me on June 8,
1914, " your dear husband looked so well and hearty.

His good-natured face beamed with happiness and health. . . . Last Monday . . . I reminded him of my appointment to dine with him on his 90th birthday. His face assumed one of his broad, glad smiles, and, taking my hand, he said, ' Tom, I mean to keep that appointment.' " Yet surely it was not a mere perverse literariness which made Walter quote to me then :—

" This is the top of life,
Henceforth the path slopes downward to the grave."

A day came when he was caught in a shower, as a result of going for a walk on the Common. The damping he received seemed to bring on rheumatic pains in his legs. He was astonished, and laughingly remarked, " I am very lucky to have arrived at my age without experiencing either gout or rheumatism." He suggested " a good old massage ; " but massage only increased his discomfort, and I was greatly alarmed when the next day he informed me that the pains in his legs had not lessened. The doctor, duly summoned, prescribed a medicine which he disliked so much that he said he would rather bear the pains than swallow any more of the remedy for them.

Then day by day an inward feeling of helplessness or premonition stayed with me. I felt he was aware of it ; but still the feeling found no utterance. We talked of any subject under the sun except his death.

Yet that feeling gagged me, so to speak, when I would fain say something brightly confident. I remember well that I wanted to tell him that the air and charm of Eastbourne would make him all right, and I began by saying, " I have a surprise for you." Even as I spoke I seemed to hear the words forming within me, " He'll never go out of this house again—except . . ."

And then I heard Walter's voice, feeble, triste : " Don't tell me yet—wait awhile." This from him, who in earlier days would have heartily responded to my announcement of an impending surprise with " Out with it ! " Melancholy had indeed taken our souls into custody.

We were near, very near then, I know, to the realization of tragedy by sense of the shadow cast by the coming event ; but we forced our tongues to ignore our forebodings, and to talk of things that do not interest the doomed.

Anticipatory gloom or premonition of evil does not necessarily attend one to the very verge of a misfortune. Mr. George A. B. Dewar, the editor of the *Saturday Review*, had just accepted an invitation from me to be present at a little gathering at The Pines on June 10, 1914. The 6th of June did not dawn for me like midnight. Walter seemed to enjoy his midday meal, and after lunch, when he suggested that I should read to him a passage out of Charles Reade's *Hard Cash*, I felt no compunction in replying that the reading could take place in the evening.

When I did return, it was to find him dead on the sofa in the drawing-room, where, at 6.25 p.m., while waiting for his secretary, Mr. Hake, his heart had suddenly ceased to beat.

If I had read to him out of *Hard Cash* at the passage he indicated, 1 should have read these words, to which a pencil mark by him draws attention :—

" At six-twenty-five the grand orb set calm and red, and the sea was gorgeous with miles and miles of great ruby dimples. . . . The passengers lingered long on deck watching the Great Bear dip and the Southern Cross rise, and overhead a whole heaven of glorious stars most of us have never seen, and never shall see in this world."

In my husband's coat pocket was the last art-work of his life—a sonnet suggested by the portrait of me by Miss Norris as seen in the drawing-room at The Pines when the crystal lamp is alight. The sonnet here printed represents the most felicitous result obtainable after consulting ten variants, none of which had definitely been preferred by the author.

SUSPENSE.

" This lamp of crystal, from its fragile tower
      Flushing her portrait through a rosy veil,
      She prizes all the more for being so frail,
So servile to the chances of the hour ;
But I, while listening in this love-warmed bower
      Of her who makes my life a fairy tale,
      Tremble to think what perils may assail
My Paradise whose flowerage seems one flower.

" Oh, should malignant Nature strike this shrine—
    Strike here, where memories of her paint the air
    With pansy-coloured eyes, with rich soft hair,
    With shapes like Psyche's, more than half divine—
    Should the fell foe of bliss now murder mine,
    Who then would hold my Paradise ?—Despair ! "

Even his last artistic thought was of me, and I have a right to accept the comfort offered me by Mr. Hall Caine, who, writing to me in 1914, after my husband's death, which for him was then " the severing of a bond that was very close more than thirty years ago," eloquently adds, " In the midst of your great sorrow you have the great joy of remembering that you were so much to so great a man."

Among the many written tributes to my sorrow a few stand out as conveying something more vivid than is to be found in formal expressions, and in the comfort which worldlings wring out of their scepticism for the benefit of the bereaved.

The Lady Archibald Campbell of Argyll wrote a letter from which I extract the following appreciation of my husband :—

" You know how in his death I lost the truest, the most valued friend and master of learning I ever knew. A more profound thinker I am sure never was. He always said he owed his conversion from materialism to transcendentalism to me. I think it was due to his patience. The practical demonstrations which we witnessed together in circles (though not in all ways edifying) he approved, seeing in them a system necessary to prepare the way to a later general acceptance of what he held to be ' the only wisdom.' In transcendental physics he foresaw the establishment of the law of continuity. I was always impressed by his large-minded view of the trivialities which discourage so many people from patient investigation. In them he saw, as I did, merely a necessary and inevitable invasion from the world behind our own of mixed intelligence under direction, whose mission was to break down pig-headed, obstinate scepticism on matters spiritual, and confute the confused conceptions of pseudo-science and, last but not least, dogmatic theology. You ask me to tell you any little incident which I can recall in his early friendship with us, when he invariably was our honoured Christmas guest. You have often heard him speak of the devotion of my children to him, and his delight in them. Of the Christmas Eves when they dressed him up in all manner of strange disguises collected from the Christmas crackers, and how, while lost in the depths of philosophical discussion, he never realized his transformation till, when he rose to go, they made him, with shouts of laughter, see himself as ' motley ' in the mirror.

" Through his joyous married life I well remember his pride in your talents, your indomitable power of application, and of conquering difficulties in the technique of the accomplishments which roused your enthusiasm.

" I wonder if, in what you are printing about him, you will remember to speak of his trenchant eloquence when talking of the worship of the ugly everywhere rampant. Was he not grand on the subject of Philistinism? How he measured up the snivelling Pharisees ! Philistines of every kind—the flirting Philistines—how they amused him ! And the ultra-respectable, all the clap-trap humbug, all the shams of life, how he saw through them all, knowing that beneath the trash lay the golden truth. I know he found the nugget of pure gold, and held on to it. I think that was what kept his body and his spirit young until the day he slipped out and away to join his poet friends in the World of Beauty. You tell me of his love for me, and I believe it. I feel how very near he is to you, and that the day cannot be far when we shall meet again."

By way of a note on the above letter I quote the present Duke of Argyll, who tells me that his recollections of Walter " go as far back as 1877 at the least, when he (Walter) used to be constantly dining at my father's (Lord Archibald Campbell's) house at 14 Beaufort Gardens, where we lived till, in 1882, we took Coombe."

Mrs. Louise Jopling Rowe wrote a letter from which, from dread of an appearance of self-display, I would have made a briefer quotation if it were not that I do not like to suppress a reminiscence which comes to me out of the heart of a friend :—

" I shall never forget the last time I saw dear Walter. It was in May 1914. You were away—at Margate, I believe. When he told me, he hastened to add, ' She has gone entirely by my wish. She didn't want to go, but I made her.' And then later, still talking of you, he said in his tender voice—that beautiful, sympathetic voice of his—' She is the light of my eyes.' How proud he was of taking you about when you were quite a little girl. I remember so well the first time I saw you with him. It was at a Private View, and he knew that my painter's eye would delight in your childish beauty. I was glad of the opportunity of painting you as a wedding gift to Walter ; and how delightfully appreciative he was ! I felt it a great honour that he, who had associated so intimately with a genius like Rossetti, should admire my work. And when he praised my poems I was up in the seventh heaven of delight ! No wonder that all who knew him loved him. And this love that one bore him makes one more readily sympathize with you in your irreparable loss."

The Rev. John Verschoyle, Vicar of Wiveliscombe, Somerset, a former editor of the *Fortnightly Review*, wrote July 29, 1914 :—

" I was very glad . . . to learn that the roses were in time for the poet's funeral departure to the ' kingdom beyond Orion '—one of his happy sayings full of imaginative truth. . . . When I saw you after your marriage, I realized that your union was an ideal one.

His spiritual personality, which had expressed itself in poetry and fiction, found in you the love it had desired so long in vain, and I rejoiced that the latter part of my old friend's life was the happiest, even after his friend of friends, Swinburne, was taken away. That would have been a blow too hard to bear if he had not had you to support him and to make life still worth living."

Miss C. Ethelreda Larter, one of those who criticized *Aylwin*, wrote from St. Mary Church, South Devon, June 9, 1914 :—

" Will you allow one who loved and revered Mr. Watts-Dunton to speak one word of the feeling for you that is in my heart. Never shall I forget the speechless pride with which he showed me your portrait on the wall. . . . It needed personal contact to realize the full riches of his mind and heart—the magnetic power that drew others to him, the joyful giving of himself that won such response from men the most diverse. . . . What I had learnt from him no words can tell. . . . You will think of his words about ' the beloved dead who are loving us still.' "

When I look at this, and many other letters, I feel that I may accept the tribute which Walter's friend of many years, Mr. Coulson Kernahan, paid when he wrote to me that I had made my marriage " a rare and radiant success." It was to Mr. Kernahan that my husband said, " My dear boy, you are almost the last of my dear friends. They are nearly all gone. Come again when you can, for 1 shall long for the sight of your face."

Of letters reflecting the philosophy of gentle unfaith none touched me more than one from the poet Lord De Tabley's sister, Lady Leighton Warren, whose death occurred in August 1914.

" I have had such trouble all my life. I know that it is no use to struggle ; just live your life as you can, and presently you will sleep if you try not to dwell on it all or the past."

But a *cri de cœur* breaks through her mood of advice, and she says :—

" What to me is so painful is the fact that the present has become the past, and nothing remains but the long vista of memory, lit by the light of another world. . . . I know what you are feeling also ; even now I feel it here so much (about my dear brother) ; every time I go into a room I expect to see him there ; every time the door opens, I fancy it may be him."

Our friend, Mr. Mackenzie Bell, offered the following tribute to my husband :—

" To Theodore Watts-Dunton

(after reading, when alone, July 31, 1914, in the sitting-room at The Pines, where he died, an unpublished manuscript volume of his poems.)

"Oh ! friend of friends, what dream I most of here,
In this lov'd haunt, alas ! now void of cheer ?

Do reveries of Rossetti flood my mind,
Great in two arts, greatest of human kind !
Or does my wing-less fancy, wandering, claim
Your friend and mine, our Swinburne, whose high fame
Will march with Shakespeare's ? Do I. wondering, muse
On your imagination's wondrous hues
In *Aylwin* ? Do I trace all tenderly
The fire of genius in your poesy ?
Or, marvelling wisely, do I here explore
The matchless riches of your critic-lore ?
No ! No ! Not thus I dream ! Not thus I dream.
Mine inmost soul is wounded, and I seem
Listening for your voice, and longing to touch
Your hand so dear ! I want you—want you much.
The aim of Grief, the archer, was so true !
My heart is pierced, is pierced—I want but you ! "

Among the offerings in verse that reached me, one,
by Miss Annie Newton of Carnarvon, touched me as
indicating that Walter's romantic novel, *Aylwin*, and
its companion poem, *The Coming of Love*, lived in the
hearts of Welsh people.

" Mournful the mountain breeze blows from Eryri,
     And that sweet crwth on the ground,
   Twine it with heather and vi'lets from Sinfi,
     List to the sad Cymric sound."

A poet whose tribute expressed in a letter to me is
worth quoting is Mr. William Dowsing, author of
Sonnets Personal and Pastoral, etc., whose poetic skill
received my husband's warm praise. Of *Aylwin* Mr.
Dowsing wrote: "I have a vivid recollection of the
atmosphere of enchantment it created for me, and in
which I lived for many months."

Mr. L. Churton Collins, in a letter generously eulogistic, informed me that his father, the eminent professor of English literature, described some of my husband's poetical work as " marvellous in its intensity of imagination and feeling."

Professor Hugh Walker was among the most eloquent of those who tried to turn my thought from the contemplation of the emptiness left by a visible joy that has disappeared to the works inspired by its personality.

" He possessed," wrote Professor Walker of my husband, " and he imparted to his writings that indefinable something without which nothing can be great— *personality*. All that he wrote conveyed the impression, not merely of a powerful brain and a keen judgment, but of a man. . . . He never made the fatal mistake of keeping the intellectual faculties in one compartment and the emotions in another. His work was the outcome of his whole being. And this, it seems to me, is the secret of its superiority to ordinary criticism, or to merely ordinarily good work in any department that he touched."

Before I end this piece of writing, in which I have already been more communicative than many in like case would be, I feel I must say a few words on my husband's attitude towards the vexed but ever fascinating subject of survival after death. It will be readily believed that the coiner of the phrase, " The Renascence of Wonder," was no cut-and-dried materialist, thinking that all present and existing things are discoverable in the chemist's laboratory.   No. He thought, on the contrary, that we stand on the edge of a vast field of knowledge, for which we have already a name—the field of psychology.   True, he made no pretence of knowing what becomes of the soul—the will—when it is separated from the flesh.   But he never lost the memory of the wonderful sights he had seen when he was in spiritistic circles, and if, as on the day when Swinburne died, his eyes asked of the Sphinx the question, " Whither ? " I know his intellect, even in his most sceptical mood, never answered, " Into the grave."

Speaking for myself, who am no occultist and have but my intuitions, my dreams, and the perceptions of one of Walter's best friends for my immediate *media* of belief in his continued existence, I can truthfully— if not with the approval of scientists—say that I know he lives.   Not to drug or *séance*, or any deviation from what the world deems the normal and sound way of life, did I resort to obtain my faith, for well I remember how he disliked the notion of my becoming, or attempting to become, any sort of machine for evoking or producing occult manifestations.   Therefore, my knowledge is not that of a full-fed soul.   But even as the yearning traveller knows that, though no ship is sailing from the coast whence he looks seaward to the shore where his kindred dwell, they are safe from the lashing leagues of water which baffle him, so I—still travelling on the plane of earthly life—know that across a wide but not impassable gulf, is the poet of philosophic mind and boyish heart whom death took but as a captain takes his passenger to a land where souls grow wise in the light of perfect day. When I meet him it will be in the pursuit or contemplation of beauty ; for beauty, so slighted by the realists and cynics, the commercial, and opportunist workers of to-day, was not only his ideal, but a living principle in his soul.

XXV.

THREE PERSONAL IMPRESSIONS.

XXV.

THREE PERSONAL IMPRESSIONS—(*a*) MR. COULSON KER-
NAHAN ; (*b*) MR. HERBERT JENKINS ; (*c*) MR. JOHN
LAWRENCE LAMBE.

THE following three personal impressions of Watts-
Dunton have been contributed at our request by
his friends Mr. Coulson Kernahan, Mr. Herbert Jenkins, and Mr. John Lawrence Lambe.

Mr. Kernahan, as is well known, was an intimate
friend of many years' standing, not only of Watts-
Dunton but also of Swinburne. His views, therefore, of
the *ménage* at The Pines are of special value and interest.
All familiar with the work of Mr. Kernahan's versatile
and accomplished pen know of his keen power of
observation. This is further illustrated in the article
we are privileged to publish. The shrewd critical
observer does not always make the most genial and
generous of friends. But Mr. Kernahan knows the
secret of combining both rôles.

No one was more pleased than Watts-Dunton by
the immediate success of Mr. Herbert Jenkins's *Life
of Borrow ;* while he often spoke about the biographer's

skilful treatment in terms of warm commendation.
This is another illustration of Watts-Dunton's generous attitude in literary matters, where so many men
(possessed of his intimate knowledge) would have been
grudging or hypercritical.

Mr. Herbert Jenkins is one of the most enterprising and forceful of our London publishers, and
in the following extracts from letters Watts-Dunton's
high opinion of him is clearly shown :—

" *October* 6, 1913.—The sudden success of your
firm is a subject which is very much engaging the attention of the literary world, of which world I have seen
many important members here of late. It does not
in the least surprise me, for few people, I think, have
a better knowledge of your business capacity, of your
insight into literature, than I have."

Again, in February 1914 : " Many thanks for the
pages of *The Renascence of Wonder* just returned by
your messenger. I can but congratulate myself on
having found a publisher of the real literary temper."

Mr. John Lawrence Lambe was an especially intimate friend during the later years of Watts-Dunton's
life, and his confidence in him is clearly shown by the
fiduciary position which he pressed him to accept.
Both Mr. and Mrs. Lawrence Lambe belonged to the
" inner circle " at The Pines, not only by reason of

their literary tastes, but because, both being accomplished musicians, their musical talent added greatly to the pleasure both Mr. and Mrs. Watts-Dunton felt in their company.

Watts-Dunton always took the keenest interest in Mr. Lambe's striking efforts to revive the poetic drama, and looked upon him as a writer of unusual power. This may be gathered from a letter written to a distinguished poet and critic *à propos* of Mr. Lambe's plays, to which he refers in terms of the highest praise.

THEODORE WATTS-DUNTON AS " A HERO OF FRIENDSHIP."

BY COULSON KERNAHAN.

I have often been asked by those who did not know Theodore Watts-Dunton, what was the secret of the singular power he appeared to exercise over others, and the equally singular affection in which he was held by his friends.

My answer was that Watts-Dunton's hold upon his friends, partly personal as it was and partly intellectual, was chiefly due to his extraordinary loyalty. Of old, certain men and women were supposed to be possessed of the " evil eye." Upon whom they looked with intent —be it man, woman, or beast—hurt was sooner or later sure to fall.

If there be anything in the superstition, one might almost believe that its opposite was true of Watts-Dunton. He looked upon others merely to befriend, and if he did not put upon them the spell not of an evil but of a good eye, he exercised a marvellous personal power, not, as is generally the case, upon weaker intellects and less marked personalities than his own, but upon his peers ; and even upon those who in the world's eye would be accounted greater than he. That any one man should so completely control, and even dominate, two such intellects as Swinburne and Rossetti, seemed almost uncanny. I never saw Rossetti and Watts-Dunton together, for the former had been dead some years when I first met Watts-Dunton ; but my early literary friendships were with members of the little circle of which Rossetti was the centre, and all agree in their testimony to the extraordinary personal power which Watts-Dunton exercised over the poet-painter. But Swinburne —and here I speak with knowledge—Watts-Dunton absolutely dominated. It was, " What does Walter say about it ? " " Walter thinks, and I agree with him, that I ought to do so and so," or " Let us submit the matter to Watts-Dunton's unfailing judgment."

Here, for fear of a possible misunderstanding, let me say that if any reader assumes from what I have just written that Swinburne was something of a weakling, that reader is very much mistaken. It is true that the author of *Atalanta in Calydon* was a greater force in intellect and in imagination than in will power and character ; but he was not in the habit of deferring to

others as he deferred to Watts-Dunton, and when he
chose to stand out upon some point or in some opinion,
he was very difficult to move. It was only, in fact,
by Watts-Dunton that he was entirely manageable ; yet
there was never any effort, never even any intention, on
Watts-Dunton's part to impose his own will upon his
friend. I have heard his influence upon Swinburne
described as hypnotic. From that point of view I
entirely dissent. Watts-Dunton held his friends by
virtue of his genius for friendship—" Watts is a hero
of friendship," Mr. William Michael Rossetti once
said of him — and by the passionate personal loyalty
of which I have never known the equal. By nature
the kindest of men, and shrinking from giving pain to
any living creature, he could be fierce, even ferocious,
to those who assailed his friends. It was, indeed, always
in defence of his friends, rarely if ever in defence of
himself—though he was abnormally sensitive to adverse
criticism—that he entered into a quarrel, and since
dead friends could not defend themselves, he consti-
tuted himself the champion of their memory or of their
reputation, and even steeled himself on more than one
occasion to a break with a living friend, rather than en-
dure a slight to one who was gone. " To my sorrow,"
he wrote in a letter, " I was driven to quarrel with a man
I loved and who loved me, William Minto, because he,
with no ill intentions, printed certain injurious comments
upon Rossetti which he found in Bell Scott's papers."

Rossetti is said to have spoken of Watts-Dunton as

"the one man of his time who, with immense literary equipment, was without literary ambition." This may be true of the Theodore Watts of Rossetti's time. It is not altogether true of the Watts-Dunton whom I knew during the last quarter of a century.

The extraordinary success of *Aylwin*, published, be it remembered—though some of us had been privileged to see it long before—in 1898, when the author was sixty-six, bewildered and staggered Watts-Dunton, but the literary ambitions which that success aroused came too late in life to be realized. Though a prodigious and untiring worker, he was unsystematic and a dreamer. The books that he intended to write would have outnumbered the unwritten volumes of Robert Louis Stevenson. Had Stevenson lived longer his dream-books would one day have materialized into manuscript and finally into paper and print. He was one of those whom Jean Paul Richter had in mind when he said, " There shall come a time when man shall awake from his lofty dreams and find—his dreams still there and that nothing has gone save his sleep." Stevenson worked by impulse. His talk and his letters of one day were like too plenteously charged goblets that brimmed over and ran to waste about stories he was set upon writing, but from which on the morrow he turned aside to follow some literary Lorelei whose lurings more accorded with the mood of the moment.

" I shall have another portfolio paper so soon as

I am done with this story that has played me out," he wrote to Sir Sidney Colvin in January 1875. " The story is to be called *When the Devil was Well;* scene, Italy, Renaissance; colour, purely imaginary of course, my own unregenerate idea of what Italy then was. Oh, when shall I find the story of my dreams, that shall never halt nor wander one step aside, but go ever before its face and ever swifter and louder until the pit receives its roaring ? "

But Stevenson worked of set purpose, and for the most part, sooner or later in another mood, went rainbow-chasing again, hoping to find—like the pot of gold which children believe lies hidden where the rainbow ends—his broken fragments of a dream that he might recover and weave them into story form.

Sometimes he succeeded ; sometimes he found that the vision had wholly faded or that the mood to interpret it had gone, and so more often he failed. But Watts-Dunton was content only to dream, and alas to procrastinate, at least in the matter of screwing himself up to the preparation of a book. That he accomplished as much as he did, especially in his later years, we owe, in great part, to the faithful and untiring friend who was subsequently to collaborate with Mr. Arthur Compton-Rickett in the present biography. I refer, of course, to Mr. Thomas Hake, " the Colonel," as he was affectionately called (on account of the likeness between the two), since the time that his cousin,

" Chinese Gordon," first held the rank of colonel in the army. What Watts-Dunton was to Rossetti and to Swinburne, " the Colonel " was in effect to Watts-Dunton himself. For seventeen long years, as personal friend and private secretary—himself a scholar and a man of fine literary judgment, as well as of fine literary gifts —he chose to devote himself to assisting Watts-Dunton rather than to furthering his own literary career and interests. It is to be hoped, now that what he held to be his duty to Watts-Dunton is ended, that the present biography will be the first of other volumes on similar lines. Mr. Thomas Hake's " Recollections," if he could be induced to write them, intimate as he was with so many of the great Victorians, would be of fascinating and singular interest.

Returning to Watts-Dunton, whose habit of pro-crastination was the despair of his friends, I remember that Francis Hindes Groome, whose father was the famous Archdeacon of Suffolk and a friend of Edward Fitzgerald, wrote to me as far back as January 1896 : " Watts, I hope, has *not* definitely abandoned the idea of a Life of Rossetti, or he might, as he suggests, weave his reminiscences of him into his own reminiscences. But I doubt. The only way I believe would be for some one regularly day after day to engage him in talk for a couple of hours, and for a shorthand writer to be present to take it down. If I had the leisure I would try and incite him thereto myself."

I agree with Groome that that was the only way out

of the difficulty. Left to himself, I doubt whether Watts-Dunton would ever have permitted even *Aylwin*, ready for publication as it was, to see the light. Of the influences which were brought to bear to persuade him ultimately to take the plunge, and by whom exerted (no less than of the reasons why the book was so long withheld), I shall not here write. Mr. Douglas says nothing of either matter in his book, and the presumption is that he was silent by Watts-Dunton's own wish. This, however, I may add, that were the reasons for withholding *Aylwin* so long fully known, they would afford yet another striking proof of the chivalrous loyalty of Watts-Dunton's friendship. One reason—it is possible that even Mr. Douglas is not aware of it, for it dates back to a time when he did not know Watts-Dunton, and I have cause to believe that the author of *Aylwin* spoke of it only at the time, and then only to a few intimates, nearly all of whom are now dead—I very much regret I do not feel free to make known. It would afford an unexampled instance of Watts-Dunton's readiness to sacrifice his own interests and inclinations in order to assist a friend—in this case not a famous but a poor and struggling one.

If his unwillingness to see his own name on the back of a book was a despair to his friends, it must have been even more so to some half-dozen publishers who might be mentioned. The enterprising publisher who went to Watts-Dunton with some literary project he " received," in the words of the late Mr. Harry Fragson's amusing song, " most politely." At first he hummed and hawed and rumpled his hair, protesting that he had not the time at his disposal to warrant him in accepting a commission to write a book. But if the proposed book was one that he could write, that he ought to write, he became sympathetically responsive, and finally glowed like fanned tinder touched by a match under the kindling of the publisher's pleading. " Yes, he would not deny that he could write such a book. Such a book, he did not mind saying in confidence, had long been in his mind, and in the mind of friends who had repeatedly urged him to such work." The fact is, that Watts-Dunton was gratified by the request, and did not disguise his pleasure ; for with all his vast learning and acute intellect, there was a singular and childlike simplicity about Watts-Dunton that was very lovable. Actually accept a commission to write the book in question he would not, but he was not unwilling to hear the proposed terms, and in fact seemed so attracted by and so interested in the project that the pleased publisher would leave, conscious of having done a good morning's work, and of having been the first to propose, and so practically to bespeak, a book that was already almost as good as written, already almost as good as published, already almost as good as an assured success. Perhaps he chuckled at the thought of the march he had stolen on his fellow-publishers, who would envy him the inclusion of such a book in his list. Possibly even he turned in somewhere to lunch, and, as the

slang phrase goes, " did himself well " on the strength
of it.

But, whatever the publisher's subsequent doings,
the chances were that Watts-Dunton went back to his
library, to brood over the idea, very likely to write to
some of us whose advice he valued, or, more likely still,
to telegraph proposing a meeting to discuss the project (I had not a few such letters and telegrams from
him myself), perhaps in imagination to see the book
written and published, but ultimately and inevitably
—to procrastinate and in the end to let the proposal
lapse.   Like the good intentions with which, according
to the proverb, the road to perdition is paved, Watts-
Dunton's book-writing intentions, if intentions counted,
would in themselves go far to furnish a fat corner of
the British Museum Library.   That he never carried
these intentions into effect was, however, due not entirely
to procrastination.

It is only fair to him to remember that his life work,
his *magnum opus*, must be looked for not in literature
but in friendship.   Stevenson's life work was his art.
" I sleep upon my art for a pillow," he wrote to W. E.
Henley.   " I waken in my art ; I am unready for death
because I hate to leave it.   I love my wife, I do not know
how much, nor can, nor shall, unless I lost her ; but
while I can conceive of being widowed, I refuse the
offering of life without my art ; I *am* not but in my
art ; it is me ; I am the body of it merely."

Watts-Dunton's life work was not literature nor

poetry, but friendship. Stevenson sacrificed himself in few things for his friends. On the contrary, he looked to them to sacrifice not a little of time, interest, and energy on his behalf. Watts-Dunton's whole life was one long self-sacrifice—I had almost written one fatal self-sacrifice—of his own interests, his own fame, in the cause of his friends. His best books stand upon our shelves in every part of the English-speaking world, but the name that appears upon the cover is not that of Theodore Watts-Dunton, but of Dante Gabriel Rossetti and Algernon Charles Swinburne. He wrote no Life of either, but how much of their life and of their life's best work we owe to Watts-Dunton, we shall never know. Their death was a cruel blow to him, but had he died first the loss to Rossetti and to Swinburne would have been irreparable. Just as to Stevenson life seemed almost unimaginable without his art, so I find it hard, almost impossible, to picture Swinburne's life at The Pines, failing the sustaining and brotherly presence of Watts-Dunton. Often, when Watts-Dunton was ailing, I have come away with a sinking at my heart lest it should be Watts-Dunton who died first; and I can well believe' that long ago a like dread sometimes possessed those who loved Rossetti. Cheerfully and uncomplainingly Watts-Dunton gave his own life and his own life's work for them, and his own best book is the volume of his devotion to his friends.

The sum of that devotion will never fully be known,

but it was as much at the service of the unknown, or of those who were only little known, as of the famous. He had his enemies—" the hated of New Grub Street " was his playful description of himself—and some of them have not hesitated meanly to hint that he attached himself barnacle-wise or parasite-wise to greater men than himself for self-seeking reasons. Borne thither on their backs—it was sometimes said—he was able to sun himself upon Parnassian heights, otherwise unattainable ; and being in their company and of their company he hoped thus to attract to himself a little of their reflected glory. My answer to such statements is that it was not their abilities, nor their fame, which drew Watts-Dunton to Rossetti and to Swinburne, but his love of the men themselves, and his own genius for friendship. Being the men they were, he would have first been drawn to them, and thereafter have come to love them just as wholly and devotedly had they to the end of their lives remained obscure.

And so far from seeking the company or the friendship of the great, he delighted in making friends in humble ranks of life. Any one who has accompanied Watts-Dunton on a morning walk will remember a call here at a cottage, a shop, or it may be an inn, where lived some enthusiastic but poor lover of books, birds, or children, and the glad and friendly greetings that were exchanged. If, as occasionally happened, some great person—great in a social sense, I mean—happened to be a caller at The Pines, when perhaps a struggling young

author, painter, or musician, in whom Watts-Dunton was
interested or whom he was trying to help, happened to
be there, one might be sure that, of the two, it would
not be the great man who would be accorded the warmer
greeting by Watts-Dunton and—after his marriage—by
his gracious, beautiful, and accomplished young wife.
What he once said of Tennyson is equally true of Watts-
Dunton himself.

"When I first knew Tennyson," he said, " I was,
if possible, a more obscure literary man than I now am,
and he treated me with exactly the same manly respect
that he treated the most illustrious people." Watts-
Dunton, who in his poems and in his conversation could
condense into a sentence what many of us could not as
felicitously convey in a page, puts the whole matter
into two words, " manly respect." Unless he had good
cause to do otherwise, Watts-Dunton, no less than
Tennyson, was prepared to treat others with " manly
respect," irrespective of fame, riches, or rank. That
is the attitude neither entirely of the aristocrat nor of
the democrat, but of the gentleman to whom what we
call " snobbishness " is impossible.

One more reason why Watts-Dunton's contribu-
tion to " Letters " in the publishers' lists runs to no
greater extent than two volumes, is that so many of his
contributions to " Letters " took the form of epistles
to his friends. The writing of original, characteristic,
and charming letters—brilliant by reason of vivid descriptive passages, valuable because used as a means of

expressing criticism or conveying knowledge—is an art now so little practised as likely soon to be lost.

Watts-Dunton's letter writing was possibly the outcome of his habit of procrastination. To put off the settling down in dead earnest to some work that he felt ought to be done, but at which he " shied," he would suddenly remember that he had a letter to write which he thought should be penned. " I must send So-and-so a line first," he would say; which line when it came to be written proved to be an essay in miniature, in which he had, carelessly and free from the irking consciousness that he was writing for publication and so must mind his words, thrown off some of his weightiest and wisest thoughts. He protested throughout his life that he was a wickedly bad correspondent. None the less he wrote so many charming and characteristic letters that could they—and why not ?—be collected they would add yet another to the other reputations he attained.

Swinburne, in recent years at least, did not share his friend's predilection for letter writing. The author of *Atalanta in Calydon* once said to me, almost bitterly, that had he in early and middle life refrained from writing and from answering unnecessary letters—unnecessary in the sense that there was no direct call or claim upon him to write or to answer them—there would be at least twelve more volumes by him, and of his best in the publishers' lists. One letter, which arrived when I was a guest at The Pines, led Swinburne to expound his theory of letter answering. It was from a young woman personally unknown to him, and began by saying that a great kindness he had once done to her father emboldened her to ask a favour to herself ; what it was I now forget, but it necessitated a somewhat lengthy reply. " The fact that I have been at some pains to serve the father, so far from excusing a further claim by the daughter, is the very reason why by any decent member of that family I should not again be assailed," Swinburne expostulated.

" She says," he went on, " that she trusts I won't think she is asking too much in hoping that I will answer her letter, a letter which does not interest me nor concern me in the least. She could have got the information for which she asks elsewhere with very little trouble to herself and none to me. The exasperating thing about such letters," he went on, getting more and more angry, " is that I feel that the letter is an unwarrantable intrusion. Out of consideration to her father I can't very well say so ; in addition to which, as one does not wish to seem merely churlish, to say so, to explain oneself, would necessitate writing at length—thus wasting more time, to say nothing of the chance of being dragged into further correspondence. It is one's impotency to make such folk see things reasonably which irritates. I have to suppress that irritation, and that results in further irritation. I am irritated with myself for being irritated—for not taking things philosophically, as Watts-Dunton does—as well as irritated with her, and the result is the spoiling of a morning's work. She will say, perhaps, and you even may say, ' It is only one letter you are asked to write.' Quite so. Not much, perhaps, to make a fuss about. But " (he pounded the table with clenched fist angrily) " multiply that one person by the many who so write, and the net total works out to an appalling waste of precious time."

My reply was to remind him of N. P. Willis's protest that to ask a busy author to write an unnecessary letter was like asking a postman to go for a ten-mile walk ; to which I added, " when he has taken his boots off."

Swinburne had never heard the saying, and with characteristic veering of the weather vane of his mood, forgot alike his letter-writing lady and his own irritation in his delight at a fellow-sufferer's happy hit. " Capital ! " he exclaimed, rubbing his hands together gleefully. " Capital ! The worm has turned and shown that, worm as he is, he is not without a sting in his tail ! "

In his later years Swinburne wrote few letters except to a relative, a very intimate friend, or upon some pressing business. The uninvited correspondent he rarely answered at all. For every letter that Swinburne received Watts-Dunton probably received six, and sooner or later he answered all. The amount of time that went in letters which in no way concerned his own work or his own interests, and were penned only out of kindness of heart, was appalling. Had he refrained from writing letters intended to hearten or to help some friend or some young writer, or to soften a disappointment, the books that are lost to us—a Life of Rossetti, for instance —might well be to the good. If a book by a friend happened to be badly slated in a critical journal—and no calamity to a friend is borne with more resignation and even cheerfulness by some of us who " write " than a bad review of a friend's book—Watts-Dunton, if he chanced to see the slating, would put work aside and sit down then and there to indite to that friend a letter which helped and heartened him or her much more than the slating had depressed. I have myself had letters from fellow-authors who told me they were moved to express sympathy or indignation about this or that bad review of one of my little books. The only effect of their letter was to rub salt into the wound, and to make one feel how widely one's literary naked- ness or even literary sinning had been proclaimed in the market-place. Watts-Dunton's letters not only made one feel that the review in question mattered nothing, but he would at the same time find something to say about the merits of the work under review which not only took the gall out of the unfriendly critic's ink, but had the effect of setting one newly at work cheered, relieved, and nerved to fresh effort.

I do not quote here any of these letters, as they are concerned only with my own small writings, and so would be of no interest to the reader. Instead, let me quote one I received from him on another subject. A sister of mine sent me a sonnet in memory of a dead poet, a friend of Watts-Dunton's and mine ; and having occasion to write him on another matter, I enclosed it without comment. Almost by return of post came the following note, in which he, the greatest critic of his day, was at the pains, unasked, to give a young writer the benefit of his weighty criticism and encouragement.

" My thanks for sending me your sister's lovely sonnet. I had no idea that she was a genuine poet. It is only in the 7th line where I see an opening for improvement :—

    " ' To *a* | great darkness and | in a | great light.'

" It is an error to suppose that when the old scansion by quantity gave place to scansion by accent, the quantitative demands upon a verse became abrogated. A great deal of attention to quantity is apparent in every first-rate line—

    " ' The sleepless soul that perished in its prime ; '

where, by making the accent and the quantity meet (and quantity, I need not remind you, is a matter of consonants quite as much as of vowels), all the strength that can be got into an iambic English verse is fixed there. Although, of course, it would make a passage monotonous if in every instance quantity and accent were made to meet, those who care for the best versification give great attention to it."

This is one instance only out of many of his interest

in a young writer who was then personally unknown to him; but in turning over, for the purpose of this article, some of the letters from him which I have preserved, I have found so many similar reminders of his great-heartedness that I am moved once again to apply to Theodore Watts-Dunton the words in which, many years ago, I dedicated a book to him. They are from James Payn's *Literary Recollections:* " My experience of men of letters is that for kindness of heart they have no equal. I contrast their behaviour to the young and struggling with the harshness of the Lawyer, the hardness of the Man of Business, the contempt of the Man of the World, and am proud to belong to their calling."

THE WATTS-DUNTON I KNEW.

BY HERBERT JENKINS.

Once when I was urging Mr. Watts-Dunton to republish in book form some of his critical essays, he replied with a laugh, and that characteristic wave of his arm—a wave of deprecation in this case—" My dear fellow, I am always being asked that. But I have not time ; I have not even time to die."

Until then I had never associated him, however remotely, with death. His spirit seemed to defy time, just as his mind refused to be saddled with the intellectual limitations of any particular generation. A casual observer might have been in some doubt as to whether this man of so many interests and occupations had ever regarded death as a serious menace to either.

That he was conscious of the flight of time he showed in a letter (November 19, 1913), in which he wrote : " When you get to be anything near my age you will find that the velocity with which the days pass over your head increases every year, and that it is impossible to keep down the work that every morning brings ; " and again (January 10, 1914) : " The fact is, my engagements increase by the cube foot, and I am not quite so young as I was." Even here he was not looking at the end, but merely the flight of time in relation to his own occupations. There was nothing about him suggestive of advanced years. His enthusiasm, that curious characteristic wave of the arm, the ready and spontaneous laugh, his keen interest in men and affairs—all spoke of youth rather than of old age.

For others he would do things as a matter of course ; but when himself asking anything, he invariably did so as a personal favour. I have never met a man more consistently courteous and kindly by nature. " I am distressed at the trouble you have been put to ; " " I must trust to your good nature to pardon ; " " I am afraid I am giving you a monstrous deal of trouble," he would write when, as a matter of fact, he was making some very reasonable request.

In speaking of his contemporaries he seemed to prefer to overlook those he did not like or with whom he disagreed. His generosity to men of the younger generation was spontaneous and whole-hearted. One day, when discussing critics and criticism, I reminded him of a remark he had made many years previously, that when work came before him for critical judgment, especially if it were the work of a young writer, he first sought what was good in it, and always made that the pivot of his criticism. " Yes," he remarked half to himself, " I have always tried to find the best in every book I have criticised."

He did not hesitate, however, when occasion arose, to express a hostile opinion, and he did so with a conviction that left no doubt in the listener's mind as to the sincerity of his view. One day we were discussing a certain man well known in the literary world whom I will call a lawyer (he was not a lawyer), and Watts-Dunton remarked, " A clever man, an exceedingly clever man, but a bad ' lawyer ; '" and, as far as he was concerned, there the matter ended.

Extremely sensitive alike to favourable and unfavourable comment, he seemed to wish to live on good terms with all. Dispute was abhorrent to him, yet he was tenacious to his purpose. His weapons were those of the diplomatist. If he disagreed with or disliked a man, he did not, as was the case with Borrow, wish to knock him down ; or, as with Swinburne, annihilate him with impassioned rhetoric. He expressed his view as a judgment rather than as an opinion, although there were occasions when his sense of moral indignation outweighed his prejudices, and he hit out vigorously.

He was greatly pained at Dr. Augustus Jessopp's extraordinary attack upon the manhood of George Borrow; and although a short time previously he had been in very friendly correspondence with the writer of the article, he felt it incumbent upon him to refute what can only be regarded as an unjustifiable attack upon the memory of a man about whom at one time Dr. Jessopp had written in the highest terms of praise. In this little incident Watts-Dunton's method was characteristic. He did not wait for his opponent himself to discover what had been written, but sent a copy of the book containing his remarks with the following letter :—

"2, THE PINES,
"PUTNEY HILL, S.W.,
"*Dec. 7, 1900.*

"DEAR DR. JESSOPP,

"I feel sure that the enclosed Introduction to the Minerva Library Edition of *The Romany Rye* will interest you, and I feel equally sure that you will not take amiss my answer to what you said in the *Daily Chronicle* about my old friend George Borrow.

"Not to have defended him from the strictures I have alluded to, would have been to fail in the most sacred duties of friendship.

"I was a long time making up my mind as to whether I could possibly let the matter pass by, as I naturally shrank from placing myself in a position of antagonism to you.

"Should I be the longer liver of the two, and should

any one through misconception assail your memory as you have assailed Borrow's, I shall again have an opportunity—a painful one—of showing what are my views of the duties of friendship.

"Looking forward to the great pleasure of seeing you,

"Believe me to be,

"Yours very sincerely,

"(Signed)   T. WATTS-DUNTON." *

It is interesting to note that there was no breach between the two men, and that Dr. Jessopp accepted the rebuke in as generous a spirit as that in which it was administered.

I found Watts-Dunton genuinely interested in the work of others, and he was always the first to write or voice his congratulations. When *Children of the Dead End* appeared, one of the first of a shoal of letters that I received was from him. "I congratulate you," he wrote, "upon your great success with the navvy poet and autobiographer [Patrick MacGill]. It is making really a sensation."

I had a great struggle to persuade him to consent to his two essays, *Poetry*, and *The Renascence of Wonder*, being reprinted in book form—a struggle that lasted for many months, involving numerous visits to The Pines, and conversations. In every one of these he talked

* This letter has been lent to me by Mr. F. J. Farrell, to whose efforts the Borrow Memorial at Norwich is almost entirely due.

tirelessly upon a hundred and one subjects, while I strove to keep the conversation in the neighbourhood of the two essays. I pointed out that the unfortunate student who desired to read them was forced, as I had been forced years ago, to spend an afternoon in the suffocating atmosphere of the Reading Room of the British Museum, which Dr. Garnett, with characteristic humour, once described to me as the finest *scientifically* ventilated building in Europe. Watts-Dunton laughed, and invariably replied, " Well, come and see me again, and we will have another talk. I am always glad to see you."

At the conclusion of each of those delightful encounters I felt that little progress had been made towards the object I had in mind. On one occasion I pointed out that never a week passed that did not bring him letters from students of literature and other admirers at home and abroad inquiring the name of a volume in which the essays appeared—a fact I had gleaned through the indiscretion of a secretary momentarily off his guard. Our talks invariably ended with, " I'll think about it."

Once I produced a copy of Swinburne's *Studies in Prose and Poetry*, and without prelude read to him the following passage :—

" The first critic of our time—perhaps the largest-minded and surest-sighted of any age—has pointed out, in an essay on poetry which should not be too long left buried in the columns of the *Encyclopædia Britannica*, the exhaustive accuracy of the Greek terms which define every claimant to the laurel as either a singer or a maker."

From that point my task was easier, and Watts-Dunton was eventually persuaded to withdraw his opposition, which he did with manifest reluctance.

When, after upwards of a year's really hard work, I finally overcame his objections to the republication of his two essays, he appeared not a little amused at himself. " For the last twenty years," he said, " I have been urged by half the publishers in London to republish those essays, and I have consistently refused." He was clearly not a little puzzled to account for his final capitulation, as, indeed, were his friends, who had previously warned me that I was courting inevitable failure.

The opinion of Swinburne obviously weighed with him as against the prayers of " half the publishers in London." He was pleased when he found that without exception the newspapers commended his determination. At the time of his death he was still actively engaged upon the work of revision.

In his work he was always the breathless pursuer. Some months before his death he wrote telling me of " the enormous pressure of work " that was upon him. " You have no idea," he wrote, " no one can have any idea, what it is. I am an early riser, and breakfast at seven, and from that hour until seven in the evening I am in full swing, with the aid of two most intelligent secretaries."

The shrewder among his friends had more than a suspicion that his methods of work were not a little responsible for this state of affairs ; but there was another reason—his kindliness of heart. He burdened himself with many things asked of him by entire strangers as well as friends; for he had brought with him from the Victorian age not its narrowness or its conservatism, but its courtesy and punctiliousness.

The world in which he lived was to him as vital as his intellectual life, and he conceived the brilliant idea of welding the two together; and the result was The Pines circle, where nothing of interest was taboo, and which centred round the personality of a man who seemed possessed of a unique capacity for friendship.

WATTS-DUNTON : AN IMPRESSION.

BY JOHN LAWRENCE LAMBE.

My friends Thomas Hake and Arthur Compton-Rickett have asked me to write a few words on my friendship with Watts-Dunton during the last two and a half years of his life.

It arose quite suddenly without any sort of introduction. In 1901 I had published my first book—a novel—and both Swinburne and Watts-Dunton wrote

to me concerning it. Ten years later, in September
1911, I committed a second indiscretion—this time six
plays in verse and prose, with introductory essays.
Three weeks after the book appeared Watts-Dunton
wrote expressing interest in it, and asked me if I could
arrange a meeting with him. He had never heard of
me then apart from my books. Ten days later I went
to The Pines, and saw him for the first time. The
following week he invited me to go again; and after
that, by his constantly repeated invitation, I visited him
alone or with my wife every few weeks until his death.
At our fifth meeting he asked me to succeed him as
executor and trustee to his beloved friend Swinburne,
in place of the late Francis Hindes Groome (who, he
told me, had been appointed in Swinburne's lifetime),
on the ground that the recent Copyright Act had given
the Swinburne copyrights a new lease of life. It was
not until after his death that I knew that I had been
appointed a trustee of his general estate.

What this friendship meant to me I cannot possibly
express. Though at the date of our first meeting my
knowledge of Watts-Dunton's critical work was almost
confined to his *Essay on Poetry*, for years I had accepted
Swinburne's view of him both as critic and friend, and
it seemed an incredible piece of good fortune that he
whose opinion on poetry I valued more than that of any
living man should be the first to stretch forth his hand
to me through the darkness. In my case even more
literally than in that of Rossetti (who was introduced to

him by Dr. Gordon Hake) he was " the friend whom my verse won for me."

Watts-Dunton's physical appearance has been described elsewhere. When I met him he had only a little eyesight left ; but he was still endowed with almost incredible powers of observation. Though partly deaf, when seated on the sofa beside him during those long conversations which frequently lasted for three hours at a stretch, and sometimes much longer, I never found the smallest difficulty or fatigue in conversing with him. His amazing brain was so active and his curiosity so insatiable that nothing escaped him, from the strategy of Radko Dimitrieff to the Tango—which he rightly prophesied would be a failure, " because the rhythm of the dance did not agree with the rhythm of the music."

He worked interminably with his secretary and reader. Every day seven newspapers were read to him, and he absorbed the contents of them all. His intellect was absolutely unimpaired, and his interest in life that of a healthy and clever boy to the very last. When he was far advanced in his eighty-first year he drove some eighteen miles in order to dine with us—which I am told was the only visit he ever paid during the last years of his life, for he had a hatred of leaving home.

He frequently spoke with deep affection of his former friends. " I don't know who was the best of them," he would say. " Sometimes I think that it was William Morris, sometimes dear Algernon, sometimes Rossetti. Swinburne was an adorable man, and he was the greatest poet of them all—greater than Shelley. People always speak of his poetry as if it were lacking in intellectual fibre. That is quite untrue—look, for instance, at a poem like *Hertha*—but twenty-five years must elapse before the intellectual side of his work will be appreciated." * Yet he was not in the least blind to Swinburne's extravagances as a critic, notably with regard to Victor Hugo. It is interesting also to observe how little influence their long residence together had on the views of either. Swinburne to the end swore by Shelley, Watts-Dunton by Keats, whose work, he said, he preferred incomparably, though he admitted that Shelley had more inspiration.†

His account of the early years at The Pines was interesting. At that time Rossetti was living at Cheyne Walk, where a bedroom was kept for Watts-Dunton, who spent a day and night there regularly every week. From Rossetti's he went on to visit Lord De Tabley, who led a solitary existence and frequently had not spoken to an outsider since Watts-Dunton's departure

* I do not hold these views. Notwithstanding an intense appreciation of Swinburne, I would rather have six lines by Shelley than all that he ever wrote, and I feel sure that Swinburne would have approved of my choice. I regard him, so far as his verse is concerned, as a very great lyrical poet, scarcely at all as a thinker. Watts-Dunton's opinion of the intellectual quality of Swinburne's work, I have good reason to believe, fluctuated considerably at different times. One cannot expect even a great critic always to agree with himself.

† In one of his buried essays he makes the illuminating remark that Nature, which was an object of contemplation to all other English poets, was a rapture to Shelley.

the week before. The next day he would return to Swinburne at The Pines. When I asked him how long he had kept up this regular and incessant round of visits, he replied emphatically, " For years."

My friends asked me also to give a criticism of Watts-Dunton's work, and I wrote quite a long article. But on consideration it seemed plain to me, owing to the position which I occupy, that I was precluded from publishing any detailed criticism. As they still kindly urge me to write a few lines, I will observe that my general view of Watts-Dunton's writings is that his claim to permanent recognition lies in the suggestive value of the vivid flashes of poetic insight which irradiate his essays. His criticism of poetry is always of the first importance. From his earliest childhood, throughout his long sojourn at St. Ives until he came to London at the age of forty, his whole being had been soaked in poetry. He once told me that in youth for three years he could not bring himself to read a line of prose. Mr. William Watson said comparatively recently that all he knew about poetry he had learned from Watts-Dunton's articles in the *Athenæum ;* adding that if these were republished they would make some of the finest reading in the world. I am convinced, however, that Watts-Dunton's literary and philosophical generalizations must be taken with caution ; that even in his best work they are apt to be vague, illogical, nay, sometimes almost contradictory.*

* As an example of what I mean, the *Essay on Poetry* opens with : "In modern criticism the word poetry is used sometimes to

He had none of the aloofness of the philosopher, and I regret the great success of *Aylwin*, inasmuch as, in my opinion, it has tended to obscure his real function, which was that of a poet's poet, a man not only poetical in himself but a most fruitful cause of poetry in other men. In this respect the list of the world's writers who can compete with him is probably a short one.

It is too early by far for me to write about Watts-Dunton's private or domestic affairs, though perhaps without indiscretion stress may be laid on the deep mutual affection that existed between him and the young wife who had loved him from the time when she was a mere girl. The hospitality of The Pines is an agreeable reminiscence, for our long talks were varied by much music on piano and violin, and also on Watts-Dunton's huge gramophone, which was a source of deep joy to him. Sometimes we danced to please him. Then came supper, with oysters from a safe sea-

denote any expression (artistic or other) of imaginative feeling, sometimes to designate one of the fine arts. . . . In classical literature Pindar may perhaps be taken as a type of the poets of energy ; Virgil of the poets of art." Later in the same essay we are told : "It was a strange conception that led people for centuries to use the word Pindaric and irregular as synonymous terms ; whereas the very essence of the odes of Pindar is their regularity. There is no more difficult form of poetry than this," etc. If so, how can Pindar represent the poets of energy as opposed to those of art ? Also, if poetry sometimes denotes "any expression (artistic or other) of imaginative feeling " and Pindar is the classical type of this meaning of the word poetry, what prevents us from asking which is the finer poetry, Pindar's *Odes* or Thackeray's *Vanity Fair ?*

bed in winter, and a perennial flow of plovers' eggs sent by Lady Leighton Warren, Lord De Tabley's sister, during their season. After supper more talk. The old house had always been a place of enchantment to me, and the pictures and furniture had been familiar from photographs years before I entered its door — which, by the way, was always left invitingly open.

The house still remains unaltered, save that fourteen tons of books have been removed from their resting-places—which consisted of every available spot between the roof and the foundations—that library which was a symbol of the patient toil and splendid achievement of those old friends, both stars of the intellectual firmament, who for so many years worked together within its walls.

XXVI.

WATTS-DUNTON : THE MAN.

XXVI.

WATTS-DUNTON : THE MAN.

IN recalling a man's personality one associates the dynamic impression less by physical externalities than by some trick or attitude—the theatrical dropping of Whistler's monocle, the Swinburnian toss of the head, the kindly twinkle of Browning's glance, and, in the case of Watts-Dunton, the intimate wave of the arm with which he made you welcome. In every one of these gestures the character of the particular man showed itself. The booming sing-song of Swinburne, distinctive as it was, seemed more accidental than incidental to the man's inner self ; but in that sudden fierce toss of the head the whole of his lyrical passion, his extravagance of moods, his ecstatic enjoyment of life, flashed into being.

One remembers the sympathetic *portamento* of Watts-Dunton's voice, his alert manner, little tricks of iteration in his speech, the small, slight figure radiating nervous vitality ; and yet obliterating all these in its inner suggestiveness was that intimate wave of the arm. The sensitive friendliness, the quick responsiveness, even the tactful *savoir-faire* of the lawyer, all seemed symbolized in that favourite gesture.

In attempting to visualize Watts-Dunton the man more thoroughly, the simple externals may be dwelt upon for a moment or so before passing to more essential matters.

Small in stature and somewhat slight in physique, he was well proportioned, with finely shaped hands and feet, and a splendid brow. In his younger days he had magnificent dark-brown eyes, that glittered brilliantly whenever he was excited. But an infirmity of vision grew upon him in later years and dimmed their lustre. Yet certain characteristics withstood all the encroachments of time, and the resonant voice and wonderful ebullience of spirits followed him down to the very end.

His speaking voice was unusually pleasing, and though with his vibrant temperament it soon became loudly emphatic, in converse it was never high and discordant, as so frequently happens with excitable people. His intonation was agreeably cultured, without being obtrusively academic ; there was no more reliable authority than he on the pronunciation of words, however recondite.

In quoting prose or verse, the voice took on a rhythmic chant—far less sing-song, however, than that of Swinburne—and with sensitive skill brought out the special prosodic points on which he wished to dwell. His memory, for verse especially, was excellent ; some writers—such as Chaucer, Shakespeare, Keats, and

Coleridge—he seemed able to quote indefinitely ; and when you mentioned a favourite poem or novel of his, he would give a long drawn *A-h-h* of appreciation.

Despite a wide and varied knowledge of English literature, he was not, in the strict sense of the term, a great scholar ; and his real strength lay neither in any profundity of research, nor in any marked originality of outlook, but in a strikingly retentive memory and in a gift for happy allusiveness.

Outside of English letters, his literary equipment, for a man occupying his position, was inconsiderable ; but he utilized with excellent effect the excursion into Oriental literature which he had taken as a student at St. Ives, and there is scarcely any writing of his where he does not turn to advantage these early studies.

Allowing for the little prejudices from which even the greatest critics have not been free, he was at his best when discussing the development of English poetry. Here his full and intimate acquaintance with English verse, his reliable memory, and his fine feeling for rhythmic beauty, made him a delightful and stimulating companion.   Again, in dealing with work of the romantic *genre*, from the Arthurian cycle to the Utopias of William Morris, he was admittedly fitted both by temperament and knowledge of his subject.   Indeed, Morris himself, an exacting authority on such matters, valued Watts-Dunton's criticism of his work as he valued that of no other contemporary critic.

In converse with him one was struck by his gift of

lucid exposition and dramatic presentment. Indeed these gifts, especially his dramatic faculty, sometimes gave the impression to those imperfectly acquainted with him, of a far more intimate knowledge of his subject than he actually possessed. He did not belong to the type of man whose gift of expression does ill justice to his intellectual powers ; and remarkable as these were in Watts-Dunton's case, it cannot be said that he was free from Macaulay's weakness for pontifical omniscience.

Yet he was an excellent listener, eagerly interested in fresh points of view, however tenacious of his own theories ; and especially when dealing with English poetry, rich in suggestive ideas.

He was a born *raconteur*, as Rossetti was never tired of reiterating, and his talent for inventing endless plots for novels—some of a thrilling character—might have made him a serious rival to Wilkie Collins had he turned the talent for sensationalism more largely to account.

A friend still living can vividly recall how Watts-Dunton once recounted De Quincey's narrative of the Williams murders to a circle of young literary aspirants, who had not at that time dipped very deeply into the works of the author of *Confessions of an Opium Eater*, with such detail and dramatic force that it seemed as though he must have committed to memory every page —a fact he once confessed he was sometimes in the habit of accomplishing.

He was a keen politician of the old Whig school, and especially interested in colonial affairs. To the very last day of his life he kept himself in touch with continental politics, and quite a year before his death, in 1914, spoke of the terrible " European conflagration " (his own words) which he foresaw was impending. He had a sound knowledge of history ; had interested himself for many years in racial problems, and was a shrewd politician of the Imperialistic type. In matters of home policy, on problems of social reform, Watts-Dunton's politics remained early Victorian. The democratic problems of the age touched him but slightly ; he looked with approval on Herbert Spencer's attitude towards State interference, and virtually endorsed that writer's social dictum that you cannot get " golden conduct out of leaden instincts."

In his early days he had received from his father a good grounding in science, and although his multifarious activities prevented him from keeping in touch with more modern developments, he never lost his interest in and fascination for the natural sciences.

On the whole, the most striking feature about his intellectual life was the intense curiosity he showed in every phase of human affairs ; the breadth and range of his interests and studies marked him out as a brilliant *causeur* rather than a profound student in any particular direction.

His Method of Work.

He had no method in the arrangement of his letters and manuscripts. They were always in the utmost disorder, piled up in his study, covering the floor as well as the chairs and tables. But this confusion never worried him. He lived in a state of cheerful chaos. On one occasion a friend who called, after the first greeting, looked round the room for an empty seat, and finding none stood somewhat embarrassed when asked to sit down. " Throw that heap of papers on the floor," said Watts-Dunton, pointing to an arm-chair beside the fire, " and help yourself to a cigarette. They won't be touched ; nobody ever touches a scrap of anything in this room."

The mantelpiece in this room was a large one, and the number of letters which he continued to pile upon it by some ingenious method was an experiment in card-building or, rather, letter-building never surpassed. The impression the sight awakened was : one letter more added must inevitably bring the whole pile pell-mell into the fender below. The time came, however, some seventeen or eighteen years before his decease, when the increase in legal and literary affairs forced him to employ a secretary, and a better method of carrying on the business of life was introduced, though even then any unusual display of method annoyed him. Indeed, on one occasion he lost his temper when his secretary ventured to suggest that a cabinet with pigeon-holes for unanswered letters would save time and trouble and lead to less friction between them.

He was a man whose enormous intellectual activity was negatived to no slight extent by ill-directed mental concentration. Having once drifted into a certain groove, he lacked the necessary impulse and force of character to escape. He had slipped into a groove in his own native town almost before the school days were over, and but for the interposition of what he would call " Harlequin Circumstance "—but for the fact that his father's firm at St. Ives began to prove less lucrative, compelling him to seek his fortune elsewhere—there is every reason to believe that his rustication would have gone on for all the remaining days of his life. Even when he came to realize in London that opportunities had been lost through letting the world slide, he failed to profit by experience and mend his ways. Instead of giving undivided attention to original work—with more than one novel practically ready by way of stock-in-trade —he allowed himself to be enticed into journalism, against the advice of many men of letters well acquainted with his stories in manuscript.

" If you had pluck enough," Gordon Hake wrote to him in a letter dated from Florence, February 15, 1874, two years before he contributed a line to the *Athenæum*—" if you had pluck enough to send in your *Gabrielle* " (this is the title by which *Aylwin* was known in those days), " at the end of the year you would be able to live where you liked. Take my word for it, you would instantly top all the novelists ; such a work is not written once in a generation. It is a great pity that you do not conquer your dislike to make the venture. But I suppose you are the victim of destiny, which holds your volition back."

Whether a " victim of destiny " or not, everything has gone to show that, in not publishing *Aylwin* earlier, he made a mistake. If he had not " topped all the novelists " of that mid-Victorian period, he would have stepped into an enviable place among them ; whereas, by delaying so long, he not only marred his novel as a work of art by over-revision, but got so far mastered by his habit of procrastination that he could never afterwards complete any other story to his entire satisfaction. Yet there is no doubt journalistic work suited his temperament, and any law business that came in his way never appeared to interfere seriously with the business of reviewing books ; and as to the writing of fiction, the mental energy was always there, but the physical portion of the work, the " mechanical," as he called it, seriously distressed him. This, however, may be said, in extenuation of his continued literary procrastinations and the curious way in which, after pursuing some project with tremendous energy for a period, he would suddenly concentrate his mind upon some other. A physician, who knew Watts-Dunton intimately, expressed the opinion that the fits of nervous exhaustion that accompanied him throughout his life were due largely to the existence of a brain too large in proportion to his muscular frame.

As a consequence, very little of his work was ever recorded in his own handwriting. Even his letters were written from dictation. This was partly attributable to extreme short-sightedness. The work, whether poetry or prose, was usually written in the first instance in pencil by an amanuensis, and then re-written in ink, the lines well apart, before he would even glance at the pages. But this neat draft once completed, he would seize upon the manuscript, a peculiar glitter lighting up his eyes, and with pencil in hand start working upon it. Seldom did a sentence escape " correction." The emendations were made with a swiftness almost incredible, and they were very frequent on every page. Whole paragraphs were often deleted or else enclosed in a circle and marked for transposition. The moment these " vital changes," as he called them, were completed, he would hand the manuscript back to the amanuensis. Every page was re-copied. Whether he chanced to be at work upon a poem or a story or some article for a literary journal, the *modus operandi* was the same ; and this process of elaboration was repeated three or four times at least. When the work was in proof the changes were no less manifest on most occasions.

It was his invariable custom for years to " start

the machinery " between five and six in the morning, even in winter. He would set light to his own library fire, boil his own egg and make his own tea, hours before the maids were about, everything needful having been left ready to hand on the previous night. But he never looked upon his literary work as other than " sport " at any period of his life. " The activity, however severe, of a born artist at his easel, of a born poet at his rhymings, of a born carpenter at his plane, is sport," as he was never tired of reiterating.

Yet he soon discovered that the writing of a novel —and after *Aylwin* was published he wrote two other novels—could never be " pure sport." Had he treated it less as a game to be taken up and put down as the mood seized him, he would probably have proved a surer artist. The canvas upon which he worked was invariably too large. The picture rapidly became overcrowded with characters and incidents. *Aylwin* grew to such dimensions as it progressed that scores of pages had to be deleted; and it was the same with those that followed. Besides, there were other enticements tempting him to continue in that journalistic groove on which he had chanced. Starting in a literary career at forty years of age—at an age when his intellectual force was at its best—he was beyond question fascinated at finding himself thrown in a somewhat sudden and unexpected manner into the very midst of brilliant literary circles where he felt thoroughly *en rapport*. Hitherto, such a contingence had seemed

to him remote, as one of the far-off St. Ivian dreams
not likely to be realized. He once, indeed, confessed
to a friend that, if the editor of any one of the London
magazines had accepted a short story or literary article
from his pen in the St. Ivian days, the event would have
been one far beyond his greatest expectations. And
yet, as it proved, in less than a year after taking up his
home in London, invitations from editors to write for
literary journals poured in upon him : as soon, in fact, as
his critical essays began to appear in the *Examiner*. One
of the earliest among these was the editor of the *Athenæum*, as already stated.

The prospect, one might almost say, obsessed him.
It was beyond his power to resist. " The business of
the novelist might, if entered into by one endowed with
exceptional pluck and perseverance, prove more re-
munerative than journalistic work. Under the happiest
conditions," as he would frequently argue, " it was all
a lottery." And so it came about, as everything goes
to show, that Watts-Dunton sank deeper and deeper as
time went on into a journalistic groove. It enabled his
active mind to rove at greater range over a variety of
topics ; it was less exacting, for he could choose his
own subjects and work how and when he liked. But by
his failure to concentrate on the more ambitious work
for which he certainly had many qualifications, he sacrificed a more permanent niche in English letters.

Beneath this mental restlessness and wilful dis-
persal of his energies, there was a shrinking from big

literary undertakings, for which he was so well equipped,
that demands a closer scrutiny than hitherto we have
given it.

When Rossetti declared that " Watts-Dunton sought
obscurity as other men seek fame," he had some show
of reason for the statement ; for even during Rossetti's lifetime he had neglected many opportunities
of publication which might have brought him both
fame and wealth. Small wonder then that Rossetti
further spoke of Watts-Dunton as being " the one
man of the time who with immense literary equipment
was without literary ambition " ; and that another
friend, Gordon Hake, writes :—

"You care not for the wreath, the dusty bays."

But more observant friends than either of these two
realized that Watts-Dunton's reluctance to publish
his work was not so easily explained, and that, so far
from not being ambitious, he was an intensely ambitious man. How then explain his perpetual hesitation
to publish ?

This unwillingness was due to two things : a highly
nervous artistic conscience, and a super-sensitiveness
to press criticism (he rarely resented even the frankest
criticism of his friends in conversation) ; while both
these factors, when probed, will be found to arise from
the basic sentimentality of his temperament.

The key to Watts-Dunton's temperament lay in his
acute sensibility. This it was that controlled not merely

his literary outlook, but his social activities and general attitude towards life.

To consider this statement in some detail. It affected his literary outlook, inasmuch as it made him exacting in his literary ideals. He was perpetually revising his own work, striving towards some exceptionally high standard, and loth to let his work be published until he had wrought it with all the skill that was possible to him. Such a characteristic in an age of hasty production, when the royalty of art is of, unfortunately, less moment than the royalties from book-making, was, of course, greatly to the honour of the hesitant. But the lifelong hesitation of the writer to allow his work to be published was due also to a horror of unfriendly criticism so acute that it can only be described as morbid. Tennyson and Browning may be instanced as illustrations of the differing attitudes that the literary artist may take towards outside criticism. Tennyson, as is well known, was abnormally sensitive ; Browning, perhaps, abnormally insensitive to criticism. Theodore Watts-Dunton out-Tennysoned Tennyson in this respect. Critical enough about his own work, he was peculiarly intolerant of even the mildest criticism from outside, resenting it as a personal affront. To avoid this as long as possible, he withheld from publication much that he positively yearned to publish. A sensitive conscience and a self-esteem fully as sensitive, combined together throughout his long life to produce a curious and unsatisfactory vacillation. And he treated most publishers as Hamlet did his father's ghost, with spirited promises and perpetual peradventures.

And if acute sensibility lay at the root of this hesitant attitude, it as surely affected the entirety of his work. Whether as a romancer or a critic, he exhibits both the failings and the merits of the sentimental temperament.

He had a full measure of that picturesque charm and dramatic aptitude of the skilful sentimentalist in letters ; but he had also, as his romances show, a taste for redundant embroidery, and for conventional values, that separates Sentimentality from Romanticism. The true Romantic builds on Reality ; the Sentimentalist is always trying to escape from it.

In his criticism, this sentimentalism is happily kept largely in check by his keen intellect ; but even here it may be seen. Agreeably so in his many pen studies of intimate friends ; less agreeably in the embarrassing discursiveness that dims the clarity of many a fine critique.

In his social life the sensibility gave rise to a strange restlessness that never permitted him to indulge in what William Morris once called " the static mood."

Here are a few extracts from some of his letters to his sister :—

" You say there is an article on Tibet in one of the papers, but you have not sent it. Please do so ; I particularly want to see it. . . . If any books come for me I should like to know."

Again he wrote about two days later : " I particularly want last Saturday's *Athenæum*. It contains an article of mine on Etheredge ; I am doing one on Congreve, and want to refer to it. There are at least four copies of the *Athenæum* in the drawing-room. . . . You might send me the St. Ives paper on Saturday with the others."

And then, almost before there was time to reply to this letter, another would be dispatched—another urgent appeal for books, more books or journals.

Finally he grows desperate.

" I very particularly want two books on Hungary or Magyarland, which are in the house. One is a book about the size of Bohn's Library which I bought about three months ago. Until very lately it was lying about on the ledge of the little Indian bookshelf near the window in the drawing-room. Its name I cannot for the life of me recall, but it is in cloth (*perhaps* a very dark green or very dark blue). It is second-hand, and looks like a circulating library book. It has a few full-page illustrations and a frontispiece. This I very urgently want at once. It may have been removed by me when Ellen Terry came, and placed on the floor or the long table of the front room. Please send it at once by the quickest post possible. The other is the book on Hungary (called either Hungary or Magyarland) I borrowed of Lord Tennyson. This is covered with a white paper covering. This also I want sending at once ; but perhaps the *other* is the more urgent."

Again, almost on the same day as that on which he asked for a volume on Hungary to be posted without delay :—

"I particularly want to refer to Scott's *Peveril of the Peak* as soon as I can," he writes. "I wish you would look for the volumes (two, I think) containing it, in Swinburne's series of the Waverley Novels, and send it *at once*—to-morrow morning if possible."

These brief extracts may give some conception of Watts-Dunton's intellectual restlessness—in other words, the acute sensibility of the sentimental temperament as it affected his mentality.

It affected his social life in another way. Companionable and affectionate as he was, he was peculiarly responsive to his environment, and was quite disproportionately distressed by those little vicissitudes that befall most men who mingle with their fellows. A tepid review of anything he had written (let alone a hostile one) was sufficient to upset him for days. He was, as men of his emotional temperament are, extremely jealous, and this was the one defect in the fine devotedness of his intimate friendships.

He was a friend of rare quality ; but he seemed at times to imagine that he had taken out a patent for friendship, and would disallow the least infringement on his fancied rights.

His name has been chiefly connected with famous

men of letters, such as Rossetti, Borrow, Swinburne ; yet his capacity for friendship was illustrated in countless ways, and some of his finest achievements in sympathy concern not the well-known few, but the unknown many. Indeed, case after case might be quoted of generosity and kindness on the part of the influential critic of the *Athenæum* to those of a less fortunate position. Let three cases suffice.

A young fellow occupying a modest post in a business firm wrote to Watts-Dunton about his literary aspirations. Watts-Dunton replied with a letter of kindly and valuable advice. The young man wrote again later on, asking if Watts-Dunton would read a novel he had written. He was told to send it ; and Watts-Dunton, finding it had promise, gave the writer an introduction to a firm of publishers. The novel was accepted, and proved an encouraging success. His correspondent never asked to see him, and, in fact, never did see him, yet without Watts-Dunton's advice and encouragement and help he might never have got his opportunity of " making good."

On another occasion Watts-Dunton befriended an artist with whom he had been on intimate terms in days gone by. This artist, a portrait painter whose genius was never recognized except by a limited circle of friends, lost heart when old age was coming upon him, and fell into evil ways. He squandered the paltry sums he received for his work from picture-dealers and pawnbrokers in drink. He drifted out of sight of all his friends ; his condition became so desperate that, homeless and without a sou, he started off to tramp through England, no one, not even his only sister, knew whither. Every one believed him dead. One day, however, there was a ring at the front door of The Pines, and a grimy-faced man, dust-ridden and in rags, inquired of the servant if Mr. Watts-Dunton was at home. Watts-Dunton was out ; but it so chanced that his sister, Mrs. Charles Mason, at this moment passed through the hall, and recognized the tramp as an artist who in better days had painted her portrait. She was deeply moved at the wretched plight into which her brother's old friend had obviously fallen. She gave him enough money to provide him with a " square meal " and a night's lodging, and told him to call again. The artist made his appearance on the following morning, looking somewhat more reputable ; and Watts-Dunton, greatly concerned when realizing his distressful condition, took compassion on him. He engaged him as an amanuensis, which proved a failure. He then hit on the idea of fitting up a room at The Pines, with easel, palette, and brush, where he might paint to his heart's content, Watts-Dunton superintending the progress of every picture with the greatest zeal, and providing his old friend weekly with an adequate sum of money to pay for a bedroom in the neighbourhood, it being understood that all " board " would be supplied at The Pines. It was, it need scarcely be recorded, clearly understood that all alcoholic habits should be abandoned.

Shut up in his studio at The Pines from nine o'clock in the morning until six o'clock in the evening, the reclaimed artist certainly led a sober, even industrious life. Watts-Dunton took as much interest in the painting of the various works of art—the subjects often suggested by himself—as a child might take in new toys. He would often stroll into the studio in the midst of literary work with his secretary, and remain absent for an hour or more.

This happened about a year before *Aylwin* was published, and one of his models sat for a fancy portrait of Sinfi Lovell.

The artist, however, who was broken in health, did not live many months after his installation at The Pines. One day he grew seriously indisposed while at his easel, and was taken from The Pines in a cab to one of the London hospitals, where he died after a few days' illness, all expenses to the last sovereign being defrayed by Watts-Dunton.

To interest oneself in the work of men like Rossetti, Borrow, and Swinburne, even to the detriment of one's own interests, may be explained on grounds other than those of disinterested friendship ; but to interest oneself in the work of the literary Tom, Dick, and Harry, as Watts-Dunton did right down to the very last days of his life, does argue a sympathetic nature of no common kind.

In the last years of his life, when he was particularly anxious to gather together some of his scattered writings, and when his capacity for work was naturally diminishing, he none the less, without a thought of how it might retard his own work, offered to read and advise upon the work of some unknown writer in whom, as was his generous wont, he had interested himself ; and the sympathetic encouragement and wise counsel given freely and ungrudgingly to this literary nobody, proved of inestimable advantage.

Here, then, in such cases like these, the sensitive sympathy and sweet kindliness of the man are seen to the fullest advantage. And without wishing to disparage the value of his tender solicitude for Rossetti during the last dark years of the poet-painter's life, or the moral revolution he wrought in Swinburne's case, it is in these unrecorded acts of friendship that the greatness of the man is the most clearly seen.

Acute sensibility, let us repeat, was essentially the keynote of his temperament. It might express itself in delicately subtle criticism, or take the form of a fit of sulks at a fancied slight ; it might be exhibited in some peculiarly gracious courtesy towards a friend, or lead him off some work he was doing into some byway that had caught his fancy. In short, the forms were protean, but the inspiration was one and the same.

While insisting on this characteristic, we do not forget that there was a highly practical side to Watts-Dunton's nature. But sentimentality and shrewd practicality, incongruous companions as they may seem, are often to be found together. Dickens is a good case in point. Sentimental to an extreme in his writings, yet his early hardships and his struggle to make a name for himself developed an " eye for the main chance " that may be readily, and should be sympathetically, understood. Watts-Dunton's condition was precarious enough at one time. His father's practice had dwindled, and the young man realized that if he was to do anything he must look keenly and carefully after his own interests.

Shrewd, cautious, tactful, he had many of the qualities that make a successful solicitor ; and having fortunately gained a footing among people famous in art and letters, it naturally followed that they sought his legal advice, and the diplomatic skill which he showed in dealing with these matters soon won for him a considerable *clientèle*. Watts-Dunton took an important part in the winding up of the famous " Morris, Marshall, and Faulkner " firm ; Madox Brown was for years one of his principal clients, and both Rossetti and Swinburne soon discovered the professional utility of this new friend.

Unlike Dickens, however, he was not really a good man of affairs ; and in his attempts to show himself a man of the world, he sometimes made mistakes that a really shrewd man of business would never have done, and, like many of his kind, he managed other people's affairs much better than he did his own.

But helpful as he was to his friends—Swinburne especially—on the business side, he is not the most happily viewed as a man of the world, for, like many

men who are three-fourths romantic and one-fourth
practical, he often confused sagacity with mere astute-
ness ; nor did he ever clearly see that imagination, which
plays so large a part in literary artistry, is equally potent
when applied to matters of practical life.

While quite obviously the friendship with Rossetti
and Swinburne brought much that was intellectu-
ally and æsthetically stimulating into Watts-Dunton's
life, it is well not to forget the other side of the
picture. Watts-Dunton's frank criticism of Rossetti's
poetry, no less than the personal services to which
reference has been made, was of real and lasting service
to the poet-painter in the last few stricken years of his
life. From the outset Watts-Dunton's friendship filled
a place of its own in Rossetti's heart, and towards the
end his craving for Watts-Dunton's presence was pathetic
in its insistence.

Writing from Bognor in 1875, he says :—

" MY DEAR WATTS,—Most welcome you will be as
soon as you can come."

Again :—

" Come as early as you can to-morrow."

Again :—

" I have no particular reason for writing, but feel
inclined to do so, and say how glad I shall be when
you can come this way."

In May 1880 he writes :—

" I now find so many evenings lonely that I am getting to feel the evil of it. If you like to bring me the Chatterton work I will see to it. I have written a Coleridge sonnet. I do not find my power of work flag if things were in every way a little livelier."

And again, at a later date :—

" I was much disappointed to miss the *welcome sight of you* this evening. I hope you are not ill. Can you fix Wednesday next ? I dare say you will not do so unless a certainty."

The most striking testimony to the influence of Watts-Dunton upon Swinburne lies less in the quality of the verse written by Swinburne during their long companionship than in the quality of the correspondence. Watts-Dunton's influence upon Rossetti was an intellectual and artistic influence. The influence upon Swinburne was almost entirely ethical. If nowhere in his later poetry he touches the " first fine careless rapture " of *Poems and Ballads* and *Songs before Sunrise*, every fair-minded critic must admit that his later work shows no falling off in craftsmanship, and assuredly has a sweeter sanity. And this sweeter sanity is even more noticeable in his correspondence. Those who have read his voluminous correspondence with Rossetti, and his still more voluminous correspondence with Watts-Dunton, will have realized the remarkable change of tone. The mocking and too Rabelaisian letter-writer of earlier years gives place to a correspondent who, with plenty of sardonic humour, takes a broader and mellower view of human life. Especially marked is his treatment of Biblical subjects (once almost entirely satirical), and in the increasing interest in Nature.

For instance :—

" I am reading the New Testament in a superb black-letter copy of Edward VI.'s version, collating it chapter by chapter with the authorized text, which hitherto I found (more often than not) inferior in direct force, and sometimes in lucidity. The older version is magnificent English—certainly, I think, better on the whole than ours. And I never saw quite such beautiful printing in my life—a blind baby might read it aloud at sight. The title-page is gone, and one leaf of preface slightly damaged, but the sacred text is (providentially) uninjured. The marginal commentary is very edifying, democratic, and Calvinistic (as, perhaps, you may be aware if ever your studies have lain in this truly blessed and improving direction). There are also large wood-cuts, greatly calculated to add to the terror and bewilderment of a student of the Apocalypse. What a strange mixture that book is of real individual imagination or passion, with unconscious imitation or echo of older and more thoroughly inspired poets. I must say it seems to me quite as often like Blake as like Isaiah."

In October 1882 he wrote from Leigh House, Bradford-on-Avon :—

" My last poem is just the length to which I usually (as in *Hertha* and the *Hymn of Man*) confine myself— 25 stanzas of 8. I have done nothing since, but have twice read through for the first time conscientiously, with great care and studious collation of texts, the whole of St. Paul's epistles—a part of Holy Writ in which I never before had made myself a thorough proficient. His immediate personal influence I think I now thoroughly understand, but am still perplexed by the survival and transmission of it in such a degree as to overshadow not only that of the other apostles, but that of Christ Himself. I have jotted down a note or two on what seem to me Paul's most distinctive characteristics as a thinker, a writer, and a man, on which I should like to have your opinion. Although my own previous views as to the religion of which he was the real founder (as surely as Columbus was the discoverer of the continent which takes its name from Amerigo), and Christ merely the godfather, are on the whole confirmed by this study, it will have to be allowed, I flatter myself, that only prejudiced ignorance—for of deliberate lying insolence I take no account—can or will ever accuse me of ignorant prejudice on the subject. (I fear this last sentence is rather Pauline in structure ; but the long-tailed entangled style of the Apostle is as catching as the mannerism of Browning or Carlyle to an unwary student.) "

And here in another letter is exemplified his boyish delight in storms :—

" This comes to assure you that we are not blown away, and to express a hope that you are not. Of course I could no more have kept within doors yesterday than I could have flown; but I never was out (I think) in quite such a storm of wind—which is saying something. I went a good long way across country in the wind's teeth, but on the return was the difficulty ; I was twice blown off my legs from behind (once nearly caught up and whirled off the ground) going right before the wind, and had to make headway by dodging and skulking under hedges. It was delicious—the wind blew in continuous fits or a fitful continuity, as if it was trying (in Hugo's phrase) to dislung itself—(*l'aquilon s'époumonne et l'autan se harasse*—What a verse that is !)—harder and more viciously at every gust. It was really rather nervous work passing under the trees, for quite considerable ones were split and dislimbed. But in the open it fully realized my idea of heaven."

Watts-Dunton, although he lived so long into the new era, was always at heart a Victorian in his sympathies and general outlook. At the same time it is true that he was interested in the thought of to-day ; in its experimental forms of art, and its note of challenge to the elder generation. No working journalist had a keener sense of to-day's literary fashions than he. No fresh writer of note escaped his observation ; none of the stupendous developments in journalism passed him unnoticed. But it must not be inferred from these facts that he had discarded, even partially, the mid-Victorianism in which he was bred. True, he was often anxious—pathetically so if the visitor was a young man—to acclaim the triumphs of the new *régime*, and to shake his head over the " prunes and prisms " of the age gone by. But when once he descended from generalities to particulars, it could be easily seen where his real sympathies lay. He would declaim against the Victorian conception of the " Dolly " woman, yet Ibsen to him was anathema, whether as a social force or an artistic influence. He would sigh over the lifeless conventionality of the Victorian drama ; none the less, Shaw to him was little more than a mountebank, and Granville Barker a freak ; and despite his admiration for the cleverness of certain leading contemporary poets and prosemen, they proved on the whole, when you came to press him, antagonistic to his sympathies. He would rather reread *Hard Cash* than essay a new Arnold Bennett. He was happier with Anthony Trollope than with H. G. Wells. Yet he was by no means blind to the merits of either Bennett or Wells.

The joy of living was very strong in him ; up to the very last he frankly delighted in the material pleasures of life, and had no trace of asceticism in his nature. He responded as much as Thackeray or Browning did to the stimulus of " good society," pretty women, and clever talk.

He once spoke to a friend of Morris as " a great artist whose life was spoilt by Socialistic tomfoolery," —the way of Collectivism was, for him, the way of "tomfoolery,"—and with a lively sense of the defects and inequalities in the social structure, warm humanitarian sympathies, and generous to a fault where his affections were touched, Watts-Dunton looked, as Bentham did, to a systematized Individualism, not to State interference, as a method of effecting social reform.

The speculative problems of the schools fascinated him. And yet his views on religion assumed no very definite shape, and he could reconcile himself neither to the pagan optimism of Meredith on the one hand, nor to the theistic optimism of Browning on the other. Tennyson's *Ulysses* more nearly voices his views :—

> " It may be that the gulfs will wash us down ;
> It may be we shall touch the Happy Isles,
> And see the great Achilles whom we knew ; "

for, as a matter of fact, questions of " fate, freewill, foreknowledge absolute," did not greatly preoccupy him, however at times they may have weighed upon his spirit. He was by temperament of a sanguine and cheerful disposition, intensely possessed of the intrinsic worth of life, as these few words of his convincingly show :—

" While there is youth in the world, this life, with all its tears, is good—good in itself and for itself— whatever there may be to follow it. Come what will, it is sweet to have lived, sweet to have enjoyed for a little while the perennial freshness of Nature."

And with that characteristic confession of faith we may leave him.

By his death his friends have lost an exceptionally loyal and generous-hearted spirit, and the world at large a critic of rare quality, a writer of wide and versatile accomplishment.

APPENDICES.

APPENDICES.

NOTABLE ESSAYS AND REVIEWS

BY THEODORE WATTS-DUNTON.

Athenæum.

Arnold, Matthew.	. *Poems of Wordsworth* . . . Vol. II.	1879
	Essays on Criticism . . . Vol. I.	1889
Blind, Mathilde .	. *George Eliot* (Eminent Women	
	Series) . . . . . . Vol. I.	1883
	Obituary Notice . . . . Vol. II.	1896
Borrow, George .	. Obituary Notice . . . . Vol. II.	1881
Browning, Robert	. *La Saisiaz* . . . . . . Vol. I.	1879
	Dramatic Idylls . . . Vol. I.	1879
	Jocoseria . . . . . Vol. I.	1883
	Ferishtah's Fancies . . . Vol. II.	1884
Canadian Poetry .	. (Lighthall's *Songs of the Great*	
	Dominion) . . . . . Vol. II.	1889
Colvin, Sidney .	. *W. S. Landor* (English Men of	
	Letters) . . . . . Vol. II.	1881
	Keats (English Men of Letters) Vol. II.	1887
Forman, Buxton .	. *Shelley* . . . . . . Vol. II.	1877
	Keats . . . . . . Vol. I.	1884
Gosse, Edmund .	. *Gray* (English Men of Letters) Vol. II.	1882
	Ferdusi in Exile . . . . Vol. I.	1886
	In Russet and Silver . . . Vol. II.	1894
Groome, F. H. .	. *Kriegspiel* . . . . . Vol. I.	1896
	Gypsy Folk Tales . . . Vol. II.	1898
	Obituary Notice . . . . Vol. I.	1902
Hugo, Victor . .	. *La Légende des Siècles* . . Vol. I.	1887

Hugo, Victor .	. .	Religions et Religion . . .	Vol. I.	1880
		Les Quatre Vents de l'Esprit .	Vol. II.	1881
		Torquemada	Vol. I.	1882
		Le Roi s'amuse (a Dramatic Criticism)	Vol. II.	1882
Jones, Ebenezer .	.	(Original Papers in three numbers)	Vol. II.	1878
Knapp, W. J.	. .	Life of Borrow	Vol. I.	1899
Knight, Joseph	.	Rossetti	Vol. II.	1887
Lorne, Lord .	. .	Psalms	Vol. II.	1877
Lowell, James Russell		Obituary	Vol. II.	1891
Meredith, George.	.	Joy of Earth	Vol. II.	1883
Miles, A. .	. . .	Poets and Poetry of the Century	Vol. II.	1893
Morris, William .	.	The Story of Sigurd . . .	Vol. II.	1876
		John Ball	Vol. II.	1889
		The House of the Wolfings .	Vol. II.	1889
		The Roots of the Mountains .	Vol. II.	1890
		News from Nowhere . . .	Vol. I.	1891
		Poems by the Way . .	Vol. I.	1892
		The Wood Beyond the World .	Vol. I.	1895
		The Tale of Beowulf . . .	Vol. II.	1895
		The Water of the Wondrous Isles	Vol. II.	1897
		The Well at the World's End .	Vol. II.	1897
		Obituary Notice	Vol. I.	1896
Robinson, F. W. .	.	Obituary Notice	Vol. II.	1901
Rossetti, D. G.	.	Collected Works	Vol. I.	1882
Shairp, J. C. .	.	On the Poetic Interpretation of Nature	Vol. II.	1877
Sharp, William	.	Earth's Voices	Vol. II.	1884
Skelton, Sir John		Comedy of the Noctes Ambrosianæ (Watts-Dunton's first Review)	Vol. II.	1876
Stedman, E. C. .	.	Victorian Poets.	Vol. I.	1888
Stephen, Leslie .		Hours in a Library . . .	Vol. I.	1879
Stevenson, R. L. .	.	Kidnapped	Vol. II.	1886
		Catriona	Vol. II.	1893
		Collected Works (Two Reviews)	Vol. II.	1897

Swinburne, A. C.	.	*A Note on Charlotte Brontë*	. Vol. II.	1877
		Poems and Ballads (Second		
		Series)	. Vol. II.	1878
		Songs of the Springtide	. . Vol. I.	1880
		Study of Shakespeare .	. . Vol. I.	1880
		Studies in Song . .	. . Vol. I.	1881
		Tristram of Lyonesse .	. . Vol. II.	1882
		A Midsummer Holiday	. . Vol. II.	1884
		Marino Faliero . .	. . Vol. I.	1885
		Study of Victor Hugo .	. . Vol. I.	1886
		Poems and Ballads (Third		
		Series)	. Vol. I.	1889
		The Sisters	. Vol. II.	1892
		Studies in Prose and Poetry	. Vol. II.	1894
		Astrophel	. Vol. I.	1894
		Balen	. Vol. I.	1896
		Rosamund	. Vol. II.	1899
Tennyson, Alfred.	.	*Lover's Tale*	. Vol. II.	1879
		Ballads and other Poems .	. Vol. II.	1880
		Locksley Hall	. Vol. I.	1887
		The Foresters	. Vol. I.	1892
		Obituary Notice . .	. . Vol. II.	1892
		Memoir (by his son) .	. . Vol. II.	1897
Thomson, James .	.	*City of Dreadful Night*	. Vol. I.	1880
Thoreau, Henry D.	.	Page's *Life and Aims* .	. Vol. II.	1877
		Early Spring in Massachusetts	Vol. II.	1882
Traill, H. D. . .	.	*Sterne* (English Men of Let-		
		ters)	. Vol. II.	1882
Ward, T. Humphry .		*English Poets*	. Vol. I.	1880
		English Poets	. Vol. I.	1881
Webster, Mrs. Augusta		*A Book of Rhyme* . . .	. Vol. II.	1881
		In a Day	. Vol. II.	1882
		The Sentence	. Vol. II.	1888
		Obituary	. Vol. II.	1894
Wells, Charles	.	*Joseph and his Brethren* .	. Vol. I.	1876

Shakespearean Essays.

New Monthly Magazine .	*The Lost Hamlet* . . .	. April	1873
Harper's Magazine .	. *Hamlet*	. May	1904

Harper's Magazine	. . *Macbeth* . . . . Nov. 1906
	Pericles . . . . . . Feb. 1909
	Cymbeline . . . . . . April 1909
Preface	*Merchant of Venice* — Complete Works of Shakespeare (George D. Sproul, New York) 1907
Introduction	World's Classics. 1910

Essays in the " Nineteenth Century."

Truth about Rossetti . . . . Mar. 1883
Tennyson : The Tributes of his Friends . . . . . Nov. 1892
Christina Rossetti . . . . Feb. 1895

Shakespeare Series in " Harper's Magazine."

Among the well-known writers who contributed to the Shakespeare series edited by Watts-Dunton which appeared in *Harper's Magazine*, there were the essays of Swinburne on *King Lear, Richard the Second,* and *Othello ;* an essay by Joseph Knight on *King John ;* one by Churton Collins on *Henry the Eighth ;* by William Sharp on *Titus Andronicus ;* by Arthur Symons on *Troilus and Cressida ;* by Mr. James Douglas on *Antony and Cleopatra ;* and by Watts-Dunton on *Hamlet, Macbeth, Cymbeline,* and *Pericles.* To each of these articles E. A. Abbey, the famous American painter, furnished more than one drawing.

The only dramatic criticism by Watts-Dunton that ever appeared in the *Athenæum* was the one on Victor Hugo's *Le Roi s'amuse.* The occasion was a memorable one. The article is dated " Paris, November 23, 1882 " :—

" I felt that the revival at the Théâtre Français of *Le Roi s'amuse,* on the fiftieth anniversary of its original production, must be one of the most interesting literary events of our time, and so I found it to be. Victor Hugo was sitting there, with his arms folded across his breast, calm but happy, in a stage box. He expressed himself satisfied and even delighted with the acting. The poet's appearance was fuller of vitality and more Olympian than ever. Between the acts he left the theatre and walked about in the

square, leaning on the arm of his illustrious poet friend and family
connection, Auguste Vacquerie. . . . Never before was seen, even
in a French theatre, an audience so brilliant and so illustrious. I
did not, however, see any English face I knew save that of Mr.
Swinburne, who at the end of the third act might have been seen
talking to Hugo in his box. Among the most appreciative and
enthusiastic of those who assisted at the representation was the
French poet who, perhaps, in the nineteenth century stands next
to Hugo in intellectual massiveness, Leconte de Lisle. And I
should say that every French poet and indeed every man of emi-
nence was there.

" Considering the extraordinary nature of the piece, the cast
was perhaps as satisfactory as could have been hoped for. Fond
as is Victor Hugo of spectacular effects, and even of *coups de théâtre*,
no other dramatist gives so little attention as he to the idiosyn-
crasies of actors. It is easy to imagine that Shakespeare in writing
his lines was not always unmindful of an actor like Burbage. But
in depicting Triboulet, Hugo must have thought as little about the
specialities of Ligier, who took the part on the first night in 1832,
as of the future Got, who was to take it on the second night in 1882.
And the same may be said of Blanche in relation to the two actresses who successively took that part. This is, I think, exactly
the way in which a dramatist should work. The contrary method
is not more ruinous to drama as a literary form than to the actor's
art. To write up to an actor's style destroys all true character-
drawing ; also it ends by writing up to the actor's mere manner,
who from that moment is, as an artist, doomed. On the whole, the
performance wanted more glow and animal spirits. The François
of M. Mounet-Sully was full of verve, but this actor's voice is so
exceedingly rich and emotional that the king seemed more poetic,
and hence more sympathetic to the audience, than was consistent
with a character who in a sense is held up as the villain of the piece.
The true villain here, however, as in *Torquemada, Notre Dame de
Paris, Les Misérables*, and, indeed, in all Hugo's characteristic works,
is not an individual at all, but Circumstance. Circumstance placed
François, a young and pleasure-loving king, over a licentious court.
Circumstance gave him a court jester with a temper which, to say
the least of it, was peculiar for such times as those. Circumstance,
acting through the agency of certain dissolute courtiers, thrust into

the king's very bedroom the girl whom he loved and who belonged
to a class from whom he had been taught to expect subservience
of every kind. The tragic mischief of the rape follows almost as
a necessary consequence. Add to this the fact that Circumstance
contrives that the girl Maguelonne, instead of aiding her more conscientious brother in killing the disguised king at the bidding of
' the client who pays,' falls unexpectedly in love with him ; while
Circumstance also contrives that Blanche shall be there ready at
the very spot at the very moment where and when she is impera-
tively wanted as a substituted victim, and you get the entire motif
of *Le Roi s'amuse*—man enmeshed in a web of circumstance—the
motif of *Notre Dame de Paris*, the motif of *Torquemada*, and, in a
certain deep sense, perhaps the proper motif in romantic drama.
For when the *vis-matrix* of classic drama, the supernatural interference of conscious Destiny, was no longer available to the artist,
something akin to it, something nobler and more powerful than the
stage villain, was found to be necessary to save tragedy from sinking
into melodrama. And this explains so many of the complexities
of Shakespeare.

" In the dramas of Victor Hugo, however, the romantic temper
has advanced quite as far as it ought to advance, not only in the
use of Circumstance as the final cause of the tragic mischief, but in
the use of the grotesque in alliance with the terrible. The greatest
masters of the terrible-grotesque till we get to the German roman-
ticists were the English dramatists of the sixteenth and the early
portion of the seventeenth century, and, of course, by far the greatest
among these was Shakespeare. For the production of the effect
in question there is nothing comparable to the scenes in *Lear* between the king and the fool—scenes which seem very early in his
life to have struck Hugo more than anything else in literature.
Outside the Elizabethan dramatists, however, there can be no
doubt that (leaving out of the discussion the great German masters
in this line) Hugo is the greatest worker in the terrible-grotesque
that has appeared since Burns. I need only point to Quasimodo
and Triboulet and compare them not merely with such attempts in
this line as those of writers like Beddoes, but even with the magnificent work of Mr. Browning, who, though far more subtle than
Hugo, is without his sublimity and amazing power over chiaroscuro.
Now, the most remarkable feature of the revival of *Le Roi s'amuse*,

and that which made me above all other reasons desirous to see it, was that the character of Triboulet was to be rendered by an actor of rare and splendid genius, but who, educated in the genteel comedy of modern France and also in the social subtleties of Molière, seemed the last man in Paris to give that peculiar expression of the romantic temper which I have called the terrible-grotesque.

"That M. Got's success in a part so absolutely unsuited to him should have been as great as it was, is, in my judgment, the crowning success of his life. It is as though Thackeray, after completing *Philip*, had set himself to write a romance in the style of *Notre Dame de Paris*, and succeeded in the attempt. Yet the success of M. Got was relative only, I think. The Triboulet was not the Triboulet of the reader's own imagining, but an admirable Triboulet of the Comédie Française. Perhaps, however, the truth is that there is not an actor in Europe who could adequately render such a character as Triboulet.

"And if it should be found that in order to render Triboulet there is requisite for the more intense crises of the piece the abandon of Kean and Robson, and at the same time, for the carrying on of the play, the calm, self-conscious staying power of Garrick, the conclusion will be obvious that Triboulet is essentially an unactable character. I will illustrate this by an instance. The reader will remember that in the third act of *Le Roi s'amuse*, Triboulet's daughter Blanche, after having been violated by the king at the Louvre, rushes into the antechamber, where stands her father surrounded by the group of sneering courtiers who, unknown both to the king and to Triboulet, have abducted her during the night and set her in the king's way. When the girl tells her father of the terrible wrong that has been done to her, he passes at once from the mood of sardonic defiance which was natural to him into a state of passion so terrible that all of a sudden a magical effect is produced: the conventional walls between him, the poor despised court jester, and the courtiers, are suddenly overthrown by the unexpected operation of one of those great human instincts which make a whole world kin.

"Now, in reading *Le Roi s'amuse*, startling as is the situation, it does not seem exaggerated, for Victor Hugo's lines are adequate in simple passion to effect the dramatic work, and the reader feels that Triboulet was wrought up to the state of exaltation to which the lines give expression, that nothing could resist him, and that the proud courtiers must in truth have cowered before him in the manner here indicated by the dramatist. In literature the artist does not actualize ; he suggests, and leaves the reader's imagination free. But an actor has to actualize this state of exaltation—he has to bring the physical condition answering to the emotional condition before the eyes of the spectator ; and if he fails to display as much of the ' fine frenzy ' of passion as is requisite to cow and overawe a group of cynical worldlings, the situation becomes forced and unnatural, inasmuch as they are overawed without a sufficient cause. That an actor like Robson could and would have risen to such an occasion no one will doubt who ever saw him (for he was the very incarnation of the romantic temper); but then the exhaustion would have been so great that it would have been impossible for him to go on bearing the entire weight of this long play as M. Got does. The actor requires, as I say, the abandon characteristic of one kind of histrionic art together with the staying power characteristic of another. Now, admirable as is M. Got in this and in all the scenes of *Le Roi s'amuse*, he does not pass into such a condition of exalted passion as makes the retirement of the courtiers seem probable. . . . For artistic perfection there was nothing in the entire representation that surpassed the scenes between Saltabadil and Maguelonne in the hovel on the banks of the Seine. It would be difficult, indeed, to decide which was the more admirable, the Saltabadil of M. Febvre or the Maguelonne of Jeanne Samary."

A FEW THOUGHTS UPON THE PEACE SOCIETY.*

It has become so fashionable of late to abuse the members of the Peace Society, that I do not see how you, as editor of a respectable journal, can creditably avoid making *one* slashing onslaught, at least, upon them. -

Not only have Mr. Cobden and his friends been " hung, drawn, and quartered," by the newspapers, from the *Times* and *Chronicle* downwards, but Lord Palmerston declares, in the House of Commons, that he considers them a " set of harmless fanatics ; " and even our immortal Colonel (that modern Hudibras, whose fame the

* Letter to Editor (*Cambridge Chronicle,* 1854).

world will not willingly let die) " would rather see the devil in the House than one of them." Indeed, the prevailing feeling through the country, as well as among the " Assembly of the wise," has dubbed the Peace Society the *Society of Fools*.

Now, Sir, " for mine own part," although not prepared to endorse *all* the sentiments uttered the other week at Manchester, yet, as soon as I heard these gentlemen classed among the numerous and respectable family of the Fools, any latent respect for them slumbering in my breast increased tenfold. For I have always had a great admiration for that most ancient though much-wronged family—a family whereof I have myself great hopes of some day becoming a member.

> " When I did hear
> The motley fool thus moral on the time,
> My lungs began to crow like chanticleer,
> That fools should be so deep-contemplative."

> " Oh that I were a fool !
> I am ambitious for a motley coat."

Like Jacques, " I am ambitious for a motley coat."

And, really, when we consider what a glorious company have ever composed this noble order of Fools, we shall be constrained to look upon it with something like reverence. If we take the catalogue of all the great and noble men the world has ever brought forth, we shall find them to have been, almost invariably, *fools*. Homer, Æschylus, and Euripides (but especially the last, as witness his tormentor, the Greek wag) were the early Fathers of the race. And, to come to our own country, Milton, Thomson, Goldsmith, Steele, and, still later, " *Mad* " Shelley, " *Manikin* " Keats, and " *Cockney* " Hunt, are a few, among a legion of the like sort, who have belonged to this lustrous family. All promulgators of new doctrines, from Galileo to the first propounders of geology—from Columbus to James Watt—have also been recognized as distinguished knights companions of the order.

But I might multiply examples *ad infinitum*, enumerating all the great philosophers, poets, and statesmen, in whose hands the fame of their country has rested, and all of whom have been *fools*.

Therefore do I think that the Peace Society loses nothing, but gains much, in being dubbed a Society of Fools. For what the world means by a fool is, one who thinks original thoughts, and acts original deeds—one who works in a groove different from his neighbours—one who endeavours to shake off the rusty shackles of prejudice and superstition, by which he, in common with all men, is enveloped. And it is natural that it should be so ; for, as the Student, in *Festus*, grandly, beautifully, says—

> " The men of mind are mountains, and their heads
> Are sunned long ere the rest of earth."

And, after all, I confess I cannot see anything so *very* ridiculous in the Peace Society's idea of international arbitration ; even though, at the present moment, it seems to be a moot question among the Fates whether Europe shall be in a state of anarchy or despotism. If all great questions had been viewed in the manner this has been—if the darkness of the present had been suffered to overshadow all hope in the future—we might still have been clothed, according to the authority of our school histories, in " the skins of wild animals." But does not all history go to prove that the " folly " of one age is often the " wisdom " of the next ?

Though, as I said before, I cannot go to the length of some of the Society's doctrines, yet I believe that, if the time is ever to come when swords shall be beaten into ploughshares, it will be brought about by international arbitration, and by no other earthly means.

THE NEW EDITOR'S BOW.*

Having been elected Editor of *Piccadilly*, I ought to say a word, I think, as to the nature of the paper, and the place which it aspires to hold among journals. Perhaps my best way of doing so is to tell the story of its origin.

It occurred to a group of people moving in that section of the world which, with charming good breeding, calls *itself* the " World," to start a little paper for themselves—a paper spiced with harmless gossip, but free from scandal—to be circulated among their own friends. and written in an amusing style, but at the same time to

* Vide *Piccadilly* (No. V.), June 13, 1878.

be tinged with as much flavour of art and culture as the " World " (whose demands in this direction are not exorbitant) might require. No attempt was made to "push" the paper in any way ; indeed, had the projectors then felt the *desire* to " push " it, they were too ignorant of the machinery of journalism to do so. They had not the faintest idea that the demand for their paper could be other than quite limited, and they were not a little surprised to find that the first number sold, if not " famously," very briskly indeed ; and, with the second number, it became apparent that something like a " hit " had been made. But so equally balanced is life— whether of man or journal—that the penalties of success are almost always as great as its advantages ; and, just as there is no such slavery as that of the successful man, so there is no such embar- rassment as that of an unpretending journal that suddenly finds itself credited with important pretensions.

It was necessary, in short, to call upon a stronger staff and a competent " man at the wheel ; " and upon the humble individual writing these lines the selection of helmsman has fallen ; and assuredly a happier selection could not possibly have been made— if we consider what are the first requisites of an editor of a brilliant paper such as this, in spite of itself, is credited with being. These requisites are, that he should be a man well seasoned in worldly knowledge—or, in the most elegant parlance of the modern draw- ing-room, " no chicken "—hard-working, systematic, and, as Mr. Carlyle would say, " simply dool." Now, all these virtues are mine, in some degree—the last in no common degree ; and here lies my special strength. Having no brilliance myself—having no preten- sions to anything like wit or humour—I am all the better qualified to gather round me the men who have. The brilliant man as a rule sees only the coruscations of his *own* brilliance ; the wit sees only the sparkle of his own repartee ; the humorist feels only the unctuousness of his own peculiar vein of humour. For instance, the boisterous, not to say somewhat vulgar, record of the break- fast proceedings described—I hope with some exaggeration— on page 12, which I admitted on account of its Rabelaisian good spirits—would as certainly have been rejected by the Marquise de Carabas on account of its lack of tone, as it would have been re- jected by the Hermit of Sark on account of its lack of philosophical calmness, and as it would have been rejected by Sir Oracle Prygge on account of its lack of practical usefulness. I, however, have accepted the article—wisely, I think—though I may observe in passing that the person called in the article Piccadilly is not really the editor of this paper (on principle I never attend such gatherings), but is most probably one of our compositors—all very intelligent men.

Hampered by no rivalry—if the "prosperity" of a contributor's joke should, by any mischance, come to grief with me, it is on account of no egotism, fussiness, or prejudice, but simply on account of that honest dulness to which I have been alluding ; yet I believe that, living as we all do—working as we all do here below—trammelled by heavy conditions, my dulness will prove to be a less serious obstacle than the dangerous brilliance of the editor I might, by ill chance, have been. My object has been to seek, regardless of personal trouble, regardless of the proprietors' expense, all the amusing writers that could be found for (my) love or (my proprietors') money as contributors to *Piccadilly*. That I have missed a good many of these, however, many gifted writers will think to be more than probable. Yet I think I may say, with some confidence, that the fifth number of *Piccadilly* is—thanks to my dulness—about the most amusing thing that has happened in London for many a day ; and, next week, when my staff are well settled down, it will be a thousand times more amusing still. This sounds like self-glorification—it is self-glorification—but I cannot help it ; I am proud of my contributors, and I am proud of *Piccadilly*.

I have no fear whatever that the other journals will take offence at these self-gratulations ; for between an amusing paper and them there can, of course, be no sort of rivalry. With the exception of the *Times* in the literary line, the *Spectator* in the metaphysical, and the *Record* in the polemic, a struggle between an amusing paper and the other journals would be as incongruous as one between England and Russia, which Cobden compared to a fight between a horse and a fish. With the exception of the three valuable organs above mentioned, I am not aware that any portion of the contemporary public press *pretends* to be amusing. John Bull, indeed— fine as are his qualities of the strictly and legitimately taurine kind —is neither a brilliant nor an amusing production ; nor, to say the truth, do I think that Nature ever intended him to be such. He

" takes his pleasures sadly : " so at least the penny-a-liners—the only people now, I fear, who read Froissart—are constantly telling us. Papers like the *World, Truth, Vanity Fair*, the *Whitehall Review, London*, the *Man of the World*, and the other five hundred social organs which it is quite needless to specialize, are exceedingly clever—very much more clever than *Piccadilly* can hope to be : the two first especially are exceedingly trenchant—exceedingly satirical—exceedingly everything—but amusing : they are too distressingly in earnest to be *that*. A man, in order to be amusing, must first be amused—highly amused—himself. He must have that appreciation of human life as a harlequinade which never comes to a man when he is " cross." It is just the same with journals. The *World* and *Truth* are always " cross " about something or another ; they cannot help it—there are so many things to be cross about—and it is impossible for a journal or a man to be cross and at the same time amusing. A woman *may* be ; but then her mouth must be so pretty that anger, while trying to spoil it, only gives a new charm to the pout. The consequence of this sourness of temper is that the journals I have mentioned—notwithstanding all their talent—are constantly lapsing into a dulness so oppressive that we fly for relief to the *Penny Pulpit* sometimes. or even to the pages of Mr. Tupper—nay, occasionally to the writing of *Punch* itself. In the rich repast of journalistic literature. to sweeten the sourness of the " socials," to soothe the gloom of the " comics," is the modest *raison d'être* of *Piccadilly*.

A play was written by Watts-Dunton in the Danes Inn period, between 1874 and 1876. at a time when he and other intimate friends were particularly interested in play-writing. This one-act farcical comedy ran through several numbers of *Piccadilly*, in the *Breakfast Yarns* columns, and was subsequently printed for private circulation. The author had intended sending it round to theatrical managers, but with his usual procrastination he put the matter off until the project had passed from his recollection.

Cleopatra's Needle had just been put up on the Embankment, and was the topic of general conversation at the moment when the play, so called, was written.

BREAKFAST YARNS.*

No. I.

THE SURPRISING ADVENTURES OF A " PERSON IN HIGH POSITION."

Adventure I.—Cleopatra's Needle.

BUTTERFLY. Pic, you're not eating the buckwheat cake.

PICCADILLY. Politeness to the gastric functions of a great paper bids me abstain, Jimmy.

BUTTERFLY. Well, you know the penalty : a yarn while the others *are* eating.

PICCADILLY. All right, Jimmy. I'll tell you a story about——

BUTTERFLY. No. We select the subject. What shall it be ?

APE. A story about the bards.

MINTO. No, no ; an Eastern story ; Hassan's Flying Donkey.

NITA NIGHTINGALE. No, *I*'ll select it. Let it be something about "Cleopatra's Needle," *that*'ll have all the talk now the war's done.

PICCADILLY. All right : Cleopatra's Needle let it be. But, mind you—you will have to keep eating buckwheat cake as long as I keep on telling the story : that's the compact.—

Well, you must know that, down in Blackfriars, in the neighbourhood of the Surrey obelisk, there is a street called Blackfriars Street.

BUTTERFLY. We don't know anything of the kind : *we* eschew low neighbourhoods ; we are not going to have a low-life story, you know.

PICCADILLY. And No. 1,006 Blackfriars Street, whose windows command a fine view of the obelisk, is occupied by a young lady, blue eyed, black eyelashed. cherry lipped, with a complexion like a peach just ripening to perfection.

BUTTERFLY. Name ! Name !

PICCADILLY. I'm glad you warned me in time. I was just going to give you her real name. Let me call her Jane Britain. She lets lodgings.

BUTTERFLY. Oh !

* *Piccadilly* (No. V.), June 13, 1878.

PICCADILLY. One morning last winter—when people were speculating as to the probable site of Cleopatra's Needle—if you had looked in upon her as she sat in her little parlour reading one of several letters, which on her return from shopping she had found on her table, you would have gathered that she was in " hot water." Letter No. 1 was from her first-floor lodger, Miss Samuelina Johnson, and ran thus :—" It is not because my property is in danger that I give you a week's notice. It is because I feel that the Johnsonian Establishment for Young Ladies can no longer be carried on with dignity, sobriety, and all the high culture for which this age is so conspicuous, in a first-floor front under which smoulders, like a female volcano, a speculator who loses." Jane, when she reached this peroration, threw herself into a chair and laughed immoderately. " And now let me see," said she, as she opened letter No. 2, " what says my third-floor back, Mr. Zerubbabel Smith, the Quaker, and secretary to the Self-abnegation Building Society." " It is not " (said the Quaker's letter) " that my property is in danger that I give thee a week's notice ; it is because thee has been speculating and lost. Speculation, Jane Britain, is the great vice of this corrupt age—in man, heinous ; in woman, shocking ; in landlady, prodigious." Jane laughed more loudly than before when she got to this climax. " These good people " (she cried, as the tears of merriment made her blue eyes sparkle again)—" these good people *are* indeed kind, to thus turn misfortune into a joke." She was proceeding to open the letters from her other lodgers when the door opened, and there entered the brawny figure of her servant Charlotte, with something in her hand which Jane thought looked like a dirty towel—a strapping wench Charlotte, with a biceps apparently made for the express purpose of " banging out a dun or throttling a bailiff."

BUTTERFLY. Let me know when she wants a situation.

PICCADILLY. " Well, mum," said Charlotte, as she stood watching her young mistress's ill-timed merriment, " for a ruined woman your sperrits is right on dreadful. There's an old Jew bailiff in the passage, askin' if his son Ichabod's got here yet. He says he's sent in by your mortgagee, Lady Threadneedle. And the printer's boy from the *Blackfriars Gazette* has just left this." Here she handed to Jane the dirty white object Jane had noticed, which turned out to be a poster, which Jane took, and, unfolding it, displayed this :—

No. 1,006 BLACKFRIARS STREET, BLACKFRIARS.

MR. JOHN MAMMON

Is instructed to SELL the above LEASEHOLD HOUSE

BY AUCTION

At the MART, TOKENHOUSE YARD,

On MONDAY, DECEMBER 16*th*.

At Two o'clock precisely.

Particulars, with Conditions of Sale, may be obtained of Messrs. DIDDLUM and TUFT, Solicitors, Gray's Inn, or of the Auctioneer.

JANE. Ah, my Lady Threadneedle, like the accomplished woman of business she is, puts into force her two remedies at once (*holds up poster*). The house my poor mother so lately left me (*voice trembles*). Let us see how we look on the hoardings of Black-friars (*mounts chair and pins poster on wall*).

CHARLOTTE. I don't believe anything ever *would* cow you (*looking off*). Here comes the rascally American inventor, on the second floor back, who brought all this ruin about.

Enter CINCINNATUS BUNKUM, *dressed in American costume, with cigarette in his mouth, and swishing a cane,* L.

BUNKUM. Wall, young woman (*walks up to poster and looks at it*). This heear looks like a genu-ine bust-up. I guess, I must just take care of my patents and skee-daddle afore the crows *settle*. So, if you'll make out my account slick, I'll go and fetch my cheque-book and pay you up. (*Turning back*) Afore I go, however, I want to ask you one question : Who's the man in the second floor front—door opposite mine—keyhole opposite mine ? (JANE *turns away in contempt*.)

CHARLOTTE. Why, that's Mr. Honour Bright, if you *must* know, a real gentleman as 'ud scorn takin' advantage of a poor young woman and cheat her out of her money. And there's no need for you to watch *him* about for fear he should find out your patents. *He* don't want your patents, *I'*m sure. Here he comes.

Enter SIR CHARLES LARKIE (*with open letter*).

BUNKUM *and* SIR CHARLES (*together*). Wall, tell Mr. Honour Bright——tell Mr. Cincinnatus Bunkum——that if I catch him spying so close to my keyhole, I'll just (*they stop and look at each other menacingly*). [*Exit* BUNKUM.

SIR CHARLES (*laughing*). So that's the great inventor, is it ? (*To* JANE) Good afternoon, Miss Britain.

JANE (*bowing*). Good afternoon, Mr. Honour Bright.

SIR CHARLES. Now, am I really to take this notice to quit as final (*showing paper*).

JANE. Yes, sir.

SIR CHARLES. It is very cruel. What have I done ? (*To* CHARLOTTE) Charlotte, you can go.

JANE. It was the greatest mistake my servant letting you the rooms at all. *I* should have seen at once that they were not for such as you.

SIR CHARLES. Not for such as I. Don't add insult to injury. I'm not good enough, I suppose, for the second floor ? Have you got a sixth ? Charlotte, my bed wants making.

CHARLOTTE (*aside*). Confound the man. [*Exit*, L.

JANE. In one sense, too good ; in another sense, not good enough. To be quite plain with you, I don't think your name is Honour Bright at all.

SIR CHARLES. Oh ! honour bright !

JANE. I perceived, as soon as I saw you, that you were the same gentleman who at the Monday Popular Concerts so far forgot yourself as to——

SIR CHARLES. Fall in love with your look of piquancy and dauntless pluck, and seek you out. Well, it is too true. I am the scoundrel in question. But is that a reason for turning me out like a dog into the streets—homeless—(for *you* are my home), and a beggar (for without *you* my soul starves) ?

JANE. Reason enough. But, if another were wanted, the bailiffs are in, and look here (*pointing to sale bill*).

SIR CHARLES. I say ! I'm very grieved for this, though—I really am. What does it all mean ? What's the amount ? I'll pay the fellows out, or else I'll go and kick 'em out (*puts his arm round her waist*).

JANE (*releasing herself*). No, sir. It's very good of you. I feel that you *are* good, in spite of looking the most impudent man in London; but, of course, it is impossible that you should pay out my bailiffs.

SIR CHARLES. Hang Mrs. Grundy. She is ubiquitous. I *did* think that in Blackfriars—but never mind : even *she* would not object to my *kicking* them out. Where are they ? (*Going.* JANE *pulls him back laughing.*) By-the-bye, what did your servant mean about the rascally American ? Has he been cheating you ? If he has, a drop from the second floor window might improve his morals, and I shall be delighted——

JANE (*with great heat*). He persuaded me to invest all my mother's legacy in his patents, and, what was worse, to mortgage the lease of this house to supply money for his schemes.

SIR CHARLES (*again putting his arm around her waist and trying to kiss her*). I'll try the window with him, and kick the bailiffs out—kick everybody out. There's no need for more than us two here. We want no servants. *I* can light the fires, and you cook, or somebody here does—a devilled kidney—(*screwing up his face*)— devilishly well !

JANE (*repulsing him*). Will you leave me, sir ? (*Looking at him*) Do leave me, now, there's a good fellow. I'm certain you are a good fellow (*he again tries to kiss her*). Oh ! if you could only make that rascally American disgorge my money, you might——

SIR CHARLES. What ?

JANE. I do so want to conquer him. And I do so want to see these bailiffs turned out with *his* money ; and, if my house *must* be sold, I want to sell it myself. Then I shouldn't care : the world's wide. and I am young. I will go to Australia, where women are not quite such a drug.

SIR CHARLES (*aside*). What a look of pluck there is in the girl's eyes ! (*To* JANE) Agreed. The Yankee's neck shall be spared in order that he may disgorge : the bailiffs shall skeedaddle, and you shall be your own auctioneer—I swear it. And *you* will keep *your* part of the compact ?

JANE (*laughing*). I will. I know I am perfectly safe.

SIR CHARLES. Don't be too confident.

JANE. I fancy you outwitting the " smartest man in America," as he is called, I believe. And he is rich, they say, as well as smart.

SIR CHARLES. Don't defy Cupid ; he is stronger than Hercules when he takes his labours in earnest. He has entered this frame. He inspires me₁ The Labours of Cupid are begun.

Re-enter CHARLOTTE, *with a boy carrying cold roast fowl, a basket of champagne, a box of cigars, and some wine-glasses,* R.

CHARLOTTE. These are for you, sir. I will take them upstairs at once.

SIR CHARLES. Hulloa ! I recollect I did order a snack at the Blue Lion. (*To boy*) You can call again for the champagne basket. [*Exit* BOY.

CHARLOTTE. The third basket of Blue Lion gooseberry-wine this week (*sets basket down*).

SIR CHARLES. The fact is there's something wrong about Black-friars air. Its action upon the throat is to produce a state of chronic thirst. Even at this moment I feel I must champagne or perish. As my moments are numbered here, would you allow me to draw just one valedictory cork ?

JANE. What are those papers you have, Charlotte ?

CHARLOTTE. A boy from the *Blackfriars Gazette* Office brought this newspaper and note, and he's to wait for an answer. (JANE *reads letter and then turns to newspaper and reads paragraph, while* SIR CHARLES *uncorks a bottle of champagne.*)

SIR CHARLES. Charlotte, glasses ! (CHARLOTTE *hands three glasses.*) Three ! Oh, yes, there *are* three of us (*fills three glasses. hands one to* JANE *as she reads, the other to* CHARLOTTE). Have you been long a drinker of champagne, Charlotte ?

CHARLOTTE (*emptying her glass with a grimace*). Long enough to know it from this.

SIR CHARLES (*aside*). Well, May Fair is impudent ; but it has no idea what it could learn from Blackfriars.

JANE. What a shame ! The lady alluded to there (*handing* SIR CHARLES *paper*) is my aunt. She's ignorant, poor old thing ! but she shan't be made a public butt.

SIR CHARLES. She shan't (*reading aloud*) :—

" CLEOPATRA'S NEEDLE : THE BATTLE OF THE SITES.—It is
" a wonderful fact that an old and wealthy lady, residing not a
" thousand miles from the Obelisk, has got the maggot into her

" head that the authorities will decide to erect Cleopatra's Needle
" in sight of the Surrey Obelisk, because, according to Dr. Erasmus
" Wilson's pamphlet, the Needle ' stood with a companion near a
" temple in the Egyptian city of On.' "   .

SIR CHARLES. I confess I don't see the joke. It's certainly the
least ridiculous site proposed yet.

JANE. The editor sends me this letter. You may as well see
that too (*hands* SIR CHARLES *letter*).

SIR CHARLES (*reading letter aloud*) :—

" *Blackfriars Gazette* Office. Dec. 1877.

" DEAR MADAM,—The paragraph I have marked has been sent
" to us. At the last moment, before going to press, it has occurred
" to me that you, as an esteemed friend and subscriber, ought to
" see the proof of the paper. I am just going out, but should you
" find the personal allusion to your aunt offensive to *yourself*, you
" can strike it out, and my compositor will fill in the space with
" something else. The bearer will wait.—Yours truly,
" JAMES BABBAGE, *Editor.*"

CHARLOTTE (*to* SIR CHARLES). They call her " Money-grubbing
Sal."

JANE. Shall I be offended ? he asks. Of course I shall (*pulls
out pencil, strikes out words with pencil*). There ! I have struck out
all allusion to my aunt, and not taken out much either (*hands paper
to* CHARLOTTE, *but* SIR CHARLES *takes it, and reads while* CHARLOTTE
and JANE *converse at back*).

SIR CHARLES (*aside*). Yes, you *have* struck out all allusion to
your aunt ! and, should the printer let it appear as it stands, there
will be all the tradesmen of Blackfriars speculating in sites for
Cleopatra's Needle near the Obelisk ! (*Reads*) " It is a wonderful
fact that the authorities will decide to erect Cleopatra's Needle in
sight of the Surrey Obelisk, because, according to Dr. Erasmus
Wilson's pamphlet, the Needle ' stood with a companion near a
temple in the Egyptian city of On.' " Well, I won't tell her. This
perhaps, may be turned to account in the Labours of Cupid, though
I don't at present see how.

CHARLOTTE (*to* JANE). Well, all I can say is, I wish you had let
the newspapers have their laugh at her, an old——

JANE. Silence, Charlotte ! You seem to forget she is my aunt.

SIR CHARLES. And, if your mistress's, mine.

CHARLOTTE. And you seem to forget that she cheated you out of the legacy you ought to have had under your grandfather's will.

SIR CHARLES. Do tell me about this aunt. I am so interested always in aunts. I've one myself—spinsterial, rich, eternal. But, Charlotte, hadn't you better take that newspaper to the printer's devil ?

CHARLOTTE (aside). Oh, yes, of course ! Wants to be alone again with her. But you can't help liking him : he's got such an impudent look. [Exit, L.

SIR CHARLES (drawing up to JANE). What is the meaning of this new maggot of the money-grub genus which has attacked—aunt ?

JANE (slyly). As you are so very much interested, I will tell you ; and then you must and shall act at once on my notice to quit.

SIR CHARLES (handing a glass of wine to JANE). Yes ; (aside) it's the look of fun dancing up in her eyes that crazes me.

JANE (laughing). Well, ever since the railway, some years ago, paid her such an enormous amount of compensation-money for the site of her house at Camberwell, her head has been quite turned about buying up sites and obtaining compensation-money ; and since she went to see the Lord Mayor's Show the other week, a money-grub, as you call it, has attacked her of a very peculiar kind in connexion with Cleopatra's Needle and the Battle of the Sites. She is very illiterate, but in Dr. Erasmus Wilson's little pamphlet about Cleopatra's Needle she is quite learned.

SIR CHARLES. How very interesting. I knew I should be rewarded if I stopped. Is she much like you ?

JANE (laughing). Well, I hope not ! But she's my only relative, and as a forlorn hope I sent for her a little while since. I am expecting her now (bell rings outside). Here she is, I dare say. So good-bye.

SIR CHARLES. Oh, if she's actually at the door. I can't be so rude as to bolt out, the moment——

Re-enter CHARLOTTE, *followed by two men carrying a package about five feet six inches high, wrapped in a packing-cloth,* L.

CHARLOTTE. These men from the Parcels Delivery Company

have brought this, and insist upon leaving it (*the men place it in middle of room*).

JANE (*going up to it, and reading address*). There's no name on the card : only the number of the house.

PORTER. Number of the house means *landlady* of the house. Are *you* the landlady, mum ? because if you are, we must leave it with you, unless you say you won't take it in.

SIR CHARLES. Yes; we're the landlady. (*To* JANE) Don't send it away.

JANE (*to* PORTER). You can leave it. (PORTER *presents parcelbook for signature.* JANE *signs.*)   [*Exeunt* PORTERS, L.

JANE *and* CHARLOTTE (*together*). Whatever can it be ? (*They and* SIR CHARLES *walk round it.*)

JANE. I certainly thought it moved. It looks to me a man.

SIR CHARLES. A man? (*feels it*). The feminine wish is father to the thought—feels more like a woman (*pulls out penknife, and thrusts it into parcel*). Breast as hard as a money-lender's (*shakes it*). It isn't a box of money. I give it up.

JANE (*to* SIR CHARLES). I wonder if it's anything of yours : not another man introduced, I hope, in a " long pack."

SIR CHARLES. Another man ! The very last thing I should introduce here ! That it's not another *woman* I perceive by the instinctive interest you show in it. Inference, it is of the neuter gender. Fetch a knife, Charlotte. (CHARLOTTE *runs, R., out, and returns with carving-knife and ordinary dinner-knife, runs to package with it, and gives* JANE *a large table-knife. They begin to rip open the cloth. An envelope falls out, which* SIR CHARLES *picks up unperceived by them, and takes to front of stage.*)

JANE *and* CHARLOTTE (*together, with excitement*). It *is* alive ! It *is* a man ! Mind how you cut. Here's his whiskers ! Here's his mouth ! Ha ! It's one of the Lord Mayor's Sphinxes ! (*They pull off cloth, and disclose a model of Cleopatra's Needle, ornamented with hieroglyphic figures painted on false sides or shutters, working with hinges. Near the top there is a face in high relief, removable for business, of an Egyptian Sphinx. The Obelisk has on one side a practicable door.*)

SIR CHARLES. Great fall in the price of gingerbread ! Lord Mayor selling off !

JANE *and* CHARLOTTE (*together*). Cleopatra's Needle, with one of the Lord Mayor's Sphinx's heads ! What can it mean ? What's in it ?

SIR CHARLES (*aside, reading paper*). Oh ! oh ! Here's a godsend. I'll pass this model off as mine, and tell her I can't leave without taking my property with me. It'll give me another day here. It's evidently something for the scoundrel Yankee upstairs (*reads while* JANE *and* CHARLOTTE *are busy inspecting Needle*) :—

" To Cincinnatus Bunkum, Esq.

" DEAR SIR,—Owing to the unexpected return of our modeller
" from Paris, we have the great pleasure to send you, a week earlier
" than we had promised, the model of your new invention, the
" Patent Walking Advertisement Obelisk, and return you your
" written instructions. We thought it well to address it to your
·" house merely—partly because the name of so famous an inventor
" might have excited the curiosity of our men, but chiefly because
" you alluded to being under the surveillance of a spy in the second
" floor of the house you live in.—Yours obediently,
" SMUDGE AND TINKLER."

(*Looks at Needle, then takes from envelope instructions.*) Ho, ho ! Now I will read the patentee's instructions, to see if Messrs. Smudge and Tinkler have done justice to Mr. Bunkum's inventive genius. (*Reads*) :—

" Each side of the Obelisk is to be furnished with a false side
" or shutter, ornamented according to pattern, upon hinges—so
" that when the sandwich man inside pulls a string they fly open,
" and disclose the true sides displaying advertisements. The
" Sphinx's face to be moveable from within, so that the sandwich
"·man can replace it by his own face at will."

So this is the last new thing in advertisement sandwiches ! Well ; the idea's so very original—that is to say, so very bunkum—that the British investors *must* come down on it as thick as flies. So, I'm a spy, am I ? I'd no idea I was anything half so clever. But to the smart man all the world is smart. He doesn't expect it home for a week ! Meantime, it shall be mine. (*Walks up to Needle.*) Where's the fastening ? Oh ! here it is. (*Touches catch, when door flies open. He enters, pulls the door to, while* JANE *and* CHARLOTTE, *in amazement, look on. He then removes from within the Sphinx's face, and shows his own, surrounded by the Sphinx's headpiece.* JANE *and* CHARLOTTE *shriek with astonishment.*)

JANE. Then that extraordinary thing *is* yours ?

SIR CHARLES. Could you doubt it ?

JANE (*laughing*). No, no. Such a whimsical thing could only have been invented by you. I never saw anything so character-istic. It really *is* yours.

SIR CHARLES. If the product of a man's own inventive brain may be called his—then the Patent Walking Advertisement Obelisk may be called mine ; otherwise, there are infernal pirating Yankee inventors roaming the earth who would no more mind peeping through my keyhole, pirating my idea, and——

JANE. Then you are not a gentleman after all, but only an inventor, like the American ?

SIR CHARLES. I am proud to find Blackfriars so apt at dis-tinctions. I am only an inventor. *Now*, may I stay ?

JANE (*bell rings*). That *must* be my aunt. Come with me, Charlotte. (*To* SIR CHARLES) If you won't leave the house, at least go to your own apartments.

[*Exeunt* JANE *and* CHARLOTTE. L.

SIR CHARLES (*coming from Needle*). That girl's turning my head fast. She's as fearless as an English lady, and as brilliant as a French—(*listens*). Hulloa ! Somebody's coming along the passage. The Yankee, most likely. I must hide this, somehow (*runs to pack-ing-cloth*). No time ! I'll get behind the Obelisk, and attack him in ambush (*slips behind Needle*).

Enter ICHABOD, *with inventory-book open, and pencil in hand,* L.

ICHABOD. I vonder vere my father is. He told me to come first and begin the inventory. I vent to the second floor, and an American came to the door with a bowie-knife, and pitched me downstairs for being near his keyhole. I hope it ishn't a madhouse they've sent us to, but it looks like it (*sees Needle*). Vy, vot ish dish ? Dish looksh *very* mad (*goes up to it, raps it, opens door*). Yesh, dish does look very mad. I vonder vot's inside (*gets into Needle, and inspects it*).

SIR CHARLES (*coming forward, and shutting door of Needle, and catching it*). Ha ! ha ! We've killed the keeper, and the cook boils in his own pot.

ICHABOD. Murder ! murder !

SIR CHARLES (*looking out of door, and listening*). There's some one else coming along the passage. This, of course, *is* the Yankee, and he'll see his invention after all before I can turn it to account (*runs to packing-cloth, mounts chair, and throws it over top of model, which now looks something like a coffin*).

ICHABOD (*kicking within*). Murder ! murder !

SIR CHARLES (*in his natural voice*). Hold your row, you fool ! The mad people are all upon us. (*Aside*) Now, I'm ready to receive my Yankee. Why, this is the parent bailiff !

Enter ABRAHAM ISAACS, *an old man, bowing to* SIR CHARLES, L.

ISAACS. Vot vash dat noish ? 1 thought I heard somebody cry murder. I vonder vere is my son Ichabod, vot I sent on here fust with the execution to take the inventory. 1 cannot find Ichabod.

SIR CHARLES. Oh, you are the bailiff ? (ISAACS *grins and bows*.) Walk in, bailiff (ISAACS *advances*).

ISAACS (*pointing to package*). Vot is dat ? It looks very like the best bed packed up to be taken off. We can't allow dat, unless you—— (*grins*).

SIR CHARLES (*confidentially*). Best bed stuffed with spoons. Shut the door, bailiff (ISAACS *shuts door*) ; bolt it, bailiff (*he bolts it*). Come along, bailiff (ISAACS *advances*). (*In a solemn, meaning tone*) Did anybody see you enter the house ?

ISAACS. No, ve always slips in vidout being seen.

SIR CHARLES. All right, bailiff. It's *my* business to take care that nobody sees you go *out*, bailiff (*stoops and picks up carving-knife*).

ICHABOD (*kicks the box*). Oh ! I shall be smothered (ISAACS *starts back*).

JEW. Vot ish dat noise ? And vy do you pick up that knife ?

SIR CHARLES (*stoops, picks up poker and sharpens knife on it.* ISAACS, *alarmed, retreats :* SIR CHARLES *moves between him and the door*). Come here on the oil-cloth (*beckons him*). I hope you're not as full as *he* was, bailiff (*pointing to package*).

ISAACS. Full of vot ?

SIR CHARLES. Blood, bailiff.

ISAACS (*aghast, pointing to package*). Den vot is dat ?

SIR CHARLES. Inside that coffin, bailiff ? It *was* a bailiff.

ICHABOD (*kicking in Needle*). Murder, murder ! Father, help !

SIR CHARLES. Don't be frightened. It seems he wasn't quite dead when we put him in.

ISAACS (*shrieking*). Who ? Ichabod ?

SIR CHARLES. Oh ! was that his name ? Well, Ichabod (*brandishing knife to Needle*). *you* spoilt our best carpet. I'll take care this one don't : come to the oil-cloth (*collars him*).

ICHABOD. They've killed the keeper ! and the cook's being boiled in his own pot !

ISAACS (*struggling violently*). Oh, a madhouse ! Murder, murder ! Let me go ! I'm very full of blood—very full of blood indeed, for an old man—fuller of blood than Ichabod ! I shall spile de carpet. I shall soak right through de floor, I shall. Murder, murder ! Let me go ! (*extricates himself*).

JANE *is heard at door*, L.

SIR CHARLES. Well, if you're so full of blood as *that*, you'll be a nuisance here. I can hear the lady of the house coming this way. I don't want the bother of sticking you ; I've stuck so many. Perhaps she might spare your life if you asked her in a proper way.

ISAACS. Vot shall I do, sir ? Vot shall I do ?

SIR CHARLES. Oh, I leave that to you. I know what *I* should do.

JEW. Vot should *you* do, sir ?

SIR CHARLES. Well, I should fall on my knees when she comes in. I should empty my pockets, lay my money on the floor before her, and say, " This will help to pay out the bailiffs." Then, in my very prettiest manner, I should ask her to let me go, and promise to never come back.

Re-enter JANE, L.

ISAACS (*approaching her, and falling on his knees*). Oh, good lady, let me go, let me go ! I vill never come back here any more—never any more ! Never, never ! Let me go, let me go !

JANE (*in bewilderment*). Certainly, you may go if you like, and I am not *particularly* anxious for your return.

ISAACS (*emptying his pockets, and laying money on floor*). This vill help to pay out the bailiffs (*rising and rushing to door*). Bless you, lady ! bless you, lady ! [*Exit*, L.

JANE (*looking at money, picking it up, and then at* SIR CHARLES). Why, what can this mean ?

SIR CHARLES. The labours of Cupid. The love-god talked to the old man so eloquently about the iniquity of his calling, that—well, you see the result of Cupid's eloquence.

JANE (*looking at* SIR CHARLES *in amazement*). Wonderful man !

SIR CHARLES (*advancing towards her*). And Cupid will win ! (*kisses her*).

JANE (*shrinking back*). But this money ! This is, of course. some mistake. I must follow this convert of Cupid's, and at least make him take back his money. [*Exit*, R.

SIR CHARLES (*goes to door*, L., *and unbolts it. Then walks up to Needle, and opens door*). Well, I'm glad one of you has escaped. I thought they would have killed the old man. What made the sheriff send you here ?

ICHABOD. This is a private madhouse, and you are the keeper ?

SIR CHARLES. With the perspicacity of your race, you have struck the nail at once.

ICHABOD. And you locked me in there to save my life ?

SIR CHARLES. Again does the Hebraic acuteness pierce to the truth like lightning. But spare your expressions of gratitude. You are quite welcome. What a strong prejudice mad people have against Jew bailiffs ! It's very strange.

ICHABOD. Then they've broken loose ?

SIR CHARLES. Yes ; I think it was the sight of your father's nose that irritated them. The mad American cried out, " Sickle, sickle ! " and sprang upon him. That's the man with the craze about keyholes and inventions, who, I believe, threatened you on the second floor with a bowie-knife for being near his keyhole. The mad old English woman, with the craze about Cleopatra's Needle and the Surrey Obelisk. followed suit ; and, last of all, the young woman with the money-craze rushed in. I just got here at the nick of time.

ICHABOD. For God's sake, let me get out of this.

SIR CHARLES. I can't. They are all over the house (*listens*). I fancy I can hear the money-maniac coming this way now, poor thing ! She mostly uses a carving-knife like that (*pointing to knife on floor*).

ICHABOD. Vot am I to do ?

SIR CHARLES. Oh, they're all easily managed, if you know them. Empty your pockets before this one, and she's as gentle as a lamb. How much money have you got about you ?

ICHABOD (*digging his hands in his pockets*). Fifty-five pounds. I have just taken it from an execution paid out.

SIR CHARLES. Well, other people's money is just as good as your own for all practical purposes. When she comes in, kneel down before her ; lay the money at her feet and say, " This will help to pay out the bailiffs." She is a *lady*, and will take it as a touchingly graceful act as coming *from* a bailiff.

Enter JANE *and* CHARLOTTE.

JANE. I can do nothing with this extraordinary old man. (*Bell rings in passage.*)

CHARLOTTE (*running off*). This must be your aunt, at last.

JANE. He positively refuses to take the money, and has gone away without it. Now, what *does* it mean ?

ICHABOD (*advancing to* JANE, *kneeling, emptying his pockets, and laying money at her feet*). This vill help to pay out the bailiffs.

JANE. Well, this is most bewildering. (*Aside*) This brilliant madcap is sending the world mad. I wonder who he is.

Enter CHARLOTTE, L.

CHARLOTTE. Your aunt is here—umbrella and all. *She's* no good. She looks as black as Newgate.

[*Exeunt* JANE *and* CHARLOTTE, L.

ICHABOD (*to* SIR CHARLES). I've got out of *that* one. She seems to know she's mad, poor thing ! Vill the others come ?

SIR CHARLES. Sure to.

ICHABOD. What am I to do ?

SIR CHARLES. All you've got to do is to go back into that Needle, and shut yourself in (*leads him to Needle, puts him inside, and removes Sphinx's face*). Here ! you see this string. If the American comes, all you have to do is to walk about, pull that string, and, whenever he speaks, say " Keyhole ! " He considers " Keyhole " to mean " God bless you." If it's the old woman with the Obelisk craze, *she's* very touchy ; your best way, perhaps, would be to stand still, and humour her by expressing your agreement with everything she says. If s'he asks a question, for instance, answer it by repeating exactly her own words. I've often found this to be the only way of humouring her. *Her* weapon is mostly—an umbrella, of the gingham species, I think ; but she *can* use her teeth.

ICHABOD. Oh, Lord ! Oh, Lord ! If I only get out of this place——

SIR CHARLES. You will never return to it, you were about to say. I cannot say that your resolution is impolitic (*going*).

ICHABOD. Oh, don't go, sir !

SIR CHARLES. I shall be back in a minute. (*Aside*) I must just go and see that there is no *exposé* with the old Jew. I hope he is clear off. [*Exit*, L.

ICHABOD (*listening to noise in passage*). Lord ! Lord ! there's somebody coming ! (MRS. THROGMORTON *is heard storming loudly in the passage and approaching. She enters*, R. ; *she is asthmatic, and carries a large umbrella.*) It's the old woman with the gingham. I've got to agree with all she says.

MRS. THROGMORTON (*storming in a very loud and angry voice*). Jist what I thought and said. Whenever nieces wants to see aunts " *very* particular," it's allus to drag money out on 'em—*allus !* Not a word do I hear from you till your house is goin' to be sold, and you're broke, then it's " Aunty, dear, come forrud ! " " Aunty, dear," *allus* means comin' forrud, and allus means bein' money-dragged. But I ain't a-goin' to come forrud, and I ain't a-goin' to be money-dragged (*sees poster*). Oh ! this is the bill, then, as she said wur up on the wall, is it ? (*goes up to poster*). She couldn't tell me neither the date nor the place of sale. Rare bisness head ! Jest like her mother as is dead and gone ; only *she* didn't set up to be the fine lady. I *will* say that for her. Eddication's a cuss (*reads poster*). Ah now ! if *this* was a-goin' to be the site of Cleopatra's Needle—and it *may* be, for the paper I bought coming along (*pulling out* " *Blackfriars Gazette* ") says they have decided to put it near the Surrey Obelisk, after all their laughing at me (*turns round and sees Needle*). Why, bless me, ain't that the moral of Cleopatra's Needle as Gover'ment's a-puttin' up all over London ?

ICHABOD (*from Needle*). It's the moral of Cleopatra's Needle as Government's a-puttin' up all over London.

MRS. THROGMORTON (*aside*). Bless me, what voice is that?
I hope my sister don't haunt this house (*moves round so as to see*
ICHABOD's *face*). It's alive! Thieves! Thieves!

ICHABOD. It's alive! Thieves! Thieves!

MRS. THROGMORTON (*in amazement*). *You* call *me* thieves? Do
you? What do you mean by calling me thieves? Of course, I'm
alive.

ICHABOD. You call *me* thieves, do you? Vot do you mean
by calling me thieves? Of course, I'm alive.

MRS. THROGMORTON (*aside*). I wonder what this means. Lord!
if it should mean that the Gover'ment's trying this very house of
Jane's for the site of Cleopatra's Needle. (*To* ICHABOD) Are you
the Gover'ment, sir?

ICHABOD. I am the Gover'ment, mum.

MRS. THROGMORTON (*aside*). Perhaps it's the Prime Minister
himself come to look at the Surrey Obelisk out of the winder, to
see if the two will match. Are you the Prime Minister, sir?

ICHABOD. I am the Prime Minister, mum.

MRS. THROGMORTON. And are you the Sphinx, too, sir?

ICHABOD. And I am the Sphinx, too, mum.

MRS. THROGMORTON. Is that the Gover'ment's Needle, sir?

ICHABOD. This is the Gover'ment's Needle, mum.

MRS. THROGMORTON (*aside*). How straightforrud he answers
questions, to be sure! And he a Prime Minister and a Sphinx!
Is this house selected as the site of Cleopatra's Needle, sir?

ICHABOD. This house is selected as the site of Cleopatra's
Needle, mum.

MRS. THROGMORTON (*with great excitement*). To be a companion
for the Surrey Obelisk, sir?

ICHABOD. To be a companion for the Surrey Obelisk, mum.

MRS. THROGMORTON (*aside*). I know'd it! I know'd it! But
to think that the site I've been lookin' arter should turn out to be
Jane's house, arter all. (*Aside, with trembling eagerness*) I must
buy it of Jane, afore she knows what's the vally on it; (*in a de-
spairing tone*) but, then, it's up for sale, and everybody will be
buyin' it, and gettin' thousands for compensation. Oh! what
shall I do? what *shall* I do? what *shall* I do? (*To* ICHABOD) Oh,
sir! I'm Jane's aunt—her only pertecter, now her poor mother's
dead and gone. This property's up for sale. There's the bill

(*pointing to poster*). It'll be bought right over the family's heads. and that'll break the family's hearts. What shall I do ? I can pay off the mortgage money, can't I ?

ICHABOD. You can pay off the mortgage money, can't you ?

MRS. THROGMORTON. Of course I can, sir.

ICHABOD. Of course you can, mum.

MRS. THROGMORTON. I can give Lady Threadneedle notice at once to pay her off before the sale. I'm Jane's aunt, sir. Of course I am.

ICHABOD. You can give Lady Threadneedle notice at once to pay her off before the sale. You're Jane's aunt, mum. Of course you are.

MRS. THROGMORTON. How straightforrud his answers are, to be sure ! And he a Prime Minister and a Sphinx ! (*Runs to table and turns over pens and paper*) Oh, but I'm such a dreadful bad writer, sir !

ICHABOD. Oh, but you're such a dreadful bad writer, mum ! (SIR CHARLES'S *footsteps are heard approaching in passage*).

MRS. THROGMORTON. Perhaps here's somebody coming as can write it for me.

ICHABOD. Perhaps here's somebody coming as can write it for you.

Re-enter SIR CHARLES, L.

MRS. THROGMORTON. I dare say he belongs to the Gover'ment, too, sir.

ICHABOD. I dare say he belongs to the Gover'ment, too, mum.

MRS. THROGMORTON (*approaching* SIR CHARLES). Oh, sir, this property as is going to be taken by the Gover'ment for the site of Cleopatra's Needle is going to be sold by a wicked old lady named Lady Threadneedle for her mortgage money, and I'm Jane's aunt, sir.

SIR CHARLES. The deuce you are ! (*Aside*) Fancy, my charmer with an aunt like this. Oh, that Beauty had no family connexions !

MRS. THROGMORTON. And I want to pay off her mortgage money, and this gentleman says he's the Prime Minister, and a Sphinx, too ; and he says of course I can pay it off if I like— bein' her aunt, and he says you belong to the Gover'ment, and he's quite sure you will be so kind as to write out the notices for me, because, he says, I'm such a bad writer.

SIR CHARLES (*looking in amazement at* ICHABOD). Well! at the long bow I thought Cupid had been just displaying a pretty firm hand ; but for real masterly archery, give me a Prime Minister, as is a Sphinx, too.

MRS. THROGMORTON. Oh, sir, please write it out at once. Here's the *Blackfriars Gazette* got wind of it, and they'll be comin' about us like a shoal o' herrings to buy it over our heads (*shows him paragraph in " Blackfriars Gazette "*).

SIR CHARLES (*taking newspaper and reading paragraph, aside*). Why, it really *is* so. The stupid compositor has actually printed the paragraph exactly as Jane altered it ; but, still, it doesn't indicate the exact spot selected for the site. Perhaps (*meaningly*) I had better indicate it for them in this elegant aunt's notice of postponement of sale. (*To* MRS. THROGMORTON) Then you are ready to pay her off ?

MRS. THROGMORTON. Yes, yes.

SIR CHARLES. Pardon me, madam ; the Government, to be a Government at all, must be practical. Did the Prime Minister (*pointing to* ICHABOD) put the financial question : How are you off for tin ?

ICHABOD. How are you off for tin, mum ?

MRS. THROGMORTON. Do you mean money ? I've just been taking my Michaelmas rents, and I've got a goodish bit just now.

SIR CHARLES. A goodish bit meaning—— ?

MRS. THROGMORTON. Three hundred and fifty-six pound, six shillings.

SIR CHARLES. Is it in the bank ?

MRS. THROGMORTON. Some's in the bank, and some's in a worsted stockin'.

SIR CHARLES. Bring the stocking here, and while the Prime Minister and I count the contents, you must send a notice immediately to Lady Threadneedle (for she, I believe, is the mortgagee) that you, as Miss Britain's aunt, are ready to pay her off. Shall I write the notice for you ?

MRS. THROGMORTON. Oh, if you would be so kind, sir. (*Aside*) I shall make thousands by this if Jane don't find it out too soon.

SIR CHARLES (*sits down and writes, reading out to himself*). " My Lady,—I beg to give you notice that I shall, within one week of this date, pay off, on behalf of my niece, Miss Jane Britain, the full amount of principal, interest, and costs, due to you in respect of your mortgage upon No. 1,006, Blackfriars Street, Blackfriars. No doubt you have heard that the house has been selected as the site of Cleopatra's Needle." (*Aside*) Lady Threadneedle is very energetic ; I am mistaken in her business capacity and rapacity if she does not fly hither to buy the site. And this notice I have been preparing for the aunt to sign (*reads*), " SALE POSTPONED ON ACCOUNT OF THE SITE HAVING BEEN SELECTED FOR CLEOPATRA'S NEEDLE," will, if posted over the sale bill, tend also to enliven the market, and prevent so valuable a property from being thrown away. Madam, if you'll sit down and sign these (*rises and directs her to take his place*).

MRS. THROGMORTON (*sitting down*). Don't look at me, please. I ain't much of a writer at the best o' times ; and now I'm a little excited, the pen won't stir if you look at it.

SIR CHARLES. Then I'll look another way.

ICHABOD. How dreadful mad *she* seems, sir.

SIR CHARLES. Dreadful.

ICHABOD. I suppose she ain't really goin' out of the house, sir ?

SIR CHARLES. Of course not.

ICHABOD. You managed her wonderful well, sir.

SIR CHARLES. Experience, nothing more. (MRS. THROGMORTON *rises.*) Have you quite done ?

MRS. THROGMORTON (*with a sigh of relief*). Quite, sir.

SIR CHARLES. Sure ?

MRS. THROGMORTON. Yes, sir. It's all done.

SIR CHARLES. That's right (*folding up and directing letters*). Now, this letter to Lady Threadneedle you must give to a hansom cabman outside. Pay him his full fare—half a crown ; tell him to drive as hard as he can to this address.

MRS. THROGMORTON. Yes, sir. I'll keep that in *this* hand.

SIR CHARLES. Then take this letter to the nearest printers.

MRS. THROGMORTON. That's the *Gazette* office.

SIR CHARLES. Tell him to print this at once, and distribute the bills. Then go home, get the stocking, put it in your pocket, and bring it to me.

MRS. THROGMORTON. Yes, sir ; I'll put *them* in *this* hand (*is going*).

SIR CHARLES. Stop a moment. Besides the stocking money have you any other loose cash in the house ?

MRS. THROGMORTON. I've got ten pounds, but it ain't loose ; it's in the bureau secret drawer.

SIR CHARLES. Ten pounds ! That's all ?

MRS. THROGMORTON. Yes, sir ; that's all.

SIR CHARLES. Then that must do, I suppose. *That* you will bring also and hand over to me as the Government's Needle fee.

MRS. THROGMORTON. Did you say Needle fee, sir ?

SIR CHARLES. Needle fee.

MRS. THROGMORTON. Oh, Needle fee, Needle, Needle fee.

[*Exit*, L.

SIR CHARLES (*aside*). Cupid is getting on. He will make the old girl disgorge the grandfather's legacy, too.

MRS. THROGMORTON (*returning*). What did you say the Needle fee was for, sir ?

SIR CHARLES. That's for advertising the postponement of the sale on the Government Needle ; like this (*opening the false sides, and showing the advertisements*).

MRS. THROGMORTON (*going*). Oh, I see, sir ; Needle fee, Needle fee.

[*Exit*. L.

SIR CHARLES. What a splendid scoundrel Cupid is making of me ! Inspired as I am, it is a shame for me to be an idle man about town when Scotland Yard is crying out for talent.

ICHABOD. It's wonderful how you managed her.

SIR CHARLES. Experience. I assure you. Should they imprison you in that Needle for only a week, you will be quite as clever with them. (*Aside*) I must follow the old woman, though, and see that she doesn't jostle her niece. [*Exit*, L.

ICHABOD. He's left me alone again (*Listens*) And, oh Lord, oh Lord, oh Lord, here comes the other madman. Here's the American as is mad about keyholes. Let me see ; vot am I to do with him ? Oh, I recollect : I'm to say " Keyhole," which, he thinks, means " God bless you," and pull this string, and valk about.

Enter CINCINNATUS BUNKUM, *with cheque-book in his hand,* L.

BUNKUM. Wall, young woman, if you've made out my account, I'll jis draw you a cheque. But let me see the figgers first. They say a Cockney gal, when she *is* smart, will jest chop down a New York gal afore she can pull out *her* chopper. (*Turns round, sees Needle ; stands transfixed by* ICHABOD'S *eyes ; walks up to it as if drawn by fascination ; then stops, and looks round room, as though to satisfy himself where he is.*) Wall, Sphinx, I don't know who you *air*, but you've chopped *me* down (*looks round room again*).

ICHABOD (*from Needle*). Keyhole! (*He moves about room pulling the string and displaying advertisements.*)

BUNKUM (*starting back*). Damnation! The second floor front!

ICHABOD. Keyhole! (*Proceeds to walk about room as before.*) Keyhole!

BUNKUM (*shaking his fist at* ICHABOD). That's the hook nose I saw against my door. A conspiracy! Come out of it! come out of it! (*Pulls out his bowie-knife.*)

> " I'll drop a slice of liver or tew,
> My bloomin' shrub, with yew."

ICHABOD (*walking about*). Keyhole! keyhole! keyhole!

Re-enter JANE *and* CHARLOTTE, L.

CHARLOTTE (*screaming*). I declare here's Mr. Honour Bright's new invention walking about!

JANE (*aside*). Oh, don't be frightened. He's put some man in it to try it.

BUNKUM (*sarcastically, putting up his knife*). So that's Mr. Honour Bright's invention, is it?

JANE. Of course it is.

CHARLOTTE. Unless you manage to steal it before he can make it safe. But I dare say you will.

BUNKUM. And what name does Mr. Honour Bright give to his invention?

JANE. The Patent Walking Advertisement Obelisk.

BUNKUM. Oh! that's what he *calls* it, is it? And what's the principle of it?

JANE. Oh, he showed us that. (*Aside*) I see how it is, I think. Mr. Honour Bright has forestalled his patent. Won't I tease him? (*Holding out her hand in an oratorical manner.* ICHABOD *keeps walking about and saying, "Keyhole!"*) We are to consider that the man inside is a sandwich man, carrying this patent Obelisk about London. The attraction of the hieroglyphics, and especially of the Sphinx's head, will be immense, Mr. Bunkum, immense. All London will be at the heels of the sandwich man. Then, at the moment when the excitement is at the very hottest, he pulls a string inside, and, presto! all the sides of the Needle fly open as they now are, and disclose advertisements paid for beforehand at enormous and unprecedented rates.

BUNKUM. Oh, that's the principle of it ! And now all I want to do is to see the great inventor and (*grating his teeth*) jest teach him carvin'.

JANE. Oh, here comes Mr. Honour Bright himself.

Re-enter SIR CHARLES, *who has overheard the last few lines*, L.

SIR CHARLES. Yes, that's the principle, Mr. Bunkum (*bell rings at outer door*. CHARLOTTE *goes to window, then returns to* JANE).

CHARLOTTE. There's the butcher's boy. He threatened yesterday that he would come to-day, and not leave without the money. He's *so* strong, and *so* shiny (JANE *and* CHARLOTTE *move towards door*).

SIR CHARLES. They *all* are—it's suet and fresh air. Shall I come and assist ? (*Kicks out his foot.*)

JANE. No, no. We shall soon be back.

[*Exeunt* JANE *and* CHARLOTTE, R.

SIR CHARLES (*taking a bottle of champagne from basket and proceeding to open it*). This is friendly, Mr. Bunkum. Take a glass of wine ? (*Pours out glass of wine, and offers it to* BUNKUM.)

BUNKUM. Wall, you seem to make pretty free with this room (*takes the glass cautiously*).

SIR CHARLES (*pouring out glass of wine for himself and drinking it*). Yes, I suppose I do, seeing whose room it is. I think you'll like this fiz, though it *is* Blackfriars—real " Blue Lion," I assure you.

BUNKUM (*looking round room*). This is *your* room—is it ? A few minutes ago it was somebody else's.

SIR CHARLES. I see you have not heard that poor Miss Britain is in difficulties.

BUNKUM. Yes, I hev.

SIR CHARLES. And that, as she can't afford to occupy her ground floor any longer, Cupid has just taken it off her hands.

BUNKUM (*sarcastically*). Wall, no, *that* I hadn't heard.

SIR CHARLES. Cupid has already begun, as you perceive, his flitting (*pointing to Needle*). Take another glass. Now that you and he are on different floors, he hopes you will be friends.

BUNKUM (*drinking the wine*). And what hev the floors to dew with Cupid's friendship, anyhow ?

SIR CHARLES. Well, to be quite candid, he thought that, for people in the same line, your *keyholes* were too near !

BUNKUM. Oh ! Cupid's an inventor, is he ?

SIR CHARLES. Yes ; having at last got quite ready for the Patent Office the model of his Patent Walking Advertising Obelisk, and judging—*inferring*—that even if you *should* have hit upon the same idea (BUNKUM *begins to rise involuntarily from his chair*), your model would (BUNKUM *stands up*), owing to your modeller being ill in Paris, not be ready for a week (BUNKUM *throws down wine-glass, exclaims " Damnation ! " and walks towards Needle, while* ICHABOD *walks about, saying, " Keyhole, keyhole "*)—having *inferred* this, Cupid thought the convenient time had come (*he coolly takes up carving-knife from floor, and slowly sharpens it on the poker*) for him to quit a too close proximity to a professional American pirate. (BUNKUM *springs round, pulls out his bowie-knife, while* SIR CHARLES *keeps coolly sharpening the carving-knife on poker, and* ICHABOD *keeps walking about displaying advertisements, and saying, " Keyhole."*)

BUNKUM (*putting up bowie-knife, but* SIR CHARLES *continues business with his*). Cuss that keyhole. I came across the river for quiet and secrecy, and I find *you !* I spotted you for the smartest man in this darned island. When I was makin' the drawing I watched you sharp ; when I talked it over with the French modeller it wasn't much above a whisper ; but I forgot the cussed keyhole till it was too late, and I found yours was stopped with plaster of Paris.

SIR CHARLES (*aside*). To keep out the draught. (*To* BUNKUM) What a singular omission ! You should have noticed Cupid's. A god who stops his keyhole with plaster of Paris understands the article keyhole in *all* its functions.

BUNKUM (*looking at* SIR CHARLES *with vexation mixed with admiration*). Wall, you *air* smart, Cupid ! You air that ! The man as chops down CINCINNATUS BUNKUM *hes* to be smart. And the man as can copy a drawin' through a keyhole *is* smart. But what air yew whetting that knife for ?

SIR CHARLES. Simply because I'm going to pitch into that chicken (*pointing to chicken*), and I thought it seemed blunt at the point, and I hate *carving* with a blunt knife (*strikes panel of door,* L., *with knife, piercing the panel through, and then withdrawing it with great velocity*).

BUNKUM. Cupid's a strong *carver* anyhow. You're right in sayin' we ought to be friends. Now, what's your game ? Is it takin' out the patent, or is it bein' bought off ? If it's bein' bought off, I'm open to treat ; for nobody can't work *that* patent only me ; but, mind, draw it mild—I ain't a-goin' to be eel-skinned and chawed up, nohow.

SIR CHARLES. Perhaps I had better dismiss my man, and then we can talk at leisure (*goes to Needle and releases* ICHABOD). (*To* ICHABOD) I think you can escape now while I hold him in conversation.

ICHABOD. Thank you, sir, for all your kindness. *He's* a dangerous customer and no mistake, but the carvin' knife scared him ! I'll go and find my father and tell him the people are all mad, and I'll go and tell the sheriff it's of no use his putting executions into madhouses.

SIR CHARLES. I should if I were you. Good-bye.

[*Exit* ICHABOD.

SIR CHARLES. Sit down, Mr. Bunkum. (*They sit down at the table.*) Nobody can work the patent, only you, Mr. Bunkum ! That sounds like vanity. I know Cupid's working *his* pretty well. A month ago he hadn't a shilling, and now he's got enough to take these rooms, besides paying off Miss Britain's mortgage money, clearing out the bailiffs, and stopping the sale.

BUNKUM. Why, your patent isn't out yet.

SIR CHARLES. Mr. Bunkum, as a smart man you are falling in my estimation every moment. Cupid didn't wait for the patent to be out, but got a month's advance of advertisement money for a forthcoming mysterious invention without a name.

BUNKUM. You air jest now sharpening the razor rather *too* fine, Cupid. What you've jest told me *is—a*—damned lie. The British public *will* stand a good deal, but they won't stand that—I've tried it. They won't stand the pig in the poke, *nohow.*

SIR CHARLES. The public *do* stand it from Cupid, however ; and, what's more, the advertising agents allow him a fixed income for Needle fees before they've seen the Needle.

BUNKUM (*throwing himself back in his chair*). Ha ! ha ! It ain't often as anybody fetches a laugh like that out of Cincinnatus Bunkum. But *yew* can—ha, ha ! ha, ha ! Wall, it's ridiculous.

SIR CHARLES. Is it ? You seem amused (*looking off*). Here's one of Cupid's *employées* coming back at the very nick of time, to save his character both for smartness and for veracity.

BUNKUM (*looking off*). One of your *employées* ? What ! that old woman with the umbrella and the basket—ha ! ha ! ha ! Wall, I like yew ; yew *can* make me laugh, *yew* can.

SIR CHARLES. One of Cupid's *employées*. Love is the only true wisdom. The little god knows that the best of all ways in this country to make money is to base your speculations on philanthropy.

BUNKUM. Wall, that's true, anyhow.

SIR CHARLES. So Cupid has turned all the widows in the neighbourhood into canvassers on commission ; and the way they go from tradesmen to tradesmen, canvassing for advertisements, with special instructions as to cash in advance, is another instance —if one were needed—of the lamentable waste of material in this country. As a touching proof that they *are* industrious British widows, they always receive the subscriptions in that old-fashioned and, alas ! obsolete British purse—the worsted stocking.

BUNKUM. Wall, yew *can* make me laugh, yew can—ha ! ha !

SIR CHARLES. I assure you the stocking is a *great* hit. Sentiment is a great factor in money-getting.

BUNKUM. Wall, Cupid is the most brilliant liar this side Kentucky, anyhow.

Enter MRS. THROGMORTON, *with basket.*

MRS. THROGMORTON (*handing* SIR CHARLES *ten pounds*). Here's the ten pounds separate. I'll give you the Needle fee fust, sir.

BUNKUM (*starting up*). WHAT !—what did you say that money was for, ma'am.

MRS. THROGMORTON. Lud, how you startle me ! That's the Needle fee, of course.

BUNKUM. The Needle fee ! and what's the Needle fee for, ma'am ?

MRS. THROGMORTON. The Needle fee ! Why, that's for the advert*is*ements.

BUNKUM (*sinking down in his chair*). Wall, I *am* chopped down. Yes, yes, I *am* chopped down, this time !

Re-enter JANE, R., *with bill of postponement in her hand, advancing to table.*

JANE. Mr. Bright, see this! (*stands amazed at the sight of* MRS. THROGMORTON).

MRS. THROGMORTON (*to* SIR CHARLES). And here's the stocking, sir (*she empties the stocking on the table, and the contents—gold, silver, and copper—roll about* BUNKUM'S *and* JANE'S *hands*).

SIR CHARLES. And how much other money have you brought me?

MRS. THROGMORTON. Three hundred pounds fifteen shillings and sixpence.

SIR CHARLES (*in a patronising tone*). Ah, very fair (*patting her on the back*), very fair.

MRS. THROGMORTON (*looking at him in amazement, aside*). What a pleasant gentleman this is! He seems to have taken quite a fancy to me! (*Sees* JANE, *aside*) Why, here's Jane! I must git her away, and buy the property on her, before she knows anything about this.

BUNKUM. You air the smartest man!—But it *must* be a plant. (*To* MRS. THROGMORTON) Then this gentleman sends you about a good deal, does he? Where hev you been to-day for him?

MRS. THROGMORTON. Well, let me see! First I went to the cabman, and gave him the letter for **Lady** Threadneedle, tellin' her that her money was ready for her as soon as she liked to have it. And then I went to the printing-office with this gentleman's letter to the printer, tellin' him to print the bills about the postponement of the sale (*she goes to* JANE, *who has retired in amazement to the back, and converses energetically with her*).

SIR CHARLES (*to* BUNKUM). The fact is, Cupid makes these old girls generally useful. They do all his errands.

BUNKUM (*looking at him dreamily*). Wall, Cupid is the smartest man in all creation.

SIR CHARLES (*rising*). Well, Mr. Bunkum, I suppose we've not much more to say to each other.

BUNKUM. Wall, yes, I guess we hev. Fust of all (*holding out his hand*), I beg your pardon for giving you the lie jest now. Second, I've been tryin' all my life tew find a man smart enough tew jine me in business. I couldn't find him, but if he's to *be* found, I think he's the owner of that Needle (*pointing to it*).

SIR CHARLES. Really, you are too kind.

BUNKUM. A man as can pirate a design through a keyhole, and work it out, and be ready for patentin' a week afore *me*, to say nothin' of gittin' John Bull to pay for advertising in a scheme without a name, and gittin' the advertisin' agent to pay a Needle fee afore ever the Needle's made, seems to me exactly the man I've been lookin' for. Wull you jine me ? Don't you think it seems a pity we should be parted ?

SIR CHARLES. But wouldn't the name of the firm look rather queer—Bunkum, Honour Bright, and Co. ?

BUNKUM. Don't see that at all. In the commarcial world Bunkum and Honour Bright are gittin' to hev pretty much the same kind of sound, I guess.

SIR CHARLES. Well, if *you* don't mind the incongruity, *I* don't. We'll join our fortunes. You've got your cheque-book with you, I noticed ; sit down (*beckons him to a table and arranges paper, pens, and ink before him*).

BUNKUM. What's the cheque-book got to do with it anyhow ?

SIR CHARLES. Really, Mr. Bunkum, we start badly, I fear. *I* bring in that (*pointing to Needle*), worth at least £10,000 ; *you* write me a cheque for, let us say, £2,000, in part of the cash capital, to be afterwards settled, which *you* bring in to balance *my* Needle.

BUNKUM (*looking at him suspiciously and yet admiringly*). Wall, you *air* smart ! (*Aside*) The patent *is* worth a long figure ; but, as a partner, your figure's longer (*sits down and writes.* SIR CHARLES *looks over his shoulder*).

SIR CHARLES. No, put it thus: Pay to Honour Bright, Esq., £2,000 as a premium for going into partnership with him. (*Aside*) Then, when the explanation about the model comes, I shan't get into any real trouble about *that* (BUNKUM *throws himself back in his chair and reflects ; then he looks at* SIR CHARLES *scrutinisingly, and signs*).

SIR CHARLES. No, don't cross it. I shall cash it at once.

JANE (*advancing to* SIR CHARLES). Mr. Bright, do tell me what makes this extraordinary change in my aunt. She puzzles me ; she's so anxious now to buy this house.

SIR CHARLES. Don't strike a bargain with her by any means ; don't do anything without me.

JANE. That I certainly will *not :* for you are, indeed, a treasure.

SIR CHARLES. Is the little god winning?

JANE. He has won.

SIR CHARLES (*advancing to her with the cheque which he has taken from* BUNKUM). Would you send Charlotte to cash this at once?

JANE (*looking at cheque*). Mr. Bunkum! (*and then looking at* SIR CHARLES). Wonderful man!

[*Exit* R., *followed by* MRS. THROGMORTON.

BUNKUM (*who has been watching them*). Wall, partner. and what does all that whisperin' mean? Is that a *very* good bit o' business?

SIR CHARLES (*mounting chair and pinning postponement poster over sale bill*). Oh! this is a separate account. Our partnership is patents only.

BUNKUM. No! (*Observing postponement poster*) I don't see that. It's a general partnership. There's no deed between us yet, but, honour——

SIR CHARLES. Among thieves, you were going to say (*descending*). But this is my best spec, and has nothing to do with the partnership. But I'll tell you what you *shall* do, if you like : you shall buy a *third* of my interest at a sum fixed—paying down, of course.

BUNKUM. Wall! (*suspiciously*) what is it?

SIR CHARLES. Read that paragraph (*hands him "Blackfriars Gazette"*).

BUNKUM (*starting up*). Site of the Needle—why, the compensation-money!

SIR CHARLES (*looking at him*). Yes, I know.

BUNKUM (*regaining his coolness*). Now, I know why you sent the notices to Lady Throgmorton. You are the— You're buying it before anybody knows, of course.

SIR CHARLES. Of course. You don't suppose I should have waited till they do know.

BUNKUM. Wall ; now—what will you let me in at?

SIR CHARLES. For a third, you know ; no more than a third. Well, I'm not a greedy man. Make the cheque for £1,500.

BUNKUM (*looking at him, and then at poster, and then at paragraph*). No, I'm damned if I'll touch *this*, anyhow.

SIR CHARLES. Now, come, that's kind of you. It would *not* have been fair. I did really consider the partnership special (BUNKUM *sits down, writes cheque, and hands it to* SIR CHARLES).

SIR CHARLES (*refusing to take it*). No, no. You declined.

BUNKUM. Yes ; business is business. You've been too smart for *me*. But I guess I'm a little too smart for *you*, this time (*lays down cheque on table*).

SIR CHARLES (*taking it up and putting it in his pocket*). Yes, you're too smart for me this time, Mr. Bunkum.

BUNKUM. If you're going to cash this at once, too, I must just go and see what my balance is (*going*). Let me ask you one question, partner. What *are* you—by profession ?

SIR CHARLES. An English baronet.

BUNKUM (*in amazement*). One of the British upper ten ? Why, I thought they were all Dundrearys, all fools.

SIR CHARLES. Not when inspired by Cupid, Mr. Bunkum.

[*Exit* BUNKUM, L.

Enter JANE, *followed by* CHARLOTTE.

JANE. The cheque is cashed ; here's the money (*lays it on table*). But what does this change mean in my aunt ? She's turned into an angel.

SIR CHARLES. All Cupid ! She's brought you this money—just to go on with (*pointing to money on table*). And look here ! I'm so sorry to trouble you again ; but this other cheque—would you kindly get that cashed too, and at once ? the branch bank will be closed shortly.

JANE (*looking at cheque*). Bunkum ! Why, what *can* all this mean ?

SIR CHARLES. Simply that Cupid has won (JANE *hands cheque to* CHARLOTTE, *who goes out*). When Fortune is very blind and won't give Cupid a turn, Cupid considers it only fair to turn the wheel for her. Follow my cue in all I say and do (*enters Needle*).

Re-enter MRS. THROGMORTON, R.

MRS. THROGMORTON. Why, where's the Gover'ment gentleman (*looks at* SIR CHARLES'S *face in Needle*). Bless me, how the Prime Minister has altered. (*Sees postponement poster*) Why, that'll bring everybody to bid against me. (*Approaching* JANE *and whispering*) My dear, I'm a-goin' to stan' your friend, for the sake of your poor mother. How much shall I give you for the house, jest to keep it away from that nasty old Lady Threadneedle, and keep it in the family ?

Re-enter CHARLOTTE, *followed by* LADY THREADNEEDLE
and FOOTMAN, R.

CHARLOTTE. Lady Threadneedle. [*Exit*, R.

LADY THREADNEEDLE (*to* JANE). Why, what does this mean, Miss Britain ? Who gave orders for this postponement ? (JANE *hands her newspaper, and points to paragraph.*)

LADY THREADNEEDLE (*starting as she reads*). Impossible ! And yet the site is so very unsuitable that it must be true (*turns round and sees Needle, but not the face*). And I declare ! (*looks at it through her eye-glass*) what does this mean ? A model of the Needle here ? (*Aside*) If this news is true, what money will be made ! (*To* JANE) I expect my solicitor here shortly. I shall be quite willing to buy the house and stand your friend.

SIR CHARLES (*from Needle*). Always look well after a purchaser that buys to stand your friend (*turns round again so that the face is not seen*).

LADY THREADNEEDLE (*looking round in amazement through her eye-glass to* MRS. THROGMORTON). What did you say ?

MRS. THROGMORTON. What did *you* say ?

LADY THREADNEEDLE (*aside*). This is done to drive me off ; but I'll buy it if it is to be bought.

MRS. THROGMORTON (*coming up to* JANE). My dear, the party to stand your friend is your own aunt by the mother's side—the clussest of *all* aunts, for father's-side aunts are *allus* disagreeable (LADY THREADNEEDLE *looks at* MRS. THROGMORTON *through her eye-glass*).

SIR CHARLES (*from Needle*). Who is this person ?

MRS. THROGMORTON (*turning round upon* LADY THREADNEEDLE). Person ! No more a person than you. Person, indeed !

LADY THREADNEEDLE (*losing her temper*). Do you know whom you are addressing ?

MRS. THROGMORTON. Oh, yes ! You're my Lady Threadneedle. You make money in a big way ; I make money in a little way. You do it genteel ; I do it low.

SIR CHARLES (*from Needle*). Wholesale rogue and retail.

LADY THREADNEEDLE (*looking round, and then at* MRS. THROGMORTON). What an extraordinary person ! But I'm not going to be befooled by a vulgar old ventriloquist.

MRS. THROGMORTON. What do you mean by callin' me a rogue ? If you come to that, there ain't much difference between you and me, except the heye-glass and the ladyship.

LADY THREADNEEDLE (*becoming very angry*). You false woman ! You know it was *you* who called *me* a rogue.

MRS. THROGMORTON. Oh, what a lie !

SIR CHARLES (*from Needle*). I'll have you locked up.

MRS. THROGMORTON (*turning upon* LADY THREADNEEDLE *in great wrath*). *You* have *me* locked up !

LADY THREADNEEDLE. You know I didn't say so, you bad, designing woman ! You know you said it yourself—you—you—you—you wicked old—old—ventriloquist !

MRS. THROGMORTON. *You* have me locked up ! There's a law for the rich and a law for the poor, else *you'd* stand a chance of being locked up yourself for comin' here and trying to cheat a poor, unpertected young female and her poor old aunt—trying to make us sell our family estate for a few hundreds when it's worth so many thousands (*turning to* JANE). I didn't mean all that, my dear, only I must shut her up.

SIR CHARLES (*from Needle*). Don't quarrel ! Both in the same boat, you know. If Throgmorton's a rogue, so is Threadneedle.

LADY THREADNEEDLE. There you are again ! You want to drive me away by your low insults, but you'll find I'm not to be beaten.

MRS. THROGMORTON. There *you* are again—callin' me a rogue. But you'll find *I* ain't to be beaten. I'll buy it over your head if it busts me ! Do you let me come and speak to my niece (*pushing* LADY THREADNEEDLE *violently*). My dear, I'll give you nine hundred pounds for the house.

LADY THREADNEEDLE. Miss Britain, I'll give you nine hundred and fifty pounds for the house.

Re-enter CHARLOTTE, *with cash*, R.

CHARLOTTE. Here's all Blackfriars coming, with posters in their hands.

MRS. THROGMORTON (*very excitedly, and pulling* LADY THREAD-NEEDLE'S *shawl*). Don't let the family be cheated, Jane. It's worth more, my dear ; it's worth a good deal more—no, not a good deal more—a *little* more. I'll give you ten hundred (*as* LADY

THREADNEEDLE *is about to speak*, MRS. THROGMORTON *flies upon her, and they fight*).

SIR CHARLES (*from Needle*). Don't fight, ladies ! As the property is going to the highest bidder, I will mount the table, become my own auctioneer, and play Mammon myself ! (LADY THREADNEEDLE *and* MRS. THROGMORTON *both turn round.*)

JANE. As the property is going to the highest bidder, I will mount the table, become my own auctioneer, and play Mammon myself (*mounting table*). (*Aside*) This is too charming. I will let him see how I can enter into his glorious spirit of fun (CHARLOTTE, *by* JANE'S *directions, hands her up a chair and stand, and a brush, to use as an auctioneer's hammer*).

MRS. THROGMORTON (*rushing up to table*). No nonsense, Jane ; no tomfoolery, Jane. Don't let it go out of the family. I'll give you another hundred—and that's the last I *will* give.

JANE (*imitating the auctioneer*). Thank you, aunt ; thank you. Another hundred bid for this fine site—going at eleven hundred, if no advance—going at eleven hundred.

LADY THREADNEEDLE. I'll give you another twenty pounds.

SIR CHARLES (*from Needle*). And that's the last I *will* give.

JANE. Thank you, my lady. Eleven hundred and twenty pounds bid for this noble site—going at eleven hundred and twenty—going at eleven hundred and twenty,—going, going, going !

MRS. THROGMORTON. Eleven hundred and thirty, and that's all I *will* give.

SIR CHARLES (*from Needle*). Eleven hundred and forty.

MRS. THROGMORTON (*turning to* LADY THREADNEEDLE). What do you mean by tellin' such a lie as sayin' you wouldn't bid no higher and go and bid directly—cheatin' me out of a ten-pound note.

LADY THREADNEEDLE. I didn't say so—you know I didn't (*advances to table to bid, when* MRS. THROGMORTON *seizes her bonnet and tears it off.* LADY THREADNEEDLE *strikes her—a scuffle ensues*).

JANE (*hilariously imitating auctioneer*). Now, Lady Threadneedle, I am quite ready to take your bid ! May I say another twenty ? Thank you, another twenty. It stands at Lady Threadneedle at eleven hundred and sixty. Going at eleven hundred and sixty if no advance ; going, going, going at eleven hundred and sixty, going at eleven hundred and sixty, this valuable property which is so shortly to become famous as the site of Cleopatra's

Needle, a model of which you see before you. Going at eleven hundred and sixty if no advance. Now, aunty dear, don't let it go out of the family at such an absurd sum. Going once, going twice, going.

MRS. THROGMORTON (*shrieking*). Another twenty, Jane ; knock it down.

JANE. Thank you, aunty dear, another twenty ; eleven hundred pounds and eighty bid for this noble site shortly to become so famous.

MRS. THROGMORTON. Knock it down.

JANE. Not yet, aunty dear, not yet. We mustn't let the property be thrown away at such a figure.

Enter MISS JOHNSON, R., *with a copy of the newspaper in her hand and poster.*

Ah, here comes another bidder ! My first-floor front—Miss Johnson. So sorry I cannot take your bid, Miss Johnson, but deposit *must* be paid down, and, without wishing to be indelicate—it must still stand at Mrs. Throgmorton at eleven hundred and eighty pounds, and it's going at eleven hundred and eighty pounds. Going at eleven hundred and eighty pounds, if no advance.

MISS JOHNSON. Eleven hundred and ninety.

JANE. Now, really, Miss Johnson, if I could only take your bid, I should really be delighted to see you make a bargain that would enable you to *leave* a first-floor front under which smoulders, like a female volcano, a speculator who loses.

Enter MR. ZERUBBABEL SMITH, R., *with poster and newspaper in his hand.*

Going at eleven hundred and ninety pounds, if no advance. (*Perceiving* Z. SMITH.) Now, I declare, here's another estimable bidder, whose bid, I regret to say, I cannot possibly take.

Z. SMITH. I assure you my bid may be taken with perfect safety. As secretary of the Self-Abnegation Building Society, I have an unlimited command of funds.

JANE. But, my dear Mr. Smith, it is not your own.

Z. SMITH. That doesn't at all signify, I assure you.

JANE. Mr. Smith, Mr. Smith, speculation is the great vice of this age.

Enter CINCINNATUS BUNKUM, R., *followed by a number of tradesmen in their aprons, who rush in excitedly with newspapers and posters in their hands. Bidding goes on furiously from all parties. Angry altercations ensue between all of them.*

JANE (*at the top of her voice*). Going at fifteen hundred and ninety pounds ; going at fifteen hundred and ninety pounds ; going, if no advance, going ! going ! going ! (*More tradesmen rush in, bidding furiously ; great uproar.*) Here they come, the brewer, the baker, the candlestick-maker (*nodding to various bidders*). Thank you, thank you. The property now stands at two thousand and eighty pounds. Going at two thousand and eighty pounds, if no advance— going ! going ! going ! What ! all done ? All done ? Well, then, it's Lady Threadneedle's, after all (*knocks down hammer*). Accept, ladies and gentlemen, my thanks on behalf of myself, no less than Mr. Mammon, whom I represent, for your patronage and courtesy, and the very spirited way in which you have been bidding up (*descends*).

SIR CHARLES (*coming from Needle*). By Jove ! that's the finest girl in London. If she'll have me, I'll marry her to-morrow, and have old Mother Throgmorton for an aunt. (*He goes up to her*) Miss Britain, I can't say how much I admire you as an auctioneer. (*Aside*) Was there ever such a piquant, brilliant, plucky— No ! I'm damned if ever there was. (*To Jane*) Miss Britain, I want to speak to you (*they converse apart*).

Enter MR. DIDDLUM, R., *with blue bag, in great haste.*

LADY THREADNEEDLE (*rushing up to him*). I've bought the site of Cleopatra's Needle.

DIDDLUM. There must be some mistake.

LADY THREADNEEDLE. No, no. Write out a cheque for the money. Never mind about the formalities till afterwards. Give her the cheque (*Diddlum sits down and writes cheque*).

DIDDLUM (*coming up to* JANE). Here is the cheque, Miss Britain (JANE *takes cheque*).

NEWSPAPER BOY (*outside*). Echo ! Echo ! Echo ! Fifth edish—on. Site of Cleopatra's Needle ! (*There is a general rush to the door, and " Echo " boy is pulled in.*)

BUNKUM (*reading " Echo " aloud*). " The authorities have at last decided that the site of Cleopatra's Needle is to be either on the Embankment, or in Parliament Square, or on Primrose Hill, or somewhere else." (*There is a general uproar and laughter, and cries of " A hoax ! "*)

DIDDLUM (*making towards* LADY THREADNEEDLE). Fraud, deceit ! We have been embezzled out of our deposit money ! (*Turning round.*) Who has done this ? Where's the scoundrel ? Where's the scoundrel ?

BUNKUM. There he is, the pirate of that Sphinx ! Damn him ! The smartest man in all creation.

LADY THREADNEEDLE (*going up to* SIR CHARLES). Who are you that have cheated me ? (*Recognises him*) Sir Charles Larkie !

SIR CHARLES. Yes, and the purchaser of the site of Cleopatra's Needle. The auctioneer took the wrong bid. It should have been knocked down to me (*takes cheque from* JANE *and hands it to* DIDDLUM). Allow me, Lady Threadneedle, to present to you my future wife. And as Cleopatra's Needle has brought about the match, I propose we have the Needle Dance.   [*Dance.*

CURTAIN.

THE KEATS LETTERS, PAPERS, AND OTHER RELICS.

[The following passage is a characteristic extract from the last piece of criticism that Watts-Dunton ever wrote. It is taken from the " Foreword" to the sumptuous edition of Keats edited by Dr. G. C. Williamson.] *

With regard to Shelley, Dr. Garnett has proved to us that no sooner had Shelley set down a word in writing than his instinct for self-criticism leapt upon him, and he began to revise it. The same may be said of all other modern poets of the first class, unless we except Swinburne. In the composition of *Atalanta*, Swinburne did, to be sure, revise a good deal, especially in the choruses ; but after the publication of that great poem, so completely steeped was his mind in the English language as a poetic vehicle that he was a veritable *improvvisatore* whose hand always " swept from left to right, fiery and final." There are long passages of his in what has

* Published by John Lane, The Bodley Head, 1914.

been called "his latest and ripest work," such as *Tristram of Lyonesse*, in which no single revision for scores and even hundreds of lines occurs. It is in Keats's work, however, which was produced in the way that Rossetti alludes to, that the importance of facsimile reproductions of his manuscripts is seen.

I will give a most striking example of the felicitous results of Keats's tentative method. If any student of English literature were asked what are the finest three lines to be found in English poetry, he would, I think, adduce lines 8, 9, and 10 in the seventh stanza of *Ode to the Nightingale :—*

> " The same that oft-times hath
> Charm'd magic casements, opening on the foam
> Of perilous seas, in faery lands forlorn."

By the side of these miraculous lines even the finest of Shakespeare's seem almost prosaic. But how were these lines originally written ? Thanks to Mr. Buxton Forman's loving labours, we now at last know that they originally stood thus :—

> " The same that oft-times hath
> Charm'd the wide casements, opening on the foam
> Of keelless seas, in fairy lands forlorn."

Never were poetical lines so transfigured by a few touches as here.

I think no more need be said about the importance of preserving facsimiles of Keats's manuscript instead of relying upon printed reproductions.

And now a word about Keats and his position as a poet— a subject upon which Swinburne and I always agreed to differ somewhat.

Year by year Keats's fame grows, and when Matthew Arnold named him in the same breath with Shakespeare he did not say a vain thing, but a wise one. As to myself, who began to be steeped in Keats at fourteen years of age, I feel sure that I should always have seen from the sonnet on Chapman's Homer, from *Endymion,* and from *Sleep and Poetry*, the foreshadowing of the great poet of the odes. The conventional talk about the futility of *Endymion* has come down to us from the unfair criticisms of Keats's own time.

It is full of poetry. When it descends into prattle. which it sometimes assuredly does, it is always the prattle of a baby Olympian.

Before I conclude this note, I must not forget to record that it
was the American Keatseans who, as far back as July 16, 1894,
erected in Hampstead Parish Church a memorial bust to the poet.
All honour to them ! I was there. Indeed, a little poem of mine,
called *To a Sleeper at Rome*, was read to the company by Mr. Edmund Gosse, who unveiled the memorial and made an eloquent
speech. I am tempted to give here a few lines of this poem, as they
embody more fully my personal feeling about Keats, and the deep
pathos of his life, than anything I could say in prose :—

"To a Sleeper at Rome.

" Thy gardens, bright with limbs of gods at play—
      Those bowers whose flowers are fruits, Hesperian sweets
      That light with heaven the soul of him who eats,
And lend his veins Olympian blood of day—
Were only lent, and, since thou couldst not stay,
      Better to die than wake in sorrow, Keats,
      Where even the Siren's song no longer cheats—
Where Love's long ' Street of Tombs ' still lengthens grey."

Twenty years have passed since these lines were read to that
assembly—twenty years ! The long " Street of Tombs " has got
longer, and lengthens out greyer than ever. It is only the man
who has reached old age, and lost friend after friend, who can
truly understand the poignancy—the ineffable pathos—of human
life.

FROM "CARNIOLA."

A Scene with Brigands on the Plains in Hungary.*

When we reached the spot where we were to sleep (which, being near a stream, had been chosen because we could take a bath in the morning), my father, whose sailor training had made him more deft in such matters than most women, soon made up among the puszta flowers two very comfortable-looking beds. They consisted of the Russian rugs which we had brought in our carriage in case an occasion for their use such as this should arise.

By the time that my father and I had thrown ourselves on our beds, with Czindól stretched on the bare ground near us, the stars had begun to turn the plains into the land of magic I loved.

"Which has the greater charm for you," I said to my father, "a beautiful woodland scene, or this ? "

"This ; though, of course, I do dearly love woodland scenery, especially if it's in England. It is the emptiness of the puszta that gives me a sense of freedom only second to what the sea can give."

"So, on the limitless sea-like plains of my native land, Sindbad himself," I said, "can dispense for a time with the sea ? "

"Yes," said he. "As to the inland woods, however deep their poetry may be, the Spirit of Romance is not there, or, if there, he is in hiding."

"Not even in the Australian bush ? " I said.

"Not even in the Australian bush. In order for that spirit to come forth and take captive the soul of the true Sindbad, something else is wanted—the sense of the infinite. Howsoever thick and green the trees may be, and however bright and winding the streams may be, a magical glimmer of sea-light far or near must

---

* Deleted by Watts-Dunton in his novel " for want of space."

shine through the branches as they wave, or there is no feeling of romance for the soul of Sindbad."

" And this is not needed in our puszta ? " I said.

" No ; for a time it is not needed here."

*   *   *   *   *

When I awoke next morning and turned my eyes away from the blinding light, I became conscious that my father was standing by my side. A bathing-towel was slung over his shoulder.

" Is there a land sight in the world," said he, " so fascinating as a sunrise over our puszta ? "

" Surely not," I said ; " surely not."

" Beloved puszta ! " said he. " There is no kind of trouble, no kind of sorrow, no kind of remorse even, which morning on the puszta or the steppes cannot soothe. I can even imagine Cain in his wanderings, or the Shiite martyr during his penance, feeling a thrill of comfort, perhaps of joy, during this one hour in the twenty-four."

He stood in silence for some time. Then he said, " There is no landscape and there is no seascape that cannot be made more bewitching by its grandeur and by its gloom, by its pathos and by its beauty, when the colours and the breezes of morning begin to stir over it."

" The day is going to be a scorcher," I said.

" A scorcher indeed ! Are you ready to take an early morning dip ? " He pointed to the water, whose sheen was glimmering between the clumps of trees, where the nightingales had held their serenade on the previous evening, and where the wood-pigeons were now cooing, and the blackbirds singing. We will go further down the stream, though ; I remember that the water is deeper there ; and, besides, we shall enjoy the bathe better after a walk. Bring your towel and join me."

" Towel ! I forgot to provide myself with one."

" I didn't forget to bring one for you."

" I suppose the well-seasoned Sindbad," I said, " forgets none of the essentials of travel ; and I have much to learn."

" Look under your blanket, and you'll find one."

Throwing my towel over my shoulder, I went with him towards the stream. As we went along he showed me a little parcel he was carrying, which he told me was our breakfast of bread-

and-meat, and pulling from his pocket a bottle of Bass, he said—

" I think with the British nectar we can make a fair British breakfast."

We then moved on, and after a brisk walk of nearly two miles we found signs of the water being deep—deep enough for a really good plunge.

" This is the kind of thing that makes life so delicious," said my father, as we swam side by side.

" Ah! so it is. But the first bathe ought to have been in the sea ; that's where father and son, and that's where two friends, ought to have their first bathe. There's no bond so strong between two friends as that of the passion for the sea. During all my life the sea has been my great comfort as well as joy ; and in the sea my life must find its close, or it will have been a failure. I mean that it's the place where a Sindbad ought to end his days : in fact, it's the best place for the nature-worshipper of any kind to die in."

When he saw me looking rather grave at these words, he said cheerily—

" Marvellous the difference between a young fellow like you and a man of my age in the way we think about death. When I was your age to confront the idea of death was almost impossible. I almost felt that, although other people might die, I might escape the common doom by means of Elijah's chariot, or something of that kind. It is the strongest of all instincts, the instinct of self-preservation, that produces this effect. The gentleman on the pale horse used then to vanish as soon as I got a glimpse of him. Now he comes cantering by my side in the friendliest way, the jolliest skeleton imaginable."

" You don't want to die, father ? "

" Certainly not ; but I live in the constant knowledge that I am now on earth only on sufferance."

On leaving the water I was startled by the appearance of three horsemen coming towards us at a canter.

My father went quietly to his clothes, and pulling out his revolver, concealed it behind his body, but cocked it.

" Brigands ? " I asked.

" Apparently," said he.

Every man was armed to the teeth, though, as they seemed to be laughing, it was difficult to say whether they were coming to attack us or whether they were merely coming to the stream to water their horses.

One of them, who was evidently the leader, was dressed in a splendid costume, and looked extremely picturesque.

My father stood and looked at them as coolly as though he were looking at an oil-painting of three brigands.

" One of them has got a lasso," I said.

As I spoke the fellow advanced before the others and threw out his lasso. It flew through the air with such amazing precision that, had its destination been my body instead of my father's, it could not possibly have missed. But my father being, as he had already told me during one of our chats, quite familiar with lasso-throwing in several countries, gave a peculiar snake-like twist to his body, and the rope fell at his feet. At the same moment he presented his revolver, covering, however, not the lasso-thrower, but the gaily-dressed chief of the band. This brought the three to a halt.

" Put down that revolver," said the leader in Hungarian.

" You are imperious, my gay cut-throat," said my father.

" Throw your money to us, and then we will go away."

" Money would be of no use to you, Istók," said my father, calmly.

" Oh, wouldn't it ? Why ? "

" Because unless you all three throw your rifles across your saddles and hold up your hands, something amusing will happen."

" What ? " said the man.

" Why, a certain famous chief will be as dead a thing in a second as can be seen between here and Debreczen."

The figure of my father seemed to combine the activity of youth and the solid strength and dignity of middle age at its most virile point ; the gigantic form as white as ivory, with the sinewy pistol-arm stretched out ; the sun making the water-drops all over him sparkle like spangles, while little streams ran down from his hair.

The chief, whom his pistol was covering, was a man almost as big as himself—fierce, grey-eyed, and naturally of a fair complexion, but with a skin as dark as the Czigánys themselves, so tanned was it by exposure to the sun and wind of the puszta.

The party stood petrified. Without any word or gesture from the chief, the rifles of the two were automatically laid across the saddle-bows, and the chief's rifle followed suit.

I have often noticed since then that, in a crisis of this kind, it is not the words spoken that cow an antagonist, but the tone in which they are uttered. No one could have doubted, from the quiet, sardonic accent of my father, that, unless his demands had been complied with in an instant, a bullet would have been safely lodged in the chief's brain.

The dead silence was broken by the words, in Hungarian, " The Englishman—the great pistol-shot—the Archduke's friend! "

INDEX.

ABBEY, Edwin, 1. 329 ; ii. 284.
Æstheticism, i. 176.
Ainsworth, Harrison, i. 65.
Anderson, G. F. R., sonnet by, ii. 195.
Animals at Kelmscott, i. 85.
—— at Cheyne Walk, i. 190.
Argyll. Duke of. recollections of Watts-Dunton, ii. 203.
Aspects of Tennyson, ii. 57.
Athenæum, The, work for, i. 118, 133. 237–253. 321 : ii. 18. 20.
Aylwin, i. 48, 49, 59, 69–71, 80, 81, 83, 84, 88, 106, 134, 181, 190, 242, 257, 273, 303–328 ; ii. 20, 124, 140, 177, 207, 218, 221, 244, 255, 258.
——, motto on title-page, ii. 69.
——, preface to. i. 304.

Balmoral : a Pendant to Lothair, i. 56–59.
Bateman, Mr. Stringer, ii. 165.
Bell, Mr. Mackenzie, ii. 155, 206.
Bells, The, i. 154, 295.
Birthday Sonnets. ii. 53, 67, 68.
Black, William, i. 115, 121–122.
Blind, Mathilde, i. 303.
Books, old, letter on, i. 41.
" Boors of Huntingdon. the," letter on, i. 39–41.
Borrow, George, i. 46–48, 314, 324 ; ii. 11, 19, 72. 75, 76, 235.

Borrow, George, a day with, ii. 89–97.
——, Watts-Dunton's relations with, ii 83, 84, 85, 86, 89–97.
Bothwell, by Swinburne, i. 108, 109, 113, 115, 125.
Braddon, Miss, Rossetti on, i. 230.
Breakfast Yarns, ii. 294–329.
Breath of Avon, The, i. 340.
Brontë, Charlotte, i. 250, 313.
Brown, Ford Madox, i. 67, 71, 105, 112, 121, 156. 157, 216 ; ii. 124, 269.
Browning, Robert, ii. 11, 21, 22–27.
——, Mrs., i. 151.
Burne-Jones, Sir Edward, i. 158, 176, 206 ; ii. 11.
——, Watts-Dunton on pictures of, ii. 13.
Burton, Sir Richard, i. 129–133 ; ii. 11.
Byron. essay on, i. 263, 268–270.

CAINE, Hall, i. 228, 229 ; ii. 201.
Cambridge Chronicle, contributions and letters to, i. 37, 38, 41, 43, 119 ; ii. 288.
Campbell, Lady Archibald, i. 157, 279 ; ii. 170, 201–203.
——, Lewis, i. 330.
Captain Singleton, essay on, i. 246–248.

Carlyle, Thomas, i. 121, 239, 246.
Carniola, i. 157, 322, 330, 332 ; ii. 139, 159, 187.
——, extract from, ii. 332–336.
Cavendish, Miss Ada, i. 147, 151.
Chambers's Cyclopædia of English Literature, contributions to, i. 257, 261, 262, 263 : ii. 144, 151.
Channel Islands, visit to, i. 114, 122.
Chapman, Swinburne's Essay on, i. 110, 114.
Chatterton, essay on, i. 263–267.
Chatto, Andrew, i. 113.
Chesson, W. H., ii. 156.
Cheyne Walk, residence at, i. 185–207.
Childhood, early, i. 17–21.
Christmas at the Mermaid, i. 285.
Clodd, Edward, i. 291 ; ii. 185.
Cockerell, S. C., i. 95.
Coleridge, sonnet on, i. 293.
Collins, L. Churton, i. 121 ; ii. 208.
Coming of Love, The, i. 257, 273–281, 304 ; 114, 176, 187.
Correspondence :—
    with Madox Brown, i. 105, 216 ; ii. 124.
    with Robert Browning, ii. 21.
    with Sir Richard Burton, i. 129–133.
    in Cambridge Chronicle, i. 39–41, 43–46, 119.
    with W. H. Chesson, ii. 156.
    with F. S. Ellis, i. 98, 99, 100.
    with Mr. Frowde, i. 331, 333.
    with Madame Galemberti, ii. 144.
    with F. H. Groome, i. 306 ; ii. 76, 81, 130.
    with Dr. G. Hake, i. 133 ; ii. 255.
    with Thomas Hardy, i. 286.
    with W. E. Henley, i. 238, 239, 243 ; ii. 70.
    with W. D. Howells, ii. 141.

Correspondence :—
    with Herbert Jenkins, ii. 214, 232, 236, 238.
    with Dr. Jessopp, ii. 235.
    with Coulson Kernahan, ii. 130, 231.
    with Sir James Knowles, ii. 14–15.
    with George Meredith, i. 277 ; ii. 64, 65, 66, 68, 138.
    with Wilfred Meynell, ii. 157.
    with Dr. John Nichol, ii. 12.
    with Dr. Patrick, i. 261, 262.
    with Christina Rossetti, ii. 47.
    with D. G. Rossetti, i. 186, 190–201, 211, 212, 213, 215, 217–221, 222, 227, 230, 266, 267 ; ii. 270.
    in St. James Gazette, i. 340.
    with George Sampson, ii. 156.
    with Secretary of Omar Khayyám Club, i. 291.
    with William Sharp, i. 192, 239, 306, 307–310 ; ii. 177.
    with Clement Shorter, ii. 84, 155.
    with W. Wray Skilbeck, ii. 15–16.
    with Mr. Spielmann, ii. 143.
    with R. L. Stevenson, i. 238, 239.
    with A. C. Swinburne, i. 134, 139, 142 ; ii. 86, 109, 116, 118, 119, 121, 127, 130–131, 272, 273, 274.
    with Miss Isabel Swinburne, ii. 137.
    in Times, i. 340.
    with Professor Walker, ii. 18.
    with Sir D. M. Wallace, i. 259.
    with William Watson, ii. 145–148.
    with Miss Theresa Watts, ii. 128.

Correspondence :—
  with Mrs. Watts-Dunton, ii.
    174–176, 178, 181, 183, 184,
    191.
  with E. S. Willard, i. 318.
  with Dr. Williamson, ii. 149.
  with T. J. Wise, i. 234 ; ii. 154.
Correspondence, Mrs. Watts-
    Dunton's :—
  with Lady Archibald Campbell,
    ii. 201.
  with Mrs. Holman Hunt, ii. 196.
  with Mrs. Lynn Lynton, ii. 10.
  with Mrs. Moulton, ii. 186.
  with Mrs. Jopling Rowe, ii. 204.
Country visiting, ii. 128.
Crawford, Marion, ii. 11.
Critical genius, i. 242 ; ii. 243,
    251.
Cromer, visits to, ii. 122.
Cymbeline, essay on, i. 339.

Danes Inn, life at, i 115, 120.
"Dante's Dream," i. 193.
De Quincey, i. 339.
De Tabley, Lord, i. 158 ; ii. 206,
    242.
Death, ii. 197 *et seq.*, 200.
Defoe's *Captain Singleton*, essay
    on, i. 246.
Dervish and the Lost Camel, The,
    i. 295–297.
Detective stories, i. 294.
Dewar, George, ii. 153, 199.
Dickens, articles on, ii. 143, 144.
Dilke, Sir Charles, i. 238.
Dinners, literary, i. 147 *et seq.*
Disraeli, study of, ii. 159.
Dixon, Hepworth, i. 149.
Douglas, James, ii. 153, 161, 169,
    221.
Dowden, Professor, i. 333, 334.
Dowsing, William, ii. 207.
Du Maurier, George, i 170.

Early literary work, i. 37.
East Anglian associations, ii. 84,
    85.
Eastbourne, visits to, ii. 126, 140.
Eastern legends, interest in, i. 294.
Eliot. George, i. 161–163.
Ellis, F. S., i. 98, 99, 100.
Encyclopædia Britannica, contri-
    butions to, i. 257, 259 ; ii 151.
Erechtheus, by Swinburne, i. 139,
    140, 141.
Essays :—
  on Byron, i. 263, 268–270.
  on *Captain Singleton*, i. 246–
    248.
  on Chatterton, i. 263–267.
  on *Cymbeline*, i. 339.
  on *Hamlet*, i. 330, 336.
  on Keats, ii. 148, 150, 329.
  The Lost Hamlet, i. 107, 334–
    336.
  on *Macbeth*, i. 338.
  on *Poetry*, i. 257, 261.
  on *The Renascence of Wonder*,
    i. 249, 257, 261 ; ii. 151, 236.
  on George Sand, i. 118.
  on Thackeray, i. 118.
  on *Two Gentlemen of Verona*, i.
    332, 333.
Essays and reviews, list of, ii.
    281.
Essays and Studies, by Swinburne,
    i. 124, 125.
Examiner, The, contributions to,
    i. 110, 115, 121 ; ii. 20, 259.
Eyesight, failure of, i. 332 ; ii.
    159.

Ferishta's Fancies, review of, ii.
    22–23.
Fitzgerald, Edward, ii. 76.
Francis, John C., i. 240.
Friendship, genius for, ii. 216, 217,
    221, 223, 224, 264, 265.

GALEMBERTI, Madame, ii. 144.
Garnett, Dr., i. 115 ; ii. 237.
German Shakespearean criticism,
i. 337.
Glyn, Miss, i. 147, 149.
Gosse, Edmund. i. 97, 116.
Groome, F. H., i. 306 ; ii. 11, 64,
68, 72, 75–83, 130, 173, 187, 220,
240.
Gypsies, encounter with, i. 30–34.
——, study of, ii. 81.

HAKE, Dr. Gordon. i. 63–71. 88
(footnote), 89, 133, 138, 147, 148,
192, 214 ; ii. 255–260.
Hake, Thomas, i. 71 ; ii. 140, 200,
219–220, 315.
Hamlet, essay on, i. 330, 336.
Hamlet, The Lost, essay on, i. 107,
334–336.
Hardy, Lady Duffus, i. 147, 149.
——, Thomas, i 286
Harper's Magazine, Shakespearean
essays in, i. 329, 336 ; ii. 284.
Harte, Bret, ii. 11, 84.
Hauteville, visit to, ii. 115.
Henley, W. E., i. 238, 239, 243;
ii. 11, 70–71.
Holman-Hunt, Mrs., ii. 196.
Horne, R. H., i. 151.
Hotten, J. C., i. 108, 109, 110, 111,
112, 113.
Howell, Charles Augustus, i. 181.
Howells, W. D., letter to, ii. 140.
Hueffer, Dr. Franz, i. 67, 71.
Hugo, Victor, ii. 115, 119, 120, 284.
Humour, sense of, ii. 160.
Hunt, Leigh, ii. 150.
Hutton, Richard Holt, on George
Eliot, i. 162.

IMPERIALISM, i. 287.
Irving, Henry, i. 147, 149, 151, 154.
Italy, visit to, i. 133–139.

Jan van Hunks, by Rossetti, i. 206,
231, 232, 234.
Jenkins, Herbert, ii. 152, 213.
——, personal recollections of
Watts-Dunton, ii. 232–239.
Jerrold, Mr. and Mrs. Walter, ii.
153.
Jessopp, Dr. Augustus, ii. 235.
Journalistic work, ii. 258, 259.
Jowett, Benjamin, ii. 11, 129.
Jubilee Greeting at Spithead to the
Men of Greater Britain, i. 285.
Juif Polonais, Le, theory of origin,
i. 154, 295.

KEATS, John, i. 152, 153.
——, essay on, ii. 148, 150, 329.
Kelmscott, visits to, i. 75–102.
Kernahan, Coulson, ii 130, 156,
205, 213.
——, personal impressions of
Watts-Dunton, ii. 215–232.
Kidnapped, review of. i. 238, 250.
King Erik, review of, i. 116–118.
King's Tragedy, The, by Rossetti,
i. 222.
Knight, Joseph, i. 67, 112, 129,
147, 149, 154, 155, 324.
Knowles, Sir James, ii. 11, 14–16,
190.
Kriegspiel, review of, ii. 80.

LAMBE, John Lawrence, ii. 214.
——, personal impressions of
Watts-Dunton, ii. 239–277.
——, sonnet by, ii. 195.
Landseer, Edwin, i. 65.
Lane, Mrs. John, ii. 156.
Larter, Miss C. E., ii. 205.
Last Talk at The Pines, A, ii. 195.
Latham, Dr. R. G., i. 63, 107.
Latymer, Lord, i. 286.
" Lavengro," a day with, i. 89–97.
See Borrow.

Law, Ernest, ii. 153.
Legal studies and work, i. 36, 37, 133, 304 ; ii. 269.
Letter writer, as, ii. 226. 229.
Lewes, George Henry, i. 161.
Leyland, i. 182.
Literary studies, early, i. 24–49, 60, 61.
London, early visits to, i. 26–28, 49, 59.
——, first steps towards literary life in, i. 53–60.
Longfellow, H. W., i. 194.
Lost Hamlet, The, i. 107, 334–336.
Lovers of Gudrun, by Morris, i. 96.
Lowell, James Russell, i. 159 ; ii. 24, 25.
Lynton, Mrs. Lynn, ii. 110.

Macbeth, essay on, i. 338.
M'Carthy, Justin, i. 121, 156.
Maccoll, i. 118, 237.
M'Ilraine, Clarence, i. 329.
Margate, visits to, ii. 139.
Marriage, and married life, ii. 165 *et seq.*
Marston, Philip Bourke, i. 148, 149–151, 155, 158.
——, Westland, i. 67, 71, 121.
——, his receptions and dinners, i. 147 *et seq.*, 155, 303.
Mary Stuart, by Swinburne, i. 141, 143.
Mason, Mrs. Charles, ii. 101, 105, 108, 142.
Meredith, George, i. 180, 277, 291, 293 ; ii. 11, 53, 63–70, 138.
——, Sonnet to, ii. 68.
Method of work, ii. 254.
Meynell, Mr. and Mrs., ii. 157.
Michael Scott's Wooing, i. 196–205.
Mid-Victorian friendships, ii. 2–86.
Middleton, John Henry, i. 94.

Midsummer holiday, the, ii. 113–131.
Miller, Joaquin, i 128–129, 147.
Minto, Professor William, i. 115, 121, 258 ; ii. 20, 217.
Mirrored Star Again, The, i. 89.
Modern literature, views on, ii. 276.
Morris, Lewis, ii. 54.
——, William, i. 75, 78, 80, 83, 90–102. 120, 147, 156, 158, 180, 206, 275 ; ii. 11, 120, 251, 262, 276.
——, Mrs William, i 194, 212 ; ii. 185–186.
Moulton, Mrs. Louise Chandler, i. 158–161, 167 ; ii. 176, 186.

Neilson, Miss, i. 147.
New Editor's Bow, The, ii. 290–293.
New Hero, The, ii. 54.
Newton, Miss Annie, ii. 207.
Nichol, Dr. John, ii. 11, 12.
Nicoll, Sir William Robertson, i. 320 ; ii. 190.
Nineteenth Century, contributions to, ii. 14, 15, 57, 143.

" Old Bell Inn," the, i. 49.
Old books, letter on, i. 41.
Old Familiar Faces, ii. 152.
Omar Khayyám Club, i. 290 ; ii. 63.
Oriental studies, i 294, 297 ; ii. 251.
O'Shaughnessy, Arthur, i. 147.
Oxford, visit to, ii. 129.

Parentage and family, i. 17. 20–21.
Paris, visit to, ii. 115–118.
Pater, Walter, i. 222.
Patrick, Dr., i. 261, 262.

Patriotic note in poetry, i. 285.
Payne, John, i. 147.
Peace Society, a Few Thoughts upon, ii. 288–290.
Personal appearance, ii. 250.
Piccadilly, i. 170 , ii. 290.
Pines, The, life at, ii. 101–110 *et seq.*, 244.
——, visitors to, ii. 11 *et seq.*, 152 *et seq.*
Poe, Edgar Allan, article on, i. 297.
Poetic work, i. 241.
——, early, i. 29.
——, later, i. 285.
Poetic Interpretation of Nature, On the, i. 134, 279.
Poetry, essay on, i. 257, 261 ; ii. 151, 236.
Poetry, and the Renascence of Wonder, ii 151.
Polish Jew, The, i. 154, 295.
Political views, ii. 253.
Poynter, Sir Edward, ii. 191.
Prayer to the Winds, i. 291.
Pre-Raphælite group, the, i. 53, 60, 63–71, 156.
Proctor, Anne B. ii. 11, 21.
Prothero, Professor, i. 102.
Purnell, Thomas, i. 121, 122, 123, 124, 147, 237.
Putney Hill, life at, i. 142, 187.

RABELAIS, Watts-Dunton on, i. 337.
Reade, Charles, i. 122.
Reading aloud as test of literary style, i. 292.
Reich, Miss Clara (Mrs. Watts-Dunton, *q.v.*), i. 317.
Religion, views on, ii. 276.
Renascence of Wonder, The, i. 249, 257, 261 ; ii. 151, 236.
Reviews, notable, ii. 281.
Rhys, Ernest, i. 320 ; ii. 154, 155.

Robinson, F. W., i. 53–59.
Roi s'Amuse, Le, review of Jubilee representation, ii. 116, 284–288
Rossetti, Christina, ii. 31–47.
Rossetti, Dante Gabriel, i. 63, 65, 147, 151, 156, 171 ; ii 216, 217, 260.
——, at Birchington-on-Sea, i. 228.
——, at Bognor, i. 211.
——, at Herne Bay, i. 216.
——, illness and death, i. 228.
——, later days, i. 211–234.
——, letters to Watts-Dunton, i. 186, 211, 212, 213, 215, 217–221, 222–227, 230, 266, 267.
——, life at Cheyne Walk, i. 185–207.
——, life at Kelmscott, i. 75–93.
——, love of animals, i. 85, 190.
——, relations with Gordon Hake, i. 63–71.
——, relations with Oscar Wilde, i. 175.
——, Watts-Dunton's friendship, i. 53, 60, 63–71, 76 *et seq.*, 185, 213–234, 324 ; ii. 34, 224, 270.
Rossetti, William M., i 147, 187, 204, 228, 229, 232, 233 ; ii. 217.
Rossetti circle, Watts-Dunton's introduction into, i. 53, 60, 63–71.
Rowe, Mrs. Jopling, ii. 188, 204.
Rubáiyát of Omar Khayyám, Fitzgerald's, i. 193, 290.

ST. IVES, influence of early life at, i. 17, 28–34, 42, 281 ; ii. 255.
St. Ives Mutual Improvement Society, letter to, i. 43–46.
St. James Gazette, i. 340.
Sampson, George, ii. 156.
Sand, George, essay on, i. 118.
School life, i. 21–34.
Science and poetry, relation between, i. 280 ; ii. 57.

Scots Observer, The, ii. 70.

Scott, Walter, i. 287.

Scott, William Bell, i. 115, 158, 187, 222.

Sea, passion for the. ii. 107. 113, 114, 121.

Seaford, visit to, ii. 123.

Sensibility, acute, ii. 260 *et seq.*

Shadow on the Window Blind, The i. 77.

Shakespeare, sonnets on, i. 339.

Shakespeare festivals, letter to *St. James's Gazette* regarding, i. 340.

Shakespearean criticism and essays, i. 281, 329–340 ; ii 283

Sharp, William, i. 192, 239, 306, 307–210 ; ii. 177.

Shorter, Clement, ii. 84, 155

———, Mrs. Clement. poems of. ii. 155.

Silas Marner, Watts-Dunton's Introduction to, i. 161.

Skelton, Sir John, ii. 11.

Skilbeck, W. Wray, ii. 15.

Smetham, i. 194.

Smith, W. Robertson, i. 258, 259, 260.

Social relations, i. 71, 147, 155, 157.

Songs of the Great Dominion, review of, i. 251.

Sonnets, i. 84, 219, 220, 287, 292, 293, 339 ; ii. 58, 67, 68, 200.

Sothern, i. 147.

Spectre in Gypsy Dell, The, ii. 64.

Spirit of the Rainbow, The, i. 84 ; ii. 194.

Stedman quoted, i. 279.

Sterne, by H. D. Traill, review of, i. 239, 244.

Stevenson, R. L., i. 238, 239 ; ii. 218–219, 223, 224.

Strong, Professor Arthur, ii 184

Survival after death, views on, ii. 208.

Suspense, ii. 200.

Swimming feats, i. 153 ; ii. 107, 122, 126.

Swinburne, A. C., as poet and critic, ii. 241.

———, attitude towards women, i. 127.

———, death of, ii. 184.

———, East Anglian associations, ii. 85, 86.

———, illness, ii. 65, 181

———, Mrs. Watt-Dunton's recollections of, ii. 180 *et seq.*

———, love of children, ii. 108, 109.

———, meeting with Joaquin Miller, i. 129.

———, meeting with Oscar Wilde, i. 175.

———, life at The Pines, ii. 101–110. 113.

———, letter to F. H. Groome, ii. 77–80.

———, letters to Watts-Dunton, i. 109, 110, 115, 124, 125, 126, 140, 143 ; ii. 86, 109, 116, 118, 119, 121, 130, 272.

———, last days, ii. 135–161.

———, on letter writing, ii. 227.

———, passion for the sea, ii. 107, 113, 121, 123, 126.

———, relations with Dr. John Nichol, ii. 11, 12.

———, Shakespearean essays and research, i. 332, 329, 330 ; ii. 129.

———, swimming feats. i. 153 ; ii. 107, 126.

———, Watts-Dunton's relations with, i. 105, 107, 108, 123, 139, 140, 158, 325 ; ii. 103, 104, 108, 135, 183, 216, 224, 268, 271.

———, *references* to, i. 21, 53, 156, 275 ; ii. 158.

Swinburne, Miss Alice, ii. 118, 119.

Swinburne family, visits to, ii. 128.

Swinburne, Miss Isabel, ii. 149.

Symons, Arthur, i. 330.

Talk on Waterloo Bridge, A, ii. 84.

"Tarno Rye." *See* Groome, F. H.

Taylor, Mr. Frank, ii. 159.

——— Tom, i. 122.

Tennyson, Lord, i. 156 ; ii. 11, 26, 226, 261.

———, article on portraits of, ii. 57.

———, *Aspects of*, ii. 57.

———, relations with, ii. 53–60.

———, sonnets to, ii. 53, 58–60.

Thackeray, essay and letter on, i. 118, 119.

Thompson, Francis, Watts-Dunton on, ii. 157.

Thoreau, articles on, ii. 83.

Three Fausts, The, ii. 71, 166.

Three Stages of Shakespeare. by Swinburne, i. 125.

Titles of novels, i. 310.

Toast to Omar Khayyám, ii. 76, 77

Traill, H. D., i. 239, 240.

Trelawney, Edward John, ii. 18–19.

Tribute to Tennyson, ii 58

Tristram of Lyonesse. ii. 120.

Truth about Rossetti, The, i. 249.

Two Christmastides, The, i. 279.

Two Gentlemen of Verona, essay on, i. 332, 333.

Two Suffolk Minds, ii. 76, 77.

VERSCHOYLE, Rev. J. S., ii. 190, 204.

Vesprie Towers, i. 322.

Vezin, Hermann, i. 151.

Volunteer movement, enthusiasm for, i. 38.

WADDINGTON, S., ii. 195.

Walker, Professor, ii. 18, 208.

Warren, Lady Leighton, ii. 206, 245.

———, Leicester. *See* De Tabley, Lord.

Watson, William, ii. 145–148, 243.

Watts, Alfred Eugene, i. 37, 59, 60, 181

———, J. K., i. 17, 23, 26, 28. 35, 36, 49, 280 ; ii. 122.

———, J. Orlando, i. 20, 59, 123, 133.

———, Miss Theresa, ii. 123, 126, 161.

Watts-Dunton, Mrs., i. 317 ; ii. 152. 244.

———, story of marriage and married life by, ii. 165–210.

Webster, Augusta, ii. 11, 17.

Wells, Charles, i. 137, 152.

Westminster Abbey, In, ii. 59.

Whistler, i. 159, 160, 167–174, 181, 182. 191 ; ii. 188–189, 193.

Wilde, Oscar, i. 168, 169, 172–180.

Willard, Edward, S., i. 317.

Williamson, Dr., ii. 149.

Wise, T. J., ii. 154, 197.

Wood Haunter's Dream, The, ii. 194.

Work of Cecil Rhodes, The, i. 287–291.

THE END.

PRINTED IN GREAT BRITAIN.

Printed in the United Kingdom
by Lightning Source UK Ltd.
110586UKS00001BA/122